THE
OLDEST
CITY

ST. AUGUSTINE
SAGA OF SURVIVAL

THE
OLDEST CITY

ST. AUGUSTINE
SAGA OF SURVIVAL

Edited by Jean Parker Waterbury

by

George E. Buker

Amy Bushnell

Robert N. Dow, Jr.

Thomas Graham

John W. Griffin

Patricia C. Griffin

Daniel L. Schafer

Jean Parker Waterbury

The St. Augustine Historical Society
St. Augustine, Florida

Contents

Illustrations and Maps

All illustrations and maps not otherwise credited are from the collections of the St. Augustine Historical Society.

The Contributors

Commander George E. Buker retired from the U.S. Navy in 1963, since which time he has earned his B.A. from Jacksonville University and his M.A. and Ph.D. from the University of Florida. A professor of history at Jacksonville University, he has written numerous articles, reviews, and two books, *Swamp Sailors* and *Sun, Sand and Water*.

Amy Bushnell holds an M.A. in Latin American studies and a Ph.D. in history, with distinction, from the University of Florida. She has written several articles on Florida's Spanish and Indian history, and a book, *The King's Coffer*, about the royal treasury in St. Augustine. A Phi Beta Kappa, Dr. Bushnell is presently historian for the Historic St. Augustine Preservation Board.

Charles S. Coomes claims no professional credits for his cartography skills, but since retiring from the Florida Power and Light Company, he has developed his map-making art to the point where his work appears in various publications. His articles on aspects of St. Augustine history have appeared in *El Escribano*, the annual of the St. Augustine Historical Society.

Robert N. Dow, Jr. is a retired newspaper editor and advertising agency executive whose avocation is Florida's history and archaeology. He has worked on prehistoric excavations and hopes soon to investigate a possible site of Fort Picolata and a nearby Confederate breastwork.

Thomas Graham, professor of history at Flagler College, is the author of *The Awakening of St. Augustine*. Born in Florida, Dr. Graham traces his ancestry back to St. Augustine's first Spanish period. He holds graduate degrees from Florida State University and the University of Florida.

John W. Griffin studied anthropology at the University of Chicago and has done extensive research on the archaeology and history of Florida. He has been Archaeologist, Florida Park Service; Chief, Southeastern Archaeological Center, National Park Service; and Director, Historic St. Augustine Preservation

Board. He is now a private consultant in archaeology and history.

Patricia C. Griffin is a native Californian with graduate degrees in social service administration and anthropology. She was on the Florida State University faculty from 1970 to 1980 and has done ethnohistorical research on the Minorcans of Florida and the history of ceremonial life in St. Augustine.

Daniel L. Schafer is Associate Professor of History at the University of North Florida. He has spent two summers in Scotland studying the James Grant papers in Ballindalloch Castle, and is preparing a book on British East Florida. His articles on that period have appeared in various historical journals. It was at the University of Minnesota that he earned his doctorate in history.

Jean Parker Waterbury is a native St. Augustinian who, after a long residence in New York City, returned to her birthplace several years ago. She currently edits *The East-Florida Gazette*, the St. Augustine Historical Society's quarterly. Other published work includes a history of Manhattan's Collegiate School, founded 1638, and articles for *El Escribano*, the Society's annual.

Preface

This is a book about St. Augustine—the book which has so often been asked for by innumerable visitors, townspeople and historians.

As part of the Centennial year observance of the St. Augustine Historical Society (1883-1983), this one-volume history of the oldest city is written for the general public. Other 20th-century publications on St. Augustine have dealt with specialized topics and separate aspects of St. Augustine's more than four centuries, intended mostly for research and reference. Here the Society aims to present the broad picture at a popular level, yet without sacrificing historical accuracy.

The Society considered two options on authorship; a single historian/author for the entire book, or a multi-author approach based on the eight periods into which the history of the city naturally divides. Study of the choices indicated there would be a problem in locating a single author familiar with the long and varied past of the area; on the other hand, there were available a number of writers with intimate knowledge of one or more of the historic periods. So, the latter option was adopted.

Eventually, eight authors were selected to prepare this volume. The Society is in debt to them for dedicating their considerable talents and valuable time to this Centennial project.

The Society owes thanks also to Charles S. Coomes as cartographer, to Joseph S. Mark for the cover design and the book's layout, to Mark E. Fretwell, to Clarissa Anderson Gibbs, and to the Society's librarian, Jacqueline K. Bearden, our indexer and final authority on source material.

> The Editorial Board
> The St. Augustine Historical Society

St. Augustine
September 1983

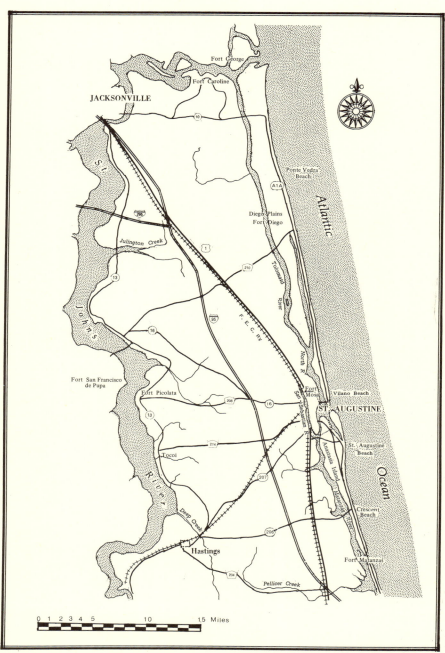

Fort George

Fort Caroline

JACKSONVILLE

St.

⑩

Ponte Vedra
Beach

A1A

⑭295

Julington Creek

Diego Plains
Fort Diego

①

⑬

Toonamo River

⑯

I95

F. E. C. RY.

North R.

Atlantic

Fort San Francisco
de Pupa

Fort Picolata

⑬

⑳8

⑯

San Sebastian R.

Fort
Mose

Vilano Beach

ST. AUGUSTINE

Tocoi

②14

②07

St. Augustine
Beach

Anastasia Island

Matanzas River

Ocean

Deep Creek

②06

Crescent
Beach

Hastings

②04

Pellicer Creek

Fort Matanzas

0 1 2 3 4 5   10   15 Miles

Map by Charles S. Coomes

The present-day environs of St. Augustine

Chapter One

The Men Who Met Menéndez
8000 B. C. - 1565 A. D.

by

John W. Griffin

He sailed northward along the coast; eight leagues
farther he discovered a good harbor with a beautiful
shoreline, which he named St. Augustine . . .

> *From Barcia's account of the 1565 voyage of
> the Spanish commander Pedro Menéndez de
> Avilés.*

The five ships anchored offshore in early September 1565
were not the first which the Indians of the village of Seloy had
seen. At irregular intervals for over fifty years similar strange
craft had appeared along the coast and the Indians had gradually
learned something about the men who lived on them. For a long
time most of the information was passed on to the Seloy from
other Indians who lived at a distance, but in recent years more
ships and more strangers had appeared in the Seloy area. In fact,
for over a year now many of these strangers had been living on
the banks of the large river to the north, only a day or two away.

At first the Indians there, like the Seloy members of the
Saturiba tribe, had welcomed these strange men with white skins
who called themselves *Français*. They had let the newcomers
build a village with a wall around it on the river bank, and they
had given the Frenchmen food and traded with them. But after a
while the Indians and the Frenchmen began to quarrel. The
French would not help the Indians in some of their wars, and the
things which the French had to trade became scarce. In the
winter the Frenchmen did not have enough to eat and in the
spring they demanded food from the Indians when the Indians
had none to spare. When the Indians refused, the Frenchmen

took the food by force. Lately, the Indians of Seloy had heard that the *Français* were hungry and discouraged and were planning to leave the country.

Only a short time ago ships had stopped near Seloy and men had asked the Indians where they might find the *Français*. These men called themselves English, and when they reached the French village they left behind one of their large ships. It was on this ship that the *Français* were planning to leave.

The Indians of Seloy knew that there were different tribes of people from the ships. There was another, beside the *Français* and the English, who called themselves *Españoles*. The ships now at anchor off Seloy were of that tribe; a message from Indians who lived along the coast south of Seloy had conveyed that information. These Indians to the south had met with the great chief of that fleet, who they said was also seeking the *Français* village. The *Españoles* chief had given these Indians many presents.

It was the *Españoles* whom the Florida Indians knew the most about. Their ships were most often along the coast, and many had been wrecked. Some people survived these wrecks, often to be taken captive by tribes in the south. Many things that the Indians could use had been salvaged from the wrecks or found scattered on the beaches. Metal ornaments worn by the Indians of Seloy had come from such wrecks. Some of these metals were highly valued by the *Españoles* who came on other ships to trade for these metals, and to rescue some of the shipwrecked people.

All of the Indians also knew of the two times when large numbers of *Españoles* had come ashore on the west coast of their land and had traveled through the lands of the Timucua tribes and into the lands of the Apalache, and then beyond. The first group had built small boats and sailed off; the second had marched north into the lands of many other tribes. Many of these *Españoles* rode atop large four-legged animals, much bigger than a deer, and could run down and trample an Indian. They knew of the death and destruction which swept through the land as the *Españoles* passed through it. They knew that often many Indian people fell ill and died very soon after the intruders had left.

They knew that more than once white men had made villages in Indian lands, as the *Français* had done, but that in every case the intruders had left, or had been driven out by the Indians.

The Indians knew all of these things and more, for, as an early Spanish historian remarked, "in those provinces news travels from cacique (chief) to cacique with greater speed than it is divulged through the mails in Europe." What they could not know was the ultimate consequence of all of these events: the destruction of a way of life that had been built through five hundred generations or more.

The first Indians entered the peninsula, today called Florida, well over ten thousand years ago. Centuries before that, their people had reached the New World across the Bering Strait and had slowly pushed farther afield until they had reached this last corner of the continent. They were hunters and gatherers without fixed homes, and with meagre material possessions.

The Florida climate was cooler then, and semi-arid. Extensive grasslands and savannahs, much like those of the African veldt today, supported large herds of game animals. The early hunters found bison and now-extinct kinds of deer grazing on the lush grasses. Mammoths were there; massive land turtles and giant armadillos lumbered across the landscape.

The few rains that fell were quickly absorbed by the sand and the porous limestone. The deep-cut rivers and the occasional sinkholes held water which attracted the animals and the hunters. The coastline lay miles seaward of today's shore, and behind it was a broad belt of uninviting dunes and coastal scrub with virtually no fresh water.

All of this changed when the Ice Age ended; the climate gradually warmed and the sea level rose. The broad reaches of grass became more restricted and many of the kinds of animals of the colder era disappeared. It was still drier than today and hardwood forests shaded areas where pines now flourish. As the seawater gradually rose, the coastal strip narrowed around this vast forest.

These changes in the landscape were slow, in most instances hardly noticeable to the human inhabitants, but as generation succeeded generation the life of the early hunters had to adapt to

Sun worship by Florida Indians was described and illustrated by artist Jacques LeMoyne, a member of the French expedition of 1564. "Every year, just before spring, Chief Outina's subjects take the skin of the largest stag, with its horns still on, and stuff it with the choicest roots. On its horns, neck and body they hang long garlands of the best fruits. Thus decorated, it is carried with music and song to an open level place and hung on a high tree with its head and breast toward the sunrise. They then pray to the sun. . . ."

Before setting off for war, heavily tattooed Chief Saturiba leads appropriate ceremonies. Artist Jacques LeMoyne described the occasion: The chief, "taking a wooden bowl full of water turned toward the sun, worshipped it, and prayed for victory over the enemy. He prayed that their blood might be poured out like the water he was about to scatter from the bowl. He then flung the water into the air and said: 'As I have done with this water, so I pray that you may do with the blood of your enemies.'"

the changing conditions. Hunters and gatherers still, they pursued smaller animals as well as the white-tailed deer which had become their staple. They foraged for nuts and acorns and berries, and discovered the merits of countless plants.

The approximate level of the present sea was reached some five thousand years ago. The rivers now ran more slowly on a reduced gradient and lakes, ponds and marshes multiplied. Forests became more patchy and diversified, and fires caused by lightning and humans created fertile clearings for new growth. The warm and moist climate ushered in the rich environment of today's Florida.

Only a small fringe of the inundated coast remained bleak. It was sculptured in new ways by offshore barriers, such as Anastasia Island, which isolated lagoons and marshes where oysters, fish and birds could thrive. In the freshwater rivers, too, shellfish were now common, and along the rivers and the coastal lagoons the Indians, year by year, added to the shellheaps which were growing into small hills.

All of these changes made it possible for the Indians to stay longer in one place, utilizing various food sources available within a limited area. A base camp could be established in a productive locality and small groups could spread out from it and return. Still, a permanent year-round residence was not practical because the natural world presented its bounty at different times and in different places. To take full advantage of resources a yearly nomadic cycle was still necessary, but the base camp could remain, awaiting their return.

With some degree of permanency more material possessions could accumulate. About four thousand years ago the Florida Indians began to make a crude but useful pottery, fashioned and fired from native clays found in small pockets along river banks and marsh edges. Earlier, it would have been of little use to them; pottery is too heavy and too fragile to serve a rapidly moving hunting community.

It was about the time of this earliest pottery that the Indians began to live along the lagoons of the St. Augustine area. Earlier there had been only brief and occasional visits to the coast, but once the lagoons had formed, rich in fish and shellfish, living there was congenial. The lower parts of many of the shellheaps which dot the shores of the Matanzas and North rivers, and which indeed underlie much of the city of St. Augustine, are the debris left by these early settlers.

As the shellheaps grew and the centuries passed many changes took place in the Indian way of life. There were no invasions of new peoples, but new ideas were borrowed from as far away as the Indian centers in the heartland of the Mississippi valley, passing from tribe to tribe in a long chain that finally reached coastal Florida. There was a modest amount of trade also. Soapstone, quartz crystals, native copper from the Great Lakes and other exotic materials reached Florida, while highly prized seashells were among the items which traveled the other direction.

The most important idea to reach these former hunters and gatherers was that of agriculture. They learned to plant, tend and harvest instead of relying on gathering nature's capricious seedings. Once the American Indian triad of corn, squash and beans was well established, people could live in a village near the fields for much of the year. Extension of the fields and the storage of some of the crop meant that villages could grow larger. More time was spent at the base village and the possessions which accumulated could be left there when small groups took to the trail to hunt for fresh meat in a retention of the ancestral pattern. Near the coast in the St. Augustine area, fish and shellfish were valuable resources at most times of the year.

Along with the new crops came new religious and ceremonial ideas, more elaborate than before and with greater emphasis on the sun as a potent force for agricultural success. With larger and more concentrated groups of people came the need to schedule agricultural work, control the distribution of stored foods and to protect the people and their resources. As a result the power of the chiefs increased, and alongside that grew the power of the priests. Ranks or social classes, ranging from nobles to commoners, came into being.

With the new ceremonial life came ideas about death and burial. Earthen mounds as sepulchers became as common in Florida as along the mid-continent river valleys, but whereas the custom was abandoned over most of the land centuries before European contact, the Indians of Florida retained the practice into historic times.

The European explorers of 16th-century Florida—French, Spanish and English—described the Indian life of northeast Florida in considerable detail. Their comments and the illustrations of the Frenchman Jacques LeMoyne are the earliest detailed observations on a North American Indian group. The writers did not understand everything that they saw and the artist had to reproduce his lost originals from memory, but used judiciously the information is priceless, and intimately tied to the immediate St. Augustine vicinity.

The village of Seloy at which the Spaniards landed to found St. Augustine was one of 30 or more villages occupied by the tribesmen of Saturiba. In turn, the tribe of Saturiba was one of perhaps a dozen tribes in northeastern Florida and southeastern Georgia who all spoke dialects of the same language, now called Timucuan, as are the tribes which spoke it. Although they shared a common basic language these tribes were not a united nation; inter-tribal warfare was commonplace. The tribe of Saturiba centered on the mouth of the St. Johns River and both north and south along the coast, including the area of St. Augustine.

Each tribe was headed by a great chief, called *holata ico* in Timucuan, but referred to by the Spaniards by the West Indian term which they applied to all chiefs, *cacique*. Each village also had a chief, subservient to the great chief. Chieftainship, tribe or village, was hereditary and all chiefs were drawn from a single clan of nobles named for the sacred white deer.

Other positions of leadership and prestige were filled from high-ranking clans, and the council which advised and aided the chief was drawn from them. Such clans were named for animals such as bear and panther, while the clans of the commoners bore such names as Dirt, Fish, and Buzzard.

The line of descent and inheritance was in all instances traced through the female, a common practice among American Indian groups but one that perplexed the tradition-bound explorers to whom the male line was the only right and proper path. Changing this system to conform to European standards would be an important goal of Spanish missionary efforts.

During the growing season, Florida Indians stored excess fruit, vegetables and grains in communal granaries. Artist Jacques LeMoyne observes, "These [crops] are gathered twice a year, carried home in canoes, and stored in low and roomy granaries, built of stone and earth and thickly roofed with palm branches and a kind of soft earth."

While the power of the chief was absolute, extending even to decreeing the death penalty, it was in practice tempered with frequent and formalized counseling. "The men do nothing without assembling and counseling thoroughly before arriving at a decision," said an early observer. At such a council the advisors would be seated in descending rank from the chief, and the ceremonial drink of cassina tea served in a conch-shell cup would be offered first to the chief and then to the others according to rank.

The leaves of the native holly *Ilex vomitoria*, which still grows abundantly near the coast, were used to brew the cassina tea; it was widely used throughout the southeast in Indian ceremonies. The Timucuans, and later the Spaniards, also enjoyed it as a beverage. The leaves provided the Timucuans with an item of trade with tribes who lived above the southeastern coastal plain, and hence outside the native range of the plant, but who nonetheless coveted "the beloved tree." The very high caffeine content of cassina tea was undoubtedly one of the reasons for its popularity.

The Timucuans were said to be "robust," "well-proportioned" and of "goodly stature," and both men and women were spoken of as handsome. Both sexes wore their hair long, but the men gathered theirs atop the head. Their ears were pierced and the most frequent ornament worn in them was made of inflated and red-painted fish bladders which "shown like pearls."

The men and women of the noble classes were intricately tattooed in azure, red and black. Paints or dyes were pricked into the skin to assure permanence. The commoners do not seem to have been so adorned. In addition to the tattooing, body painting associated with war and ceremonies was also practiced, apparently by both nobles and commoners.

The nearly nude, but ofttimes decorated bodies of the Indians were minimally covered with loincloths of deerskin which were "paynted cunningly with sondry colors." Women sometimes wore deerskin clothing, but more frequently used a skirt-like garment of Spanish moss.

Bird feathers were a favored item of personal adornment, and necklaces of shells were worn by both men and women.

A Florida Indian, considerably Europeanized by an unknown artist, uses a fish weir to catch what appears to be a mullet, to this day a prime eating fish in the St. Augustine area.

Wristlets and anklets of shells and other natural products were common. Some copper ornaments of native North American metal had been present in prehistoric times, but now gold, silver and lesser metals, salvaged from the wrecks of European vessels and traded northward, added quantity and variety to Timucuan jewelry. Large discs or gorgets of metal adorned the chests of the important men, and "many of the men wore round, flat plates of gold, silver, or brass, which hung upon their legs, tinkling like little bells."

The villages in which these people lived were located near rivers or lagoons, and at least some of them were surrounded by a palisade of upright logs with a single narrow entrance protected by a guardhouse. In the center of this protected area was a large structure, "much like a large barn," capable of holding several hundred people. This is where the important council meetings were held and where the chief resided. All around the sides of the rectangular great house was a platform or bench which could be used for sitting or sleeping; in at least one instance the platform rested on large round wooden pillars painted red, yellow and blue.

The ordinary houses filled the area between the great house and the palisade, apparently scattered in no regular plan. They were small, circular or oval, and made of timbers stuck into the ground and bent inward to form a dome-shaped roof, all of which was covered with thatch from the abundant palm trees. The doors faced south as a protection from the cold north and northeast winds of winter. The Indians used the huts for little more than sleeping, most activities being carried on outside.

The public warehouses or granaries were especially important for it was here that surplus crops and foodstuffs were held for future use. Such a granary was "low and roomy . . . built of stones and earth and thickly roofed with palm branches and a kind of soft earth." Distribution of food was regulated and fair— "no one fears being cheated."

While shrubs of cassina holly were sometimes transplanted near the houses, most farming took place outside the village. The fields were cleared in the spring by burning, and rabbits and other small animals which had moved into the weedy tangle were captured as a side product. Then the women planted the seeds of corn and beans in holes poked into the cleared field. The corn would be the major crop, but in addition beans, various pumpkins and squashes were raised. When the first crop reached maturity in June some of the corn was eaten in the green stage, but much of it was allowed to ripen fully to be gathered and stored in the community granary. A second crop would then be planted in the same fields for a fall harvest. Such heavy use of the land must have dictated that the fields be moved frequently. The resulting fallow fields would have certainly added to the bounty of berries which could be gathered. Wild grapes along the edges of the woodlands also were there for gathering.

Giant live oaks stood near the village of Seloy and in the late fall the Indians could harvest vast numbers of sweet acorns. Also nearby were groves of palm trees; the Timucua must have known and used the palm hearts, or "swamp cabbage," but no explorer mentioned the fact. There were other plants to be gathered and such creatures as box turtles and gopher tortoises could simply be picked up and carried home.

The bay upon which Seloy was located gave access by canoe both north and south to a vast land of water and marsh teeming with life. The abundant clams and oysters were collected at low tide by the women and children. Most fishing, on the other hand, was done by the men.

Some fish were caught on hook and line, and some were speared or shot with bow and arrow, but most of the catch came from the use of nets and fishweirs. A highly efficient method was stopnetting, in which a net stretched across a tidal channel traps the fish as they move outward on the ebbing tide. Even less laborious, after the initial construction, was the fishweir. These traps, ingeniously built of poles and reeds, could capture vast quantities of fish as they sought to run seaward on an outgoing tide. The fish were then dipped from the end of the weir where they had concentrated.

While hunting was a year-round activity, it became more intensive in the winter when, with the year's crop harvested and stored, the natives dropped back into the foraging pattern of their ancestors. It was then that the Indians went "for three or four months into the woods where they make little huts of palm leaves and live on acorns, fish which they catch, oysters, deer, turkeys and other animals which they hunt." When spring neared the people returned to their village and made ready the fields for another year.

Cooking was simple. Most of the foodstuffs at one time or another went into the large clay pots of the Indians, for the one-pot meal was standard fare. Gruels of corn or acorns, with varied additives, were a staple. Meats were broiled over the coals of the fires, or were smoked. While the fires were usually renewed from embers, a new one could be quickly made by rubbing two sticks together.

Ritual and ceremony attended and surrounded every aspect of life, and was nowhere more prominent than in matters relating to food. Before hunting the all-important deer, a Timucua would pray to the antlers of a previous kill and he would not partake of his own kill since he believed that this would prevent future success. Putting the liver and lungs of the deer in cold water would also prevent a future kill, as would throwing out the bones instead of hanging them up or putting them in the thatch of the house. In the spring, one of the most important ceremonies involved the offering of the skin of a stag to the sun.

A series of beliefs had to do with the first harvesting of a plant or capture of an animal. The first acorns or fruits collected were not eaten, nor was the first corn from a new crop. The first fish from a new trap was released nearby to insure future catches, and a sorcerer or priest received the first deer killed by a hunting party. All of these "first fruit" rites were in effect offerings to the gods or their representatives. The extension of this principle to humans was shocking to Europeans: The first-born male child was offered as a sacrifice to the chief, most probably in his role as a representative of more supernatural powers.

The Timucua were fond of gambling, but much of their recreation was more active and utilized the skills needed in hunting and warfare. Proficiency with the bow and arrow became a sport as well as a tool for survival. Their bows were described by an Englishman from the land of the longbow as stronger than those of other Indians and Africans and "not greatly inferior to ours." There was a strenuous game which involved throwing a small hard ball at a small square target atop a pole.

Endurance running was popular. After a long run the Indians were "sweating and trembling with pain, and making all sorts of contortions . . . their outcries attest that they are wild and happy and many will fall to the ground exhausted." The women would throw water on them, and when they were revived somewhat it was time to make a bet and take another run.

Dancing was recreational although it was most often cere-monial; it was a group activity and usually of long duration. Rhythm was marked by a drum or by sticks beating upon a stone. Rattles made of gourds or the shells of box turtles added their sounds as did whistles of reeds. The music of a group of twenty pipers impressed European ears as "making the wildest kind of noise, without any harmony or rhythm, each blowing with all his might as if to see who could blow the loudest."

Warfare seems to have been common even before the coming of the Europeans. Raiding parties staged nighttime forays against enemy villages, igniting the tinder-dry palm-thatched roofs with flaming arrows before drifting back into the forest. For a full-scale assault a chief called upon his subject villages and assem-bled his fighting force. After a ceremony praying for victory the entire party set off for enemy territory, adorned in war paint. When the forces clashed it was not in formal battle, but in a series of skirmishes and forays. Enemy casualties were dragged off, scalped and often dismembered, with the arms and legs carried back with the scalps to be displayed on tall poles in the victors' territory.

War clubs of hard wood were used by the Timucua, but the major weapon was the bow and arrow. They were adept at shooting with their arms on either side of a tree, giving them considerable personal protection. They would pick up spent arrows and reuse them; the Europeans learned to pick up the arrows during a conflict and break them to prevent reuse, a practice which infuriated the Indians because when the arrows

"The Indians hunt deer in a way we have never seen before," says artist Jacques LeMoyne of this scene he drew in 1564. "They hide themselves in the skin of a very large deer which they have killed some time before. They place the animal's head upon their own head, looking through the eye holes as through a mask. In this disguise they approach the deer without frightening them."

Feasting was a favorite activity of Florida Indians and was recorded by artist Jacques Le-Moyne. "There is a time of year," he writes, "when the natives feast each other. For this purpose they choose special cooks. These cooks take a great round earthenware pot (which they bake so well that water can be boiled therein as easily as in our own kettles) and put it over a large wood fire. The place where the cooking is done swarms with activity."

were all gone the fighting had to cease. Their arrows were tipped with points of stone, bone or even hard wood. After meeting with Europeans they used "peaked points of knives, which they having gotten of the Frenchmen, broke the same, and put the points of them in their arrows' heads."

This was the way of life of the Indians of the village of Seloy and their Timucuan kinsmen at the time of contact with the Europeans, a contact which began at some unknown date one side or other of the year 1500. Which European first reached these shores, or when, is uncertain; the earliest accounts are so vague and incomplete that advocates for particular voyages and voyagers can argue endlessly.

There are some who say that John and Sebastian Cabot penetrated this far south in 1497 and 1498, and Amerigo Vespucci, the controversial Florentine for whom America was named, is credited by some with a voyage in 1497 which could have reached Florida. Whether any or all did is open to question, but it is virtually certain that someone, perhaps many, knew these coasts before Juan Ponce de León's official "discovery" in 1513. There are two lines of evidence. First, the peninsula is unmistakably represented on several maps prepared before 1513. Secondly, the hostile reception which Ponce de León received in southern Florida strongly suggests that he had been preceded, probably by unrecorded slave raiders.

If it is uncertain that Ponce de León was the discoverer of Florida, it is equally uncertain whether or not he reached the coast and landed in the vicinity of St. Augustine. And, he may or may not have been seeking a Fountain of Youth. Yet despite all of these uncertainties the fact remains that Ponce de León did bestow the name Florida upon the land, and did leave, albeit at second or third hand, an account of his voyage. Ponce de León must retain the distinction of being the "official" discoverer of Florida.

Ponce de León left Puerto Rico with three ships on March 3, 1513, following a generally northwesterly course which carried him through the Bahama Islands and onward. Almost a month later, on April 2, land was sighted and the explorers dropped anchor a league offshore. "Believing that land to be an island,

Juan Ponce de León, discoverer of Florida in 1513. Located in St. Augustine, this bronze statue is a replica of the original which, since the early 1800's, has stood in the plaza of San Juan de Puerto Rico near the cathedral where the explorer is buried.

they named it *La Florida*, because it appeared very delightful, having many and fresh groves, and it was all level, and also because they discover'd it at the season, which the Spaniards call *Pascua Florida*." The discovery during the Easter season must have played the greater part in the selection of the name by a pious 16th-century Spaniard despite its almost afterthought placement in the narrative.

The place of the historic landfall is not known. That it lay somewhere between the mouth of the St. Johns River and Cape Canaveral seems reasonably certain. Relatively convincing cases can be made for several spots, including St. Augustine.

Concerning the five days that Ponce de León spent along the coast he had just discovered, the narrative says only that "he went ashore to get information, and take possession." The narrative does not say that he entered a harbor or inlet, or that he met any Indians, although both of these events are specifically mentioned later in the narrative as Ponce de León proceeded southward along the Florida coast where he entered several rivers, encountered groups of hostile Indians and left a hewn inscribed stone which has never been found. Ponce de León's discovery of the Gulf Stream where the "water ran so swift it had more force than the wind," was as important as his discovery of Florida. This river in the ocean soon became the preferred homeward route of treasure-laden ships from the newly conquered lands of New Spain (Mexico) and the Caribbean, passing between the island of Cuba and the Florida reef, and then between the reefs of the Bahamas and the shore of Florida, before turning eastward for the run to Spain.

In 1521 Ponce de León made a second expedition to Florida, this time directly to the lower west coast where he was met in force by hostile Indians. In the fighting, Ponce de León was wounded by an arrow and shortly thereafter died in Cuba from its effects.

Other men and other vessels probed the Atlantic and Gulf coasts in voyages of discovery, crudely mapping the shores.

The Florida peninsula was to witness a major Spanish expedition in 1528. Panfilo de Narváez, a one-eyed veteran *con-*

quistador, under a patent from the king which made him *adelantado* of all lands from the Mexican border to the Cape of Florida, commanded five ships, which landed four hundred men and eighty horses on the west coast, perhaps near Tampa Bay, in April 1528. Narváez's goal was settlement and gold, and pursuit of the latter would determine the location of the former. His expedition worked its way north and west, fighting the summer climate and the Indians whom they had alienated immediately upon landing. In the fall they reached Apalache, near present Tallahassee, and lived on the Indian harvest while fighting off its owners. The expected relief ships did not arrive on the coast and in desperation, the Spaniards built crude barge-like boats in which to flee the inhospitable land. In these the survivors sailed off to repeated disasters and the eventual survival of only four men, who reached Mexico City in 1536, eight years after the landing in Florida.

The disaster of Narváez did not deter others who desired to repeat the fabulous conquests of Mexico and Peru, and who were ever drawn by the faintest rumor of riches. Hernando de Soto had become wealthy with Pizarro in Peru and at age thirty-nine bore a royal mandate to "conquer, pacify, and people" the lands between Mexico and Cape Fear in North Carolina; he was also given the governorship of Cuba. De Soto mounted a larger and better organized expedition than his predecessor. He had over six hundred men and two hundred horses, and even a herd of pigs to drive on the march. Equipment and supplies were ample; some would be left behind as the march progressed northward from its Florida west coast base. De Soto pushed through the western Timucuan territory with the same harsh disregard for life and property that had marked the Narváez advance, and perhaps even more harsh because of the greater Indian resistance in response to their treatment of a decade earlier. The Spaniards wintered in Apalache in 1539-40, having taken over a large Indian village, but no treasure could be found and the Spaniards pushed on, first north, then west, in a trail of destruction and constantly diminishing capability, to the shores of the Mississippi River. Here De Soto died and was buried in the mighty river he had discovered, and the remainder of his force wandered aimlessly before 311 survivors finally reached Mexico.

At the Indian town of Cofitachequi, near present Augusta, Georgia, the De Soto expedition recorded evidence of a greater killer than their weaponry, although they did not know how to interpret it. They found "great townes dispeopled, and over-growne with grasse," and in a neighboring town, charnel houses "filled with bodies of people who had died of the pestilence." Such epidemics mark the introduction of new diseases among a previously unexposed population.

Even with the failure of two major expeditions, interest in Florida was not curtailed. An attempt at peaceful missionary activity in 1549 ended with the murder of Fray Luis Cancer, one of the five Dominican friars who had landed on the Florida west coast. Ten years later, in 1559, the most ambitious attempt at colonization up until that time reached Pensacola Bay, having come from Mexico under the leadership of Tristan de Luna y Arellano. Thirteen ships bearing five hundred soldiers, a thousand colonists, and quantities of all necessary foods and supplies, sailed into Pensacola Bay in August. An unusually early hurricane struck before the ships were unloaded, but after the colonists were ashore; the destruction was immense and the losses irre-placeable. After this ill-fated beginning, disaster followed disaster and the colony was abandoned in less than two years.

This latest debacle finally convinced the Spanish crown that Florida was not worth the effort, and on September 23, 1561, Philip II decreed that there would be no further effort to colonize Florida. But within six months French ships were underway, destination Florida, and the Spanish prohibition would soon be set aside.

The scene now shifted back to the Atlantic coast, ignored except as the site of shipwrecks and the recovery of salvage since the days of Ponce de León.

A French expedition led by Jean Ribault, a devout Protestant seaman seeking new lands, and possible solutions to the growing Huguenot-Catholic conflict in France, reached the Florida coast in the vicinity of present St. Augustine at the end of April 1562.

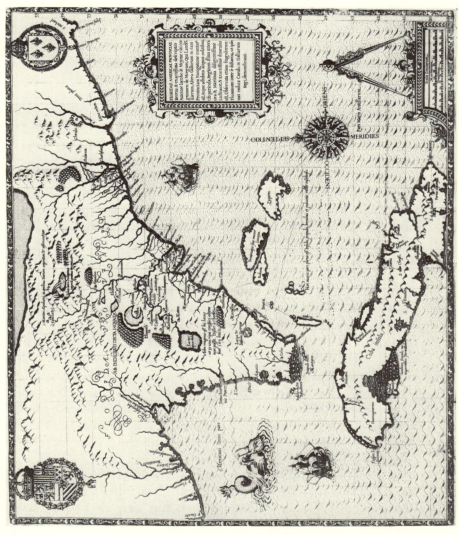

An early map shows the French concept of Cuba, Florida and the southeastern area of what is now the United States. It was drawn by Jacques Le-Moyne, cartographer and artist of the French expedition to Florida in 1564.

After setting up a stone monument on the banks of the St. Johns River, Ribault explored the coast northward, leaving a small colony, Port Royal, in what is now South Carolina. Promised reinforcements did not arrive because of unsettled European conditions and these settlers abandoned the colony.

Two years later, however, a larger expedition of French Huguenots under René de Laudonnière reached Florida and settled on the St. Johns River, or River of May as they called it. Here they built Fort Caroline, but seemingly made little effort to begin farming activity, relying rather on trade with the Saturiba for much of their food, beyond what they had brought with them. Again, reinforcements and supplies which had been promised from France did not arrive, and by the following summer the colony was disintegrating because of food shortages, personality conflicts, and general disillusionment. The Indians had become disenchanted with the Frenchmen, adding to the white men's fears.

At this juncture the arrival of John Hawkins, Elizabethan slave-trader and sometime privateer, seemed salvation to Laudonnière. With money, ammunition and cannon he bought a ship from Hawkins in which to depart for France, but before he could make arrangements to leave, the long-awaited relief arrived on August 28, 1565 in the person of Jean Ribault, returning to the St. Johns River, this time with a sizeable force.

The French Huguenot activity in Florida had not escaped Spanish attention. Not only did Ribault and Laudonnière threaten what was considered Spanish land, but they also led hated "Lutheran heretics."

At the news of Ribault's first settlement at Port Royal, Philip II had commissioned one of his most able naval commanders, Pedro Menéndez de Avilés, to oust the French and to settle Florida.

To gather his expedition took many months, and it was not until the summer of 1565 that Menéndez could sail, coincidentally only a little after Ribault's second voyage had started. The Frenchman tarried along the way, and ran for nearly two weeks along the Florida coast before anchoring off the River of May. Menéndez, with only five of his ships (the rest had been scattered by the stormy Atlantic) was in sight of the Florida coast on August 28, the same day that Ribault reached Fort Caroline.

In the next few days while Ribault was engaged in unloading, the Spanish ships worked their way northward along the coast, pausing to note and name the harbor of St. Augustine before moving on to confront the anchored vessels of Jean Ribault off the mouth of the St. Johns River. Nothing beyond shouted taunts and insults transpired at the first meeting. The French ships slipped their anchors and disappeared into the dark, and the five Spanish ships dropped back along the coast to anchor off the port which they had named St. Augustine.

It was September 6, 1565. The lives of the Indians of the village of Seloy, and the village itself, would never be the same again.

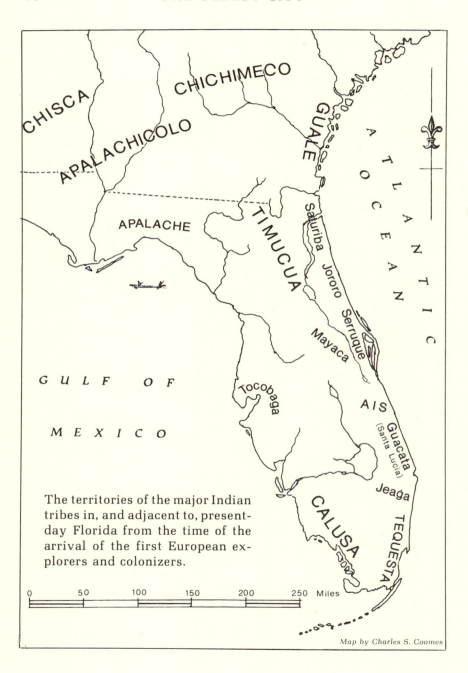

CHISCA

CHICHIMECO

APALACHICOLO

GUALE

APALACHE

TIMUCUA

Saturiba

Jororo

Serruque

Mayaca

ATLANTIC

OCEAN

GULF OF

MEXICO

Tocobaga

AIS

Guacata
(Santa Lucia)

Jeaga

CALUSA

TEQUESTA

The territories of the major Indian tribes in, and adjacent to, present-day Florida from the time of the arrival of the first European explorers and colonizers.

```
0      50     100     150     200     250  Miles
```

Map by Charles S. Coomes

Chapter Two

The Noble and Loyal City
1565 - 1668

by

Amy Bushnell

The harbor named for Saint Augustine, Bishop of Hippo and patron saint of Pedro Menéndez's home town of Avilés, presented both shelter and challenge. The shallow bar across its inlet, even at high tide, would admit only the smaller Spanish vessels, those with a draft under sixteen *palmas*. His 900-tun flagship, the stately *San Pelayo*, must be anchored out in the channel, exposed to enemies and storms. By the same token, of course, the harbor was safe from French galleons.

The camp would command the inlet and take advantage of the terrain, being placed where rivers and estuarine marshes formed a narrow peninsula with access by land from the north only. The first company to disembark would fortify it by digging a trench around the council house of the village of Seloy, near the mouth of the North River. This structure would serve as a temporary warehouse as well as fort, for in the ships' holds were the supplies for a colony, including 200 fishnets, 6 tons of iron, 8 church bells, a medicine chest and 24 reams of paper.

Clearly this was no haphazard adventure. Admiral Pedro Menéndez de Avilés, an Asturian bred in the seaports of northern Spain, was a veteran of combat and naval strategy. He and his brother Álvaro Sánchez had served their turns as captain general of the yearly treasure fleet of the Indies, although they were known to hold the interests of their corsairing clan above the king's mercantile regulations. Menéndez and another brother, Bartolomé, had in fact been charged with smuggling by the royal House of Trade, established in 1503 in Seville to regulate trade and passage to America, and had spent their share of time in the House of Trade jail.

Yet Philip II, upon learning of Jean Ribault's intrusion at Port Royal in present South Carolina, brushed aside all objections and made a three-year contract with this *norteño*, naming him *Adelantado* of Florida—a kind of lord of the marches, who at his own expense would carve out a conquest and become its lord proprietor. Menéndez was not the first to be so honored. Behind him stretched a line of luckless adelantados, each with his special commission, half a century back to the discoverer Juan Ponce de León. Menéndez's charge was to drive out all French interlopers from the lands claimed by the king between Terranova (New-foundland) and St. Josephs Bay on the Gulf of Mexico.

Before he could set sail, intelligence came that Ribault's lieutenant, René de Laudonnière, with a larger group had built Fort Caroline near the mouth of the St. Johns River and was expecting reinforcement. Military preparations escalated before this added threat. The king added his financial backing to that of Menéndez and his seafaring brothers, nephews, cousins and assorted in-laws. The expedition, as finally mounted, was too large for one seaport to handle, and separate fleets sailed from Cádiz, Asturias and Vicaya toward a rendezvous in the Canarries.

Pedro Menéndez, reaching the archipelago first, pressed on to Puerto Rico without waiting for the smaller fleets. Storms in the Atlantic scattered the vessels with him, but again he pushed on toward Florida, with only five of his ships and some six hundred people, including twenty-six women and their children. It was his aim to reach Fort Caroline ahead of the French under Jean Ribault, but Ribault's fleet arrived sooner. There was an inconclusive encounter at the St. Johns bar, with the French ships easily outrunning the heavily laden Spanish ones. This was why Menéndez had fallen back to this other harbor, which he had reconnoitered and named earlier, and why his men were hurriedly making camp and throwing earthworks around Seloy's council house. French scouts had noted their location and a counterattack was expected.

Notwithstanding the need for haste, the admiral's landing was duly marked, for the Spanish were a ceremonious people, understanding the purposes of panoply and ritual. On the eighth of September, 1565, as the Indians stood and watched, Pedro Menéndez de Avilés, Adelantado, Governor and Captain General of Florida, stepped from his launch with his gentlemen, announced by trumpets and artillery. Chaplain Francisco López de Mendoza Grajales walked forward to greet him, carrying a cross and intoning the *Te Deum Laudamus.* The company knelt to kiss the cross and, while banners hung limp in the sultry air, heard a mass in honor of the Nativity of Our Lady. Then Menéndez, notary by his side, took possession of Florida in the name of His Most Catholic Majesty and as lord of the land received the fealty of his captains and the officials of the royal treasury. The Saturibas of the vicinity played their role to perfection, kneeling before the cross, kissing hands, and trying their teeth on Spanish hardtack.

On that day St. Augustine, scarcely more than a ditch and a pile of barrels, became a Spanish municipality. This was no empty formality, for the Spanish system of government was one of city-states. A Spaniard identified himself, not with a province or a kingdom, but with a city. During the Reconquest of Spain, drawn out over centuries, each military camp the Spaniards laid out or city they reclaimed from the Moors became a center for land granting and government, with a hinterland extending to that of the last municipality. The adelantado's contract with his prince required him to found, fortify and populate at least two such cities as the bases from which to explore and conquer the great land of Florida, his to govern from the east Gulf coast around the Keys and up the Atlantic coast to chilly Newfoundland. It was with these settlements in mind that Menéndez had enlisted over one hundred farmers in the enterprise and had carefully recorded the secondary trades of his soldiers, from the 21 tailors and 16 carpenters to the one man who could make hats.

Ceremonies were quickly concluded and the Spanish returned to the urgent task of offloading the *San Pelayo* so she could go south to Santo Domingo before the enemy arrived. Arms and ammunition were put ashore, but the bulk of the foodstuffs was still deep in the hold when Menéndez ordered the crew to make sail. The great galeass set off for Hispaniola with Ribault and the French fleet in pursuit just hours behind. Menéndez had a second reason for hurrying off his flagship. Long experience in Caribbean waters told him that a hurricane was brewing. His only son, Juan, had been lost off these coasts in such a storm.

Knowing it would be days before Ribault could beat back against the wind to attack St. Augustine, the adelantado and a column of five hundred fighting men marched forty miles north to the French base at Fort Caroline, with burly Basque axemen clearing the way. Rain fell in sheets, streams rose and in places the men walked through water up to their chests, holding their weapons overhead. They arrived on the twentieth of September before dawn. Most of the French sentinels, left behind by Ribault because they were ill, had gone inside out of the rain.

Menéndez's men forced the main gate and burst into the fort. Some forty-five of the defenders escaped over the palisades, among them Laudonnière and the artist Jacques LeMoyne. The Spanish cut down the others in their nightshirts, sparing only women and children. The next day Indians brought in more Frenchmen found hiding in the woods and some of these were held for ransom. Not knowing where Ribault would reappear, Menéndez left most of his men to guard the captured supplies in the fort, which he renamed San Mateo, and returned to finish fortifying St. Augustine.

A week later, Indians brought him startling news. On the beach eighteen miles south of St. Augustine were many Frenchmen. Three of Ribault's ships had been wrecked in the vicinity of present-day Ponce de Leon Inlet and the survivors had walked up as far as Anastasia Island. With one company of soldiers Menéndez went to confront the "Lutherans." Through an interpreter he informed them that he had taken their fort and as their enemy was bound to exterminate them. The Frenchmen, with no alternative but to starve, surrendered, and Menéndez, who had neither guards nor provisions for over a hundred prisoners, put them to the sword.

Soon there was even less food on hand, when Fort San Mateo, Spanish for less than a month, burned to the ground along with the captured provisions. The adelantado gave orders to rebuild it. A second group of castaways was reported below St. Augustine. They were from Ribault's flagship, the *Trinité*, grounded

intact near Cape Canaveral. When given the same choice as the
first group, half of these Frenchmen turned back the way they
had come. The others surrendered and again most of them were
killed, this time including Ribault. The inlet south of Anastasia
Island has been known ever since as Matanzas, "the Slaughters."

As soon as a ship could be spared Menéndez sent the fifty
Huguenot women and children from Fort Caroline to Puerto
Rico. Learning that the remaining French survivors were at
Cape Canaveral trying to refloat the *Trinité*, he took two
hundred fifty soldiers down the coast and seized their fort,
capturing seventy-five of the defenders. Leaving most of his
soldiers and prisoners at Indian River in Ais territory, he sailed
south to Havana to be rejoined by the rest of his expedition.
There he collected his scattered ships and proceeded to the
Florida Gulf coast to make contact with the Calusa Indians.

In less than three months the adelantado, aided by bad
weather, had rid Florida of the dangerous and schismatic French
and had established three beachheads: San Mateo, St. Augustine
and Ais. In these little forts, however, the first winter was a
starving time. At all three places food reserves ran short, and
from the southernmost one came tales of cannibalism. Supply
ships sank and soldiers mutinied, those of Ais moving south to a
new site, Santa Lucía. In the palm-thatched hovels of St.
Augustine and San Mateo people died of a disease that may
have been due to contaminated water, since the soldiers who
drank boiled sassafrass tea upon Indian advice were said to
remain well.

In the spring Menéndez returned to the east coast with the
ships and settlers who had missed the fall rendezvous. With them
he founded a settlement at Santa Elena on present Parris Island in
South Carolina. This place, more centrally located than St.
Augustine and having a better harbor, was to be his headquarters
and the first capital of Florida. Withdrawing the garrison at
Santa Lucía, he left a few troops in Guale, along the Georgia
seacoast, and a hundred fifty men each at San Mateo and St.
Augustine.

The natives of Seloy village were no longer lightheartedly
kneeling and kissing hands. The novel strangers had overstayed

their welcome. A lone soldier fishing with a handline was easy to drown; a settler foraging for swamp cabbage made a good target. The Spanish cattle, kept on an island, were wantonly killed despite the war dogs set every night to guard them. St. Augustine's first fort was set on fire, reportedly by flaming arrows, and partly destroyed. When the Spanish started a second fort, perhaps too near the water, the sea began to eat under it even before it was finished, and the palisades were dug up and moved some distance back.

These forts are thought to have been located more or less near the site of the present castillo. Made of tree trunks, earth and fascines, which were bundles of branches, the earlier ones, like Fort Caroline, were triangular in plan. The fort that was moved back from the water's edge was at the same time enlarged to accommodate the gear of a larger garrison, for Admiral Sancho de Archiniega had arrived from Spain with mountains of supplies and a thousand men, reinforcements sent by Philip II. Half of the total troops Menéndez divided among his forts in Florida; the others he used to strengthen the defenses of ports in Puerto Rico, Hispaniola and Cuba against attack by a rumored French fleet.

When the alarm passed, the extra manpower was reassigned to the task of exploring the lands, seacoasts and waterways of Florida. The St. Johns River was followed upstream to where the Indians closed it off with sharpened stakes. Captain Juan Pardo led expeditions from Santa Elena far into western Alabama, leaving small garrisons along his route. Pedro Menéndez Marquez, a nephew of the adelantado, explored the Atlantic coast up to Newfoundland, and the Gulf coast as far as River Pánuco on the borders of New Spain, today's Mexico. Lieutenants carried forward these explorations because the king had called his most important naval advisor back to Spain for a new assignment.

Before leaving, the adelantado took stock of what he and his kinsmen had so far accomplished. In outposts along the coast of south Florida, Jesuits were beginning the work of conversion. There were three fledgling settlements, each with a deputy governor and a substantial garrison. A supply network of a hundred fifty men and ten vessels ranged as far as Yucatan for corn, salt meat and cassava. To guide his lieutenants in his absence, Menéndez issued the Ordinances of Governance, Florida's first European code of laws, and to develop his towns into full-fledged municipalities he set up councils, or *cabildos*, with the power to collect taxes and distribute lots.

The oldest part of St. Augustine may date from this time. Auger surveys and test excavations have shown where it was laid out, on the highest available ground between the Matanzas and San Sebastian rivers. The original grid pattern can still be seen south of the plaza where the streets are narrow and the blocks small. The lots were 44 by 88 feet, the *peonía* size recommended for commoners by the 1563 Ordinances for Town Planning. Each lot had its own well lined with end-to-end barrels to keep the sand from caving in, and near the well was the current trash pit, for Spanish refuse was buried. The houses were still nothing special—half-timbered structures of wattle and daub with cypress supports and straw or palmetto thatch—but for so new a frontier the town showed promise.

At court, the king rewarded his adelantado with incomes and honors, had him sit for a portrait by Titian, and made him governor of Cuba in addition to Florida. Ordered to design and command an armada for the defense of the Indies, Menéndez began to build twelve great ships to be named for the twelve apostles.

In Florida the conquest was going badly. The two forts in Saturiba territory, St. Augustine and San Mateo, were subject to constant assault. French privateer Dominique de Gourgues appeared off Cumberland Island, made contact with the natives and helped them to destroy the rebuilt Fort San Mateo and its outlying batteries. As hostilities spread, the Spanish began to classify Florida as a land of living war. At the outposts of the interior the soldiers were driven out or massacred; so were the ones in south Florida. Weighing converts against martyrs, the Jesuits left in 1571. They had failed to make headway in south Florida, or in Guale and Santa Elena, or still later in their mission at Axacán on the Chesapeake (where after another thirty-six years the English would plant Jamestown).

Pedro Menéndez de Avilés, appointed by the Spanish crown "Adelantado, Governor and Captain General of Florida," founded St. Augustine in 1565.

In Spain, Menéndez contracted to make a second conquest, this time of the Gulf coast around to Pánuco. He found time to recruit more farmers for Santa Elena, mostly among Spain's *labradores*, or sharecroppers. To encourage the settlement of persons of noble blood so the new colony could be suitably governed, he asked for royal offices in Florida for the members of his clan. He also arranged for Franciscan friars to take the place of the Jesuits. But he was never to see the results of his endeavors, for he died in 1574 at the shipyards of Santander.

Already the Council of the Indies had begun taking steps to convert the Menéndez family's lord proprietorship to a regular Crown colony. As early as 1570 financial arrangements had been clarified and a subsidy instituted similar to the one supporting the Menéndez armada. In theory at least, the king's soldiers and seamen in Florida would be entitled to regular wages, to be paid from the revenues of some more solvent colonial treasury.

At the adelantado's chosen capital of Santa Elena, Indian attacks forced the settlers to abandon first their farms, then their fort, and take refuge in St. Augustine. It was 1576, and the eleven-year-old settlement to which they fled was in a poor state. The eighty ablebodied men in St. Augustine had been unable to protect their homes from Timucuan assaults. All the houses had been torn down and a hundred women and children were sheltered in the fort.

At this crucial time the Council of the Indies named as governor Pedro Menéndez Marquez, despite his record in Cuba of able chicanery for the clan. The new governor prefabricated a fort in St. Augustine, took it up to Santa Elena and reestablished the northern garrison. The Indians of the Santa Elena area were forced to make peace and hand over some prize captives, the survivors of a French shipwreck who had been living among them as military advisors. Menéndez Marquez, practical rather than visionary, reduced the scope of conquest by abandoning for the time being his family's claims to Pánuco, the Chesapeake and distant Newfoundland. St. Augustine was his seat of government and the headquarters for his constant campaigns. For St. Augustine the governor obtained a license to send one ship a year to Spain with exports not to exceed two thousand ducats in value, a small but significant breach in the House of Trade monopoly of New World commerce. It was

Menéndez Marquez, not his famous uncle, whom the local people remembered as the conqueror of Florida.

In the 1580's there was, at long last, peace with the local Indians. St. Augustine's three hundred inhabitants began to set out fruit trees in their yards, graze cattle on the commons, and plant corn in their assigned garden plots. A soldier standing his six-hour watch on the second story of the rectangular wooden fort must have found it pleasant to look south across the commons toward the weathered church, and beyond the church-yard to the town with its flowering orange trees and its hundred or so closely-spaced houses, opening onto their piazzas instead of onto the narrow, lane-like streets, and then to look left toward the bayfront, with a frigate unloading at the wharf and fishnets drying in the sun. The church bell sounding the hours for prayer, and the smaller bell of the fort marking the watches told the soldier how long it would be until he was seated in his favorite tavern, listening to a few songs accompanied by guitar, gambling a little and companionably arguing with his friends over a cup of wine.

The town was not left in peace for long. In 1586 Sir Francis Drake, with 42 vessels and 2000 men, stopped by St. Augustine en route to England after the sack of Cartagena. Faced with these odds the Spanish buried their artillery in the sand and withdrew to the woods, in the confusion forgetting to take with them the royal coffer containing the payroll. Before Drake's men could get from the fort to the town, Indian looters had sacked it. The natives ventured back to barter and invite the English to stay, but the pirates, finding nothing else of interest, cut down the orange trees, trampled the gardens, burned the houses and left.

Drake's raid had an unforeseen consequence. The settlers of Santa Elena, who had twice rebuilt their own town, were ordered to move to St. Augustine, consolidating the forces in Florida. They were recompensed by the Crown for the loss of their corrals, granaries, gardens and houses in Santa Elena. New fields were cleared and planted at St. Augustine, and a new section of lots was laid out, probably west of town. This time most of the houses were built of vertical boards, rough and unpainted, but an improvement over wooden sticks daubed with clay. The "noble and loyal city," as St. Augustine was called on occasions of ceremony, was now the sole city of Spaniards in Florida. As a fortified settlement in a military district upon which it was dependent, it came under the classification of a *presidio.*

Before the people from Santa Elena could settle in, the town was once again flooded with refugees. Five galleons of the treasure fleet had been wrecked on the Florida coast and hundreds of castaways came for shelter in St. Augustine. Food reserves were insufficient for the emergency, and the town was visited by a famine which was relieved by the Christian Indian *cacica,* doña María Meléndez, who ruled her people from the mission pueblo of Nombre de Dios and was married to a Spanish soldier. The Council of the Indies thanked her for the gifts of corn with five hundred ducats' worth of red cloth, an important trade commodity.

The Indians of Guale had corn in their granaries, and their land also produced medicinal herbs: sassafrass and sarsaparilla (china root), regarded as specifics for syphilis. In the late 1580's a campaign was launched to bring their district into the Spanish orbit. To convert the Guales the number of Franciscans in Florida rose in six years from five to fourteen, and most of the friars were stationed in Guale.

Without Pedro Menéndez in Spain to recruit colonists, Florida no longer received families of settlers, only bachelor soldiers. In the social scheme of 16th-century Europe, a company of soldiers was formed under the leadership of a captain and each member received a share of the spoils of battle according to the assets he brought the company in horses, weapons and armor. When there was no booty the men drew, through their captain, a pittance of wages. It was highly unusual for one to settle down somewhere and raise a family. In Florida, however, some soldiers did double duty as colonists who contracted permanent unions and increased the population.

In the early years the Crown made an effort to encourage

Spanish marriages at the presidio by having the governors bring
with them a dozen or so Spanish women of good reputation. Yet
there were not enough women to go around, and most of the
soldiers in 16th-century St. Augustine continued to live in mess
groups, or *camaradas*, of four or five men. Possibly a third of
the households in town included a female, and perhaps half of the
women were Indians, whose food-finding and cooking skills
made them admirable mates. Archaeological remains show that
in the domestic sphere, Indian cooking ware and methods
predominated in an outwardly Spanish town. By the turn of the
century, when births had brought the sex ratio nearer to equili-
brium and intermarriage between Spaniards and Indians began
to be discouraged, a good proportion of native-born St. Augustinians, though they liked to forget the fact, were part Indian—
technically, *mestizos*.

Other ethnic elements existed in the little town. Black slaves of
the king worked on the fortifications almost from the beginning.
The well-to-do had slaves of their own; most of these were
black, but some were Indians enslaved in a "just war" somewhere else in the empire, and in the early days a few may have
been Moorish. The Spanish empire was a cosmopolitan one, in
which religious orthodoxy mattered more than national origin.
St. Augustine had its share of European diversity. Many of the
best skippers and pilots in town were Portuguese; at least twice
the resident surgeon was French, and at one time a single ship
introduced an Irish priest, six German artillerists and an English
fifer.

In 1597 Florida received a third strong governor: Gonzalo
Méndez de Canzo, trained in the Menéndez armada. Governor
Méndez instituted regular gifts to the Spaniards' Indian allies and
in return asked for a yearly levy of laborers to raise corn in the
presidio environs. It was an extension of the Indians' own system
of communal fields, by which they supported their chiefs and
healers and provided for widows and orphans. Perhaps it was
the governor's wife, doña Magdalena de Luaces y Estoa (described in her travel papers as having a "good figure and large
eyes"), who suggested that he build a horse-drawn grist mill to
relieve St. Augustine women of the interminable task of grinding

corn for the day's ashcakes and thickened stews. Méndez also opened a public market, repaired the church, and built a small hospital complete with a chapel and an elderly black female nurse. There was still much fever in town, which he attributed to the water.

While the governor himself was ill, rebellion broke out among the wild Surruques to the south and the Guales of the town of Tolomato to the north. In both cases, he thought, the unrest had been fomented by the French whose ships continually visited the coasts to trade with the Indians for amber and sassafrass. In 1599, the same year that Spaniards were burning the towns of Guale and Surruque rebels, their own city was devastated. First a fire swept through the Franciscan friary and some sections of town, then the sea rose during a hurricane and carried away many houses. In that storm a sheltering island in the harbor disappeared and most of the Indians of a nearby village were drowned. The sandbar shifted to make the inlet even more shallow. Until the time of modern dredging the harbor would be closed to any ship of over a hundred tuns except, perhaps, a flat-bottomed Dutch flyboat.

The compounded disasters gave Governor Méndez an opportunity to rebuild St. Augustine his way. South of town he laid out more lots. North of town he marked out a plaza large enough for a parade ground and around it built a guardhouse, a warehouse-treasury, and a governor's house. To add to the cultivable land he drained the swamp called "El Gran Mosquitero." In order to finance this ambitious program, the governor used the royal share of local tithes, tapped the fund called "goods of the deceased" (from soldiers who died intestate), and levied a contribution on the citizens whose homes were still standing. For loggers and sawyers he used the 56 slaves of the Crown, an unknown number of sentenced convicts, some of them former rebels from Guale, the not-too-willing two hundred fifty soldiers of the garrison, and extra shifts of Indians, the latter paid a stipulated amount of trade goods: red cloth, iron knives or fat glass beads.

The friars, who like the Indians were paid in goods rather than money, were fortunate that their small allowances kept pace with the cost of living. In the late 1590's the price of imported foodstuffs, especially wheat flour, began to soar. The soldiers, whose daily ration was limited to what two and a half *reales* would buy and whose wages were rigidly fixed by the Crown, became increasingly dependent upon local foods to feed their families. A soldier's issue of bread (which he liked to soak in vinegar and olive oil and eat with radishes and onions) and his salt meat and wine, having become too valuable for everyday consumption, may have been bartered for family necessities.

The common folk ate Indian corn, kidney beans and pumpkins, stewed up with local fish, shellfish and wild game—often the opossums or raccoons caught raiding their gardens—and seasoned with onions, garlic and red peppers. Their drink, like the Indians', was the caffeine-rich cassina. For treats they had the oranges, peaches, pomegranates, mulberries, grapes and figs that grew abundantly in their fenced yards. Only a royal official or a moneylender could afford expensive imported delicacies such as quince paste, hazelnuts or chocolate.

In Spain, reports to the Council of the Indies of rebellions and natural disasters revived an old discussion about whether or not to continue supporting a presidio in St. Augustine. Cuban governor Pedro de Valdés, commanded to make an investigation, sent his son Fernando to Florida to take the testimony of veteran friars, soldiers and officials. The decision, apparently by default, was to leave things as they were. It was 1602, and the "noble and loyal city" was becoming a place of some standing, as colonial places went. There were eighty families there, according to Governor Méndez, and each family owned from two to ten cows. The Crown might look for tax revenues from the colony, thought some experts, for the original royal treasury officials, drawn from the Menéndez family enterprise and armada, had been replaced, and the treasury's built-in idiosyncracies had been tempered by the recent visit of a royal auditor.

The death of Queen Elizabeth I of England in 1603 heralded a period of peace in Europe among the kingdoms of Spain, France and Great Britain. In the New World, unemployed soldiers and seamen turned determinedly to piracy, making any voyage by sea an adventure. Pedro de Ybarra, a Basque gentleman on his way to be governor of Florida, was pursued by several English vessels in the Caribbean. He escaped in his ship's launch and was tossed about on the open sea for five days only to be captured by the same pirates when he reached shore. They robbed him and dropped him off in a deserted Cuban cove. Living off of crabs, snails and wild fruit, Ybarra walked to Havana, borrowed a shirt and a frigate from the governor of Cuba, and continued to his post.

The new Basque governor's efforts to fix a personal monopoly on the amber and sassafrass trade brought him into conflict with royal officials, Franciscan friars, Cuban traders and French merchant seamen who, since their country was at peace with Spain and no corsairs were being licensed, were technically trespassers and pirates. One of the St. Augustine skippers on a routine run trapped a shipload of Frenchmen trading with the natives at the Savannah River. Ybarra awarded himself fifteen hundred ducats prize money for the ship and distributed the twenty-one French prisoners among his Indian allies to be fed. The law required that they hang, but Ybarra hoped the Crown would relent and let him collect the ransoms. Furthermore, St. Augustine was expecting its first episcopal visit; the mighty arguments of Bishop Juan de las Cabezas Altamirano would surely restore the Huguenot heretics to the bosom of the Church and save their souls.

Ybarra had been urging the Crown to arrange this episcopal visit in order to bring the independent Franciscans into line, for some of them were openly defiant of civil authority. Father Gerónimo de Celaya's inflammatory preaching against the governor's amber monopoly was provoking the Indians to rebellion and the soldiers to mutiny. Father Alonso de Peñaranda, Ybarra's own confessor, was circulating the rumor that the governor was a defrocked friar.

Bishop Altamirano arrived in Florida in 1605, having survived several pirate scares and a hurricane that carried the ship sent for him far into the Cuban mangroves. What may have been the same storm had flattened and flooded much of St. Augustine, where the bishop's first act was to use the episcopal share of

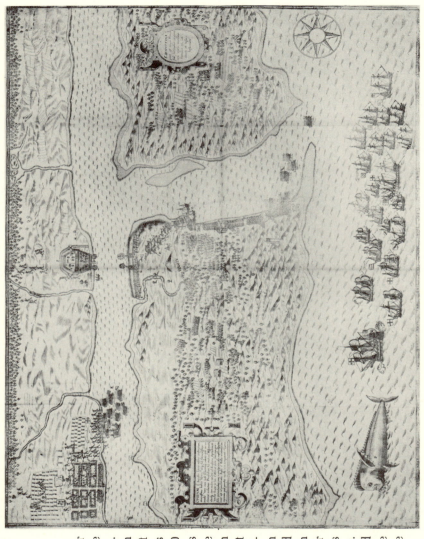

In 1586 Sir Francis Drake attacked St. Augustine with an English fleet of 42 vessels carrying 2000 men. In this map by Baptiste Boazio, the main part of the fleet is shown offshore, while in the channel and before the town (upper left) other smaller vessels discharge troops. Drake captured and burned the town and the fort.

parish tithes (probably in the form of dried beans and corn) to feed the homeless. In St. Augustine and Nombre de Dios he confirmed 370 Spaniards who were Florida-born, or *floridanos*, and 273 Indians.

The other pressing business was to deal with the pirates, on whom the Crown had refused to set ransom. Altamirano and the French-speaking Ybarra labored earnestly for the Huguenots' souls and were gratified when all but one of the condemned men returned to the Church to die Catholics. The executions were an edifying event in good 17th-century style, with the town's religious brotherhoods supplying processions and burials.

St. Augustine experienced a religious revival. There was agitation for a local branch of the Holy Office of the Inquisition to deal with any other schismatic pirates, but the bishop regarded this as an unnecessary luxury for so small a place. Ybarra considered the proposal a Franciscan scheme to introduce contraband to the colony as was done in other parts of the Indies where, claiming to represent the Inquisition, friars boarded incoming vessels and sealed boxes of imported goods under the pretext that they contained prohibited literature. More likely they were boxfuls of expensive clothing, a form of property prized by all classes of society because it was splendid and portable.

The mother country, hardpressed by Dutch rebels in the Spanish Netherlands, was undergoing a period of xenophobia. Between 1609 and 1614 the Moriscos, industrious people of Moorish descent, were expelled from Spain. In the New World, authorities were ordered to report all resident aliens, even the Portuguese, who from 1580 to 1640 shared the same royal house. In St. Augustine, which in 1607 had 28 Portuguese residents, 6 Germans, 20 Frenchmen and 2 Flemings, such a request was barely noted. A frontier town could not be particular about origins if it wanted the population to grow.

Juan Fernández de Olivera, arriving to be governor in 1610, marvelled at how few settlers there were in Florida, a country abundant in deer, wildfowl, fish, wild fruits and cultivated legumes. "The only bad thing about this land," he declared, "is the bad name it has been given!" St. Augustine in those days had the reputation of a place of exile for unruly officers and trouble-making friars. It was, moreover, something of a penal colony, with condemned criminals in evidence, rowing galleys and hauling firewood. Many of the soldiers also had records, for in order to fill the roster of the garrison, the Crown often swept its peninsular prisons clean of debtors and petty thieves, while the Viceroy of New Spain supplied vagrants and rioters of mixed blood and doubtful parentage. Even a conscript of good character was considered tainted by low class origins.

In any case, the frontier land of Florida was not the first choice of an emigrant who had heard of the rich kingdoms of New Spain and Peru. The English colonies, by contrast—first Virginia and Bermuda, then Massachusetts Bay and Barbados, and then Jamaica and Charles Town—exploded in population because Englishmen and Scots had nowhere better to go.

Governor Fernández had missed the colony's first forty-five years, when Florida was truly a land of living war. It had not been an easy mission field, the Franciscans wrote to the Crown. From the first, the Indians had hated Spaniards and mocked religion. They had exterminated good livestock as though it were vermin and rooted up unfamiliar trees and plants, "wishing to leave no trace nor smell of us." Heretic foreigners interested only in trade had been welcomed more warmly than the missionaries who were sacrificing to save native souls.

Things had finally begun to change. On Cumberland Island and the Guale coast, missions were rooted as firmly as in the Timucuan villages near St. Augustine. In them the Indians learned to read and write and attended prayers and singing school. A gunboat campaign against the warlike Indians of the Gulf coast had stopped their riverine raiding of the frontier, and it had become possible to open new missions among the Timucuan tribes of central Florida. It was understood that mission advance must be accompanied by military presence; as soon as Governor Fernández had soldiers to spare, the friars intended to extend conversions into the rich region of Apalache, around present Tallahassee, and some of them were already learning the Apalache language. In recognition of this progress

the Florida mission field was raised within the Franciscan Order
to the rank of province and joined to Cuba as the Province of
Santa Elena.

Members of the St. Augustine garrison were frequently de-
tached to mission stations as bodyguards for the friars. They also
did terms of duty on board ship, making the frequent trips to
Havana and Vera Cruz for supplies, to Spain with dispatches, or
to show the flag and trade along Florida's miles of coastline.
After a storm the presidio boats were sent out to scour the coast
for the survivors of shipwreck and, perhaps as importantly, for
salvageable cargoes and ships' artillery. It was in this sense that
St. Augustine was essential to the yearly Fleet of the Indies
which sailed majestically up the Gulf Stream well out of sight,
sixty miles off shore. The town's little harbor functioned as a
station of the Spanish coastguard, the only one along six hundred
miles of strategic sea lane.

Ensign Juan Rodríguez de Cartaya was carrying messages to
Spain in 1613 in the St. Augustine-built frigate *San Juan Bautista*,
when his men sighted a huge Portuguese *naõ* listing to her side,
sails lowered. She was a dreaded plague ship. Two hundred of
her five hundred-man crew had died and been thrown over-
board; the others, too weak to man the pumps or raise the sails,
had drifted with the ship out of the East Indian trade route
skirting Africa to the return route from the West Indies. Rodríguez and his crew, at the risk of their lives, climbed the
steep ladder, put the naõ in order and sailed her to Sagres in
Portugal, towing their frigate like a pull-toy behind them. Philip
III, king of Portugal and Spain, rewarded their heroism as was
fitting.

In the southeast also the plague was beginning to spread,
perhaps carried ashore by rats; they lived on sea-going ships by
the thousand. In the next four years half of the sixteen thousand
converted Indians in Florida and uncounted numbers of other
natives died of the plague in this unidentified form. Friars
hurrying with the Viaticum from one deathbed to another urged
that the survivors be gathered into fewer towns, closer together.
Spaniards did not escape the scourge. Franciscans died, as well

as soldiers, and seamen's places were filled only with family men or Indians, for anyone else would desert at the first foreign port. The beautiful land of Florida seemed accursed.

Ironically, it was only after this demographic disaster that the Spanish were successful in raising cattle in Florida, grazing them on the old fields of deserted villages. The cargo limit of St. Augustine's yearly ship-of-permission was raised from two thousand to three thousand ducats' worth of "fruits of the land," mainly cured cowhides. Buildings in the small town still looked little like what we see now. The houses of rough lumber decayed within a few years and were replaced by others of the same sort or of "tabby," a mixture of lime, sand and shell aggregate poured into board forms around vertical poles. Here and there was a roof of shingle instead of thatch, but St. Augustine had not yet entered the picturesque age of plastered coquina.

In the 1620's, while Pilgrims struggled with the rocky soil of New England, settlers in Florida were combatting pirates and hurricanes. The great storm of 1622 was responsible for the loss of many ships between the Keys and Bermuda. For years thereafter the Spanish were salvaging bullion from the wreck sites. Dutch and English corsairs, aware of these operations, hung about Cape Canaveral like sharks, waiting to chase the returning frigates onto the shoals. Indians of the coast below St. Augustine welcomed and traded with these interlopers as they came ashore for wood and water; they gave short shrift to a Spanish castaway. No help could be expected from the Crown, embroiled in the Dutch wars. Instead, St. Augustine found its reinforcements and war matériel diverted to other garrisons. Its subsidy, cut to the bone, fell several years behind. It was a time of short rations and even shorter wages. More than one supply ship attempting to elude the corsairs ran aground on the St. Augustine sandbar. The low point was reached when the Dutch corsair Piet Heyn captured the entire Fleet of the Indies off the coast of Cuba with the 1627 subsidies for all the Caribbean; there was no money to replace them.

Harassed from the sea, the Spaniards in Florida turned their energies inland. The Franciscans made dramatic, unapproved entrances into new territory with banners flying and escorts of arquebus-armed Indians. There was a resurgence of exploration.

During the term of Governor Luis de Rojas y Borja alone, three successive parties of Spaniards and Indians were sent to check out old tales of silver and gold mines, hills with diamonds, and lagoons of freshwater pearls. The third expedition relocated fabled Cofitachequi, which De Soto had visited and robbed eighty-two years earlier. But the 1620's were to be a period of contraction in the New World, not expansion, and the Crown refused to give Rojas y Borja permission to extend the Florida conquest two hundred leagues northward into the land of the pearls.

An eyewitness observer of St. Augustine about this time reported that the fort was little more than a stockade, with walls so dry that firing one of the guns would have set them aflame. In times of danger the women and children were sent among the Indians. Those natives, the writer continued, were the most enviable ones in the New World, since in Florida there were no workhouses or mines and no service except a little in the soldiers' fields, for which the Indians were paid. They did not owe any tribute; instead the king spent thousands of ducats a year on gifts for them, while the friars cared lovingly for their souls. It was a mystery to him how the natives could be dying off in Florida in the manner of Indians elsewhere.

In truth, the Indians near St. Augustine were beginning to find the Spanish something of a problem, one which increased as their own numbers declined. Because Florida had no beasts of burden, Indians were drafted to carry goods on their backs, sometimes as far as seventy leagues to the farthest missions of Timucua. Every expedition or campaign meant another call for baggage carriers and auxiliary warriors. Uprisings were dealt with severely. The people of Tolomato village, whose fathers had started the Guale rebellion in 1597, were still in exile, digging a canal to open an inland waterway north from St. Augustine to the missions of the coast. In 1627, at the ferry town of San Juan del Puerto near the old site of Fort Caroline, a cacica had her warriors free her brother from some Spanish soldiers, then escaped into hiding. She was tracked down, brought to the presidio for trial, and hanged. Her supporters were condemned to hard labor in Havana, with their ears docked.

The depopulation and decline of the missions near St. Augustine was offset in 1633 when Governor Luis de Horruytiner approved the evangelization of Apalache, a land both populous and fertile. Its northern Gulf port, he said, would provide the Fleet of the Indies with a refuge from storms and corsairs and would serve as a supply depôt for the distant Timucuan missions. The food supply for St. Augustine's some five hundred inhabitants would be assured. Boatloads of corn would leave the Apalache port, be rowed up the Suwannee and Santa Fe rivers to a point near present Gainesville, and from there be carried overland to the capital.

What Governor Horruytiner did not mention was the growing market of Havana, a short week's sail from the proposed port. In the advance of Christianity and the extension of the king's domains, Horruytiner had scented a personal profit and he was not wrong. His descendants, allied to the important floridano family of the Florencias, remained prominent in Florida for the next hundred thirty years, sharing in the lucrative Gulf trade. The officials of the royal treasury, similarly connected with the Florencias, neglected their account books and applied themselves to trade and to ranching.

The Franciscans, deeply in debt for the travel expenses of new missionaries, saw in Apalache not only a fresh mission field but a way out of their financial difficulties. Their efforts to keep soldiers out of Apalache Province were not solely to protect neophyte converts from evil examples and exploitation. The friars intended to be the middlemen for marketing that province's agricultural surplus and to devote the profits to their own worthy projects. This intent brought them into bitter conflict with each succeeding governor, a conflict that would last as long as the missions themselves.

Horruytiner's last year as governor, 1638, was notable for two disasters: the worst storm to hit St. Augustine in thirty years, and the kidnapping of the Florida subsidy by none less than the king. Philip IV, in desperate financial straits on account of the Thirty Years' War, ordered the captain general of the fleet carrying the Caribbean subsidies to bring them to him in Spain and to give the waiting garrison agents promissory notes instead of money for their creditors and payrolls.

Map of late 16th-century St. Augustine, drawn by an unknown cartographer. At right center is the wooden fort, at left is the village of houses with vertical board walls and thatched roofs. A wooden wharf extends into the Matanzas River.

The result in Florida was financial chaos. For the next thirty years there was almost no circulation of money. Merchants in Havana raised their prices to Florida buyers and supplied them with inferior goods. Speculators bought up the dubious certificates that the soldiers received in lieu of wages, for as little as a third of face value. The soldiers of the presidio and all tradesmen who depended on their business fell hopelessly into debt. When currency again became available, the wary subsidy agents spent it in New Spain to forestall a second seizure, while the skippers of Florida's supply ships learned to avoid Havana, where the presidio's creditors waited at the docks to impound cargoes.

The government in Madrid had little time for the problems of Florida. Iberia itself seemed to be splitting apart in 1640, with both Portugal and Catalonia in rebellion. Small and unprofitable colonies must shift for themselves. In St. Augustine there followed years of famine when the corn harvests failed and no ship brought relief. The wooden fort rotted, artillery rusted, and the soldiers went wrapped in blankets for lack of coats.

Without their regular presents from the Crown the Guale Indians, who had never liked to live in towns year-around, began to drift off to inland hunting grounds. Unfamiliar bands of Indians displaced by English activity to the north wandered into Spanish territory. These were the Chiscas, or, more generally, the "Chichimecos," a catch-all term for barbaric marauders that the Spanish had learned in New Spain. The governor hoped to control these nomads with a frank invitation to serve the presidio as mercenaries. Instead, the Chiscas united with the four out of five Apalache chiefs who in 1647 were still not Christian, and killed three friars and the deputy governor with his family. Francisco Menéndez Marquez, a floridano and an official of the treasury, defeated the rebels with the aid of sixty Timucuans and obligated them, Christian and non-Christian alike, to labor service at the presidio.

With this conquest of Apalache the Florida provinces reached their fullest extent. Later attempts to expand the borders by placing missionaries farther south in Mayaca and Jororo, northwest in Apalachicola, or southwest in Calusa territory, were unsuccessful. Only the provinces of Guale, Timucua and Apalache achieved administrative maturity within the Spanish system, each of them consisting of a loose federation of Indian pueblos speaking the same language. The chiefs of the towns in a province met occasionally in council to deliberate on common problems.

The Franciscan friars lived by twos in the major towns of a province and visited the lesser ones. They, too, had a provincial council. The deputy governor commanded a garrison detachment in the most important town, where he coordinated military matters and labor assessments with the chiefs, purchased and stored provisions for St. Augustine, and conducted quiet commerce. Small settlements of floridano families grew up around the garrisons. Farther out, the floridanos leased Indian lands and bred horses or ranched. This spreading out of the Spanish-speaking population has been under-reported since, wherever a floridano lived, he remained a citizen of St. Augustine and a member of the one church parish. What else would he be, when that was the only town of Spaniards east of Santa Fé?

Someone who spent more time on his estates than in St. Augustine on the job was Governor Benito Ruíz de Salazar y Vallecilla. Ruíz had earned the governorship of Florida by contracting to build a five-hundred-tun galleon for the Crown and he hoped to recoup his costs by large-scale agricultural production on the Gulf coast, as near as possible to Havana. As one of his ventures he started a wheat farm beside the Aucilla River, and to keep all the profits at home, sent to the Canaries for millstones and a miller to make his wheat into flour. The tithes from farms like this, he boasted, would soon be enough to support an abbot.

He would learn that economic enterprise in Florida was always at the mercy of war, weather and disease. The fleet that left Vera Cruz for Cuba in the spring of 1649 carried mosquito larvae in its water casks, and they bore yellow fever. The epidemic killed one third of the inhabitants of Havana and moved north. Unlike earlier diseases, which had concentrated on the native population, this one bore down on the Spanish. Central authority at the presidio all but disappeared. Many, perhaps most, of the friars died of the "black vomit," as did the two company captains, the two treasury officials, the sergeant major and Governor Ruíz.

The interim officers, all floridanos, met and elected one of their number, Pedro Benedit Horruytiner, who repaid them with forty-four promotions creating, among other things, twenty-two new captains. When Interim Governor Horruytiner went out of the city so much as to visit his cornfield, the fort banner dipped in salute and a salvo was fired. At the request of the Franciscans, who wanted no other Spaniards in the provinces, Horruytiner dismantled the Ruíz farms, selling slaves, horses, oxen and tools for half their value. He also withdrew the garrison from Apalache, leaving the friars and chiefs free to trade with the Dutch and English. Without a military presence on the Gulf, foreigners would take over coastal commerce there as they already had in the Caribbean. The next royal governor put the garrison back.

Yellow fever in Florida was followed by an epidemic of smallpox in which every one of the royal slaves died. Of two hundred Timucuans who one year came to their labor service, only ten survived to return home. As if this were not enough, a windstorm beat down the ripening corn in the fields and there was a famine. The seventy Franciscan missionaries in Florida, taking stock in 1655, could count only twenty-six thousand Christian Indians left in their thirty-eight missions.

In that year, 1655, Oliver Cromwell's forces captured Jamaica, sending a thrill of terror through the Spanish Caribbean. Even if the English were content with one island there would now be no rest from their privateering. No help could be expected from the king, who had again kept back part of Florida's money. To strengthen the defenses of St. Augustine, Governor Diego de Rebolledo called up five hundred Guale and Timucuan auxiliaries. The Guales arrived without provisions and were rationed on mouldy hardtack. The Timucuans, reminded to bring seventy-five pounds of corn apiece, strenuously objected. Their chiefs could not be ordered to bear burdens for they were noblemen, exempt like the Spanish *hidalgos* from common labor. They could lose this status only by committing a crime. Rebolledo, impatient with these distinctions, repeated his order with threats.

The chiefs of Timucua rose in rebellion, killing seven soldiers. The Guales, declining to help the governor punish them, announced that the biscuits were making them sick and went home. The rebellion spread, with the tacit approval of many friars. Throughout Timucua Province towns were deserted and bands of hungry people wandered about sacking mission buildings and rustling cattle. Disease, starvation and wholesale emigration were what really ended the "Great Rebellion," although Rebolledo brought it to a formal end by executing eleven ringleaders. The friars, however, had the last word. In response to their letters the Crown ordered the arrest and punishment of Rebolledo for provoking the natural lords of the land to rebellion and cruelly hanging them.

In the year 1659 an epidemic of measles visited Florida and, by one estimate, ten thousand Indians died of that disease alone. The survivors in Timucua Province were gathered into towns along the transpeninsular road to operate the ferries and maintain the overland link with Apalache. That province's produce was more essential than ever to St. Augustine, from which, like a colony, it was trying to break away.

A band of Chichimecos went on a rampage in Guale, burning churches and killing Christians. They had been set in motion by white settlements to the north and were one of many such shock waves to strike the Spanish provinces. There was little to deter them. By the 1660's Florida was becoming a hollow peninsula, virtually deserted between St. Augustine and Apalache except for the cattle ranches from which hides and tallow were exported to Havana.

The population of St. Augustine, on the other hand, had recovered and was gradually growing. There were seven hundred inhabitants in the city, of whom three hundred were on the garrison payroll. Only one hundred thirty of that number were common soldiers, for included in the payroll were the mariners, the officers, the treasurer and accountant, a surgeon, barber and apothecary, a smith, armorer and locksmith, the rations notary, the slave overseer, the chaplain, the parish priest and his assistants, and 43 of the 70 friars.

The English were making contacts among the Indians of the

southeast to prepare the way for a new colony, "Carolana." One of the scouts was the physician John Henry Woodward, who could understand five Indian languages. The Spanish governor was surprised to receive a letter from him in Latin requesting baptism and political asylum. Indians brought Woodward to town, where parish priest Francisco de Sotolongo, a graduate of the University of Mexico, made the learned doctor his guest for the period of catechism.

There was another foreign doctor in town, the French surgeon Pierre Piquet. When war was declared between France and Spain in 1667, Piquet took passage on a supply ship leaving Florida. Off the coast of Cuba the ship was seized by Jamaican privateers to whom Piquet offered interesting information. A military engineer from New Spain, using native divers at the wreck of a treasure ship, had recovered a number of silver bars which were even then in the royal coffer at St. Augustine.

The privateers, led by their captain, Robert Searles, sailed the captured ship up to the bar at St. Augustine as though she were returning with supplies. When the presidio launch came out to greet her, they kicked the crew below deck. In the dead of night a hundred cutthroats landed on the wharf below the plaza. Before the town was awake they had seized the guardhouse and the counting house, complete with 138 marks of silver. There were only 120 soldiers present in St. Augustine and their sergeant major, Nicolás Ponce de León II, took most of them with him into the woods while the privateers killed 60 persons in the streets, including Ponce's youngest daughter.

Governor Francisco de la Guerra y de la Vega slipped out a side door of his house and ran to the fort with the enemy at his heels. For what it was worth the fort was held, but the rest of the town was sacked. Captain Searles allowed the ransom of part of his prisoners, the wives and daughters of principal citizens, but refused to release St. Augustine's Indian, free black or mestizo residents, even those with Spanish fathers, saying that his license from the governor of Jamaica permitted him to sell as a slave anyone who was not a fullblooded Spaniard. The privateers took Dr. Woodward with them when they left town. They did not burn St. Augustine, which to the inhabitants meant only one thing: They would be back shortly to occupy it.

Parish priest Sotolongo laid the blame for the disaster squarely on Governor Guerra. For three years the bachelor governor had shamelessly kept a woman in his house. Because St. Augustine had tolerated this public sin, said the priest, God had visited the town with a drought, a storm, two ships lost, and this pirate attack, all in one year. The governor was guilty as charged. A royal appointee was forbidden to marry into the local families during his term, but this had not kept don Francisco from falling in love. His mistress was the highly connected doña Lorenza de Soto y Aspiolea, who bore him three children out of wedlock, each one adopted by the couple as a "child of parents unknown." Within a week of the next governor's arrival, don Francisco and dõna Lorenza were married.

This marriage of a floridana to a man from somewhere else was in the St. Augustine tradition. Between 1658 and 1670, 86 percent of the women whose marriages were recorded in the parish register were native born, but only a third of the men were, the rest being drawn about equally from the poorer regions of Spain (mainly Andalusia), and her other colonies (mostly New Spain).

The Searles raid of 1668, combined with the colonization of Carolina, persuaded the Council of the Indies to give Florida a larger share of the defense budget. A masonry fort for St. Augustine was something that had been proposed for seventy years and for which funds had been allocated, only to be diverted to more urgent needs as soon as they arrived. This time the Council resolved not only to approve the money for construction, but to increase the subsidy by the wages of 50 additional soldiers and to pay the 43 friars from other sources. This decision marked a new direction. Even so, it would be four more years before the multiple levels of the imperial bureaucracy could translate the Council's resolution into cash money, live troops, and a day of groundbreaking for the new stone fort.

Coquina quarrying on Anastasia Island has changed little over the centuries. The unique shell stone was dug by Indians and slaves to build Castillo de San Marcos and in the 19th century the workmen shown here used the same methods to cut and pry out the coquina.

Chapter Three

The Castillo Years
1668 - 1763

by

Jean Parker Waterbury

Nine months after the March 1669 decision to build the stone fort, the man who was to put that decision into action was appointed governor of Florida. Manuel de Cendoya had gotten as far as Mexico on his way from Spain to his new post when news came in mid-November from St. Augustine of a new English settlement, Charles Town. Despite that active threat, it was not until April 1671 that Cendoya finally obtained his needed men and funds for the fort and sailed for St. Augustine.

He reached the presidio in July and officially took over the province from Governor Guerra. The long process of constructing a stone fort started almost at once.

The basic material would be coquina, a shell stone soft enough to be quarried with pick and axe, but which hardened when exposed to the air over a period of time. Cendoya recruited Indians for his labor force, and set them to work on nearby Anastasia Island, hacking at the thickets and palmettos to get at the unusual stone which underlay so much of the island. Once quarried, the coquina was ferried across the bay; kilns for reducing oyster shells into the needed lime were built on the shore near the old fort.

St. Augustine had not seen so much activity since the night the pirates ransacked the town.

Finally in the fall of 1672 enough stone was cut, enough lime waited in barrels and construction could begin. Cendoya and the engineer, Ignacio Daza, with other worthies, voted that the castillo should rise just north of the old fort, opposite the inlet. Its design was the basic and traditional square, its four corners marked by bastions. Ground was broken for Castillo de San Marcos on Sunday afternoon, October 2, 1672.

Construction projects, the world over, are subject to inter-ruptions and delays. The castillo was no exception. There were illnesses among the Indians and late arrivals of the subsidy and other payments from Mexico; Daza the engineer and Cendoya the governor died within days of each other, and the great storm of 1674 dealt a serious blow to the town and the old fort when the waves, pounding at the rotting walls, brought the guns crashing down.

In May 1675 Pablo de Hita y Salazar arrived as the new governor. The new fort, he could see, was strong in some aspects: The northeast bastion was almost finished, the north curtain rose its full 20 feet, the east was 15 feet high and the south, 12. A good look to the west, and Hita set his priority. There, from the fort courtyard, one could look straight out into the woods. A moat came first: With the dirt dug from that, an earthwork was raised, faced with coquina to make it seem more substantial than it was.

Not long after his arrival, Hita had the unusual good fortune to learn directly about his widespread province, for Bishop Gabriel Díaz Vara Calderón of Cuba had recently returned to St. Augustine from months of travel among the Florida missions, west to Apalachicola and north along the Guale coast. Calderón was about to leave for Havana, but before he went, he and the governor must have sat late at night talking of Florida and its fortunes.

The bishop had come to St. Augustine the year before on the first episcopal visit in nearly sixty years, and what he had seen he would report to Queen Regent Mariana.

"It (St. Augustine) is almost cut off by an arm of the sea which surrounds it and buffets it, leaving it half submerged from hurricanes as it lies at sea level," he noted. He wrote of the weather, "very cold in winter, with freezes, and excessively hot in summer." There were other negative aspects: "The soil is sand and therefore unproductive; no wheat grows, and corn only sparsely and at the cost of much labor. Thus the inhabitants are compelled regularly to depend for their sustenance upon the products of the province of Apalache. The section does not produce any sort of raw material which could attract trade, and has no resources other than the government allowance which it awaits each year. . .''

However, with Indian labor, slaves and themselves, Floridians began to contribute to their food supply toward the end of the 17th century. Moving out from St. Augustine, they established cattle ranches west of the presidio, beyond the St. Johns River, farther out into the savannahs of central Florida, and on into Apalache. There was need for more beef as St. Augustine's population grew, and so the ranches prospered.

Pirates remained a fact of life for Florida, and St. Augustine caught their attention twice in the 1680's. A band of three hundred marauders landed near Matanzas Inlet in March 1683 but were discouraged after being caught in an ambuscade on Anastasia Island. Three years later the highly successful French pirate, Nicholas Grammont, tried his luck. He too was turned away in a skirmish, this one below Matanzas Inlet.

In both instances the pirates then sailed north to the St. Augustine inlet, but the walls of the stone castillo, in plain view from the sea, cancelled their attack plans. Castillo de San Marcos was successfully defending the town even in its unfinished state.

The comings and goings of pirates were short-lived crises; the less visible but ultimately more lethal enemy presence was growing to the north as the English moved down the Guale coast. Not only did the traders incite the Indians to destroy the Spanish missions, along with the missionaries, but they also penetrated far into the interior, opening up new possibilities for profitable Indian trade.

It was in answer to such encroachment that Governor Juan Márques Cabrera in August 1686 sent a force out from the castillo, augmented by loyal Indians and mulattoes; they destroyed the little English settlement at Port Royal in Carolina and moved on to deal with Charles Town. There a sudden storm so battered their ships that the attackers withdrew before any shot was fired.

Actions of the next governor, Diego de Quiroga y Losada, epitomized the uncertainties of Florida's future as a Spanish stronghold. By August 1687 the short rations on which the garrison and the town had been subsisting reached so low a point that within hours of Quiroga's arrival he dismissed the workmen at the castillo. There was no food for them.

Despite the troubles with the local Indians, whose allegiance was constantly under pressure from English traders, Quiroga hoped to develop Apalache as the granary for all Florida. To prove his point, it was corn from that area, received the next spring, which made possible a resumption of the castillo work.

If Apalache was to provide food, it would have to be defended, and to that end, in 1690 Quiroga established a block house on the Apalachicola River, only to order it destroyed and its small force withdrawn when St. Augustine was again threatened by pirates. The pirates never came, but the Apalachicola enterprise was abandoned.

Quiroga was at heart a builder, and St. Augustine was sadly in need of building. The presidio's population had grown with the arrival of the workmen for the castillo and more soldiers for its garrison; the early area of settlement, along the highest part of the peninsula between the Matanzas and the San Sebastian rivers, was crowded; soldiers and laborers began to move north, nearer the castillo.

A sorry official residence faced the plaza, in such a state when Quiroga arrived that His Excellency had no place to lay his head. A master carpenter said later that he had "repaired a passage where his lordship could just put his bed," but could do no more, "because there was no material for anything else." Other houses, official and private, were in the same or worse condition, their wooden frames invaded by insects and rot.

Coquina would last, Quiroga knew from even a brief inspection of the castillo walls, but that stone was reserved by royal decree for the fortifications. He petitioned the king, with attached testimony, for a relaxation of the ruling.

Juan Caleno, superintendent of the quarry for 18 years, swore before a notary that "the whole island (Anastasia) is a quarry, and have enough to build all the works of Your Majesty that might present themselves, and to fill all this post with houses of stone and four other cities and forts. . ."

Without waiting for official permission, Quiroga began selling raft loads of coquina rubble to the soldiers for their own small houses. Work began on the Governor's House and other important buildings around the plaza, using coquina blocks for the first floor walls, and wood when a second story was required.

It has been said that it was at this time that the "Stone Age" came to St. Augustine.

Troubles to the west and north continued with Indians and the English, but in St. Augustine there were enough crises right at hand to claim daily attention.

Petty as they might seem today, the troubles were worthy of report to the Crown, surviving along with accounts of greater events.

Friction between the parish priests and curates and the Franciscans was never far below the surface. In 1690 it erupted at the convent on what is today's St. Francis Street, when the head of the Franciscans refused to allow the priest, his clergy and their cross into the convent for two burials. In the first instance, the priest gave way rather than cause an open break, but when the wife of former Governor Hita y Salazar died later that spring, it was another matter. Custom decreed that the parish clergy should accompany the deceased to the burial, but the friars held to the letter of the religious law and informed the priest that when he tried to attend the funeral, he and his cross would be stopped at the door again.

Early the next day, Governor Quiroga stepped in. The heat of late May was bringing matters to a head, for the body was decomposing. Because of that, and because the governor had "interfered," the friars sent word that the priest and the parish cross would be allowed in the convent.

It was not many hours later that the priest, with the governor and townspeople, appeared at the convent entrance with the body and the cross. Despite the earlier agreement, again they were refused admittance. It took a reminder from the governor that he spoke for His Majesty the King and, as governor, he said the priest and the parish cross should enter the convent; the Franciscans could appeal where they liked.

On that note the priest, his cross, clergy and people entered the convent, placed the body in the convent's chapel, and with the governor, withdrew, Quiroga and his scribe to write a full report for the king.

A brief relaxing of tensions with the Carolina colony came in the mid-1690's, with the agreement that for the return of Spanish Indians captured by the Carolinians, any English shipwrecked on Florida shores could be free to go their way.

The English Quaker, Jonathan Dickinson, and his party were early beneficiaries of that agreement in the cold winter of 1696. Wrecked near Jupiter Inlet in September, the men and women who had been en route to Philadelphia now made their precarious way up the coast, harassed by most natives, occasionally aided by others. Half starved and freezing cold, they reached St. Augustine in mid-November, to be received there by Governor Laureano Torres y Ayala. "Seeing how extremely cold we were," Dickinson reported, the governor treated the party to Spanish wine and then sent them to the kitchen, the only warm room in the house, to thaw out.

Torres invited the Dickinson family and others to stay with him, the Quaker's *Journal* records, and townspeople "took such as they were mind to quarter in their houses . . . we perceived the people's great kindness" in providing clothes for the destitute party.

While the governor was arranging for canoes and an escort to take his visitors to Carolina, the Quakers went "all over the town and in many houses where they were kindly received and such as the people had they would give them."

Before long the little group of English were on their way up the inland waters, and St. Augustine settled back to its accustomed tensions of privation and poverty.

At the far edge of the Spanish colonial empire, St. Augustine was at the far edge, too, of Spanish cultural life. With barely enough food and barely enough money, the presidio was never able to enjoy the fiestas and amusements which gave a degree of relief to the rigors of colonial life elsewhere.

But on occasion, and by royal edict, the little town could celebrate a new monarch, or a royal marriage or birth. Ordered by the king, such celebrations had to be meticulously reported to Madrid.

Philip V had come to the throne in 1700, but it was not until January 1702 that Governor Josef de Zúñiga y Cerda officially proclaimed the event to the people of St. Augustine. To observe the occasion the town sparkled with candlelight, dancing and a considerable amount of eating and drinking at the governor's expense.

But before such gaiety, there was a formal ceremony, carefully practised in advance. The governor praised the new king, and then from one side of the plaza came the shout, *"Castilla Florida, Castilla Florida, por el rey católico, Don Felipe Quinto!"* Those stationed across the plaza had the easier role; their shouts were limited to *"Viva, viva, viva!"* After this exchange had been repeated three times, the dancing and drinking could commence.

Having cheered up his presidio in January, Zúñiga called on the people in March to observe the death of Philip's predecessor, Charles II, two years before.

Two days were set aside for the mourning; black crepe hung on buildings, and the parish church bell tolled from before daylight until 10 o'clock at night. There were masses said and there were the usual eulogies, all reported in detail to Madrid.

No matter what could have been said about Charles II in St. Augustine's parish church that March of 1702, it could not have matched the consequences of his death. That event had given immediate promise of a realignment of European powers unequaled in recent memory, for his successor, Philip V, was the grandson of the French king. The English particularly feared the potentials of a combined French-Spanish power in Europe and

North America. Locally that meant increased English forays into Florida while in St. Augustine, as one subsidy after another failed to arrive, there was often a state of near starvation.

That same March, Governor Zúñiga addressed an appeal to Philip. While the Council of the Indies studied his lists of desperately needed arms and munitions, the English in Carolina were gathering actual arms and munitions, an early move in what would become known as Queen Anne's War. The fiery Carolina governor, James Moore, in August argued for "the taking of St. Augustine before it be strengthened by french forses," and gathered several hundred Indians and somewhat more English, with supplies and fourteen vessels. Part of his force, under Colonel Robert Daniel, was to go up the St. Johns River, debark and march across country to attack St. Augustine from the west. Governor Moore would take the major part of the fleet through the St. Augustine inlet.

News of the English approach reached the presidio in October. Zúñiga, able administrator and soldier that he was, would have need of all his skills in the next weeks.

The English burned and destroyed the Spanish fort and mission at Amelia Island on their way south from Charles Town and seized the defenses at the mouth of the St. Johns in the first week of November, each disaster reported to Zúñiga and each day finding him organizing and improvising to meet the attack. Precious time was taken on November 1 to write once again to the Crown of St. Augustine's weaknesses and need for aid. When it was all over, Zúñiga succinctly reported to his king:

> "I collected in this fortress all the supply of corn from the harvests of the neighboring settlers, . . . and a large drove of cattle on the hoof was brought in and lodged in the moat, to extend the supplies of salt meat, together with some flour and biscuits. . ."

Such supplies would be essential. No provisions had been received in the town since August, and somehow the people would have to be fed in the castillo. Shelter was another essential. With planking and shingles originally intended for the

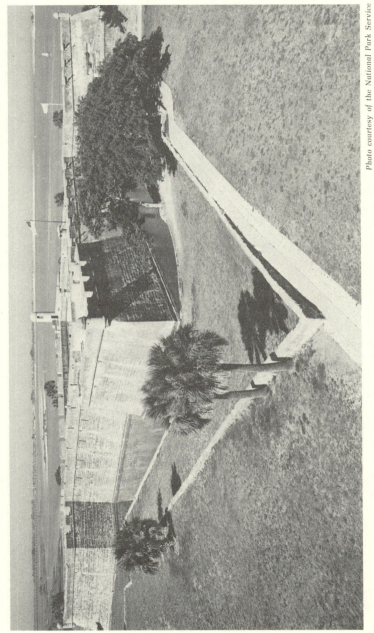

Photo courtesy of the National Park Service

For over 300 years, Castillo de San Marcos has dominated the skyline and life of St. Augustine, frightening off pirates, sheltering townspeople in the 1702 attack and the 1740 siege, and today, under the aegis of the National Park Service, attracting visitors from all over the world.

church and the treasury, rough quarters were constructed in the crowded courtyard.

On the ninth of November, fifteen hundred persons had reached the fort. On the tenth, Colonel Daniel's force came out of the pine woods to the west and bypassed the castillo by following the San Sebastian River south, to come into town near the Franciscan convent. There the English set up headquarters.

The drove of cattle Zúñiga had ordered provided one bit of pleasant excitement to offset the fears of that day: The sound of thudding hooves brought the St. Augustinians up to the castillo ramparts, to cheer on a bravado display of soldiers-turned-cowboys stampeding some one hundred sixty head of cattle through scattering Carolina troops and into the moat.

Moore's ships had come into the harbor and about this time his troops were landing, to take up positions through the town. Zúñiga realized they could fire effectively from some of the houses near the castillo, and he ordered a sortie to burn the closest buildings. The siege was under way.

Traffic in and out of the fort was never completely halted in the weeks ahead. Work crews moved out to cut marsh grass for the horses and cattle, troops left on brief forays, and Zúñiga's messengers came and went.

For some days all was fairly quiet. The four Carolina cannon proved ineffective against the thick coquina of the castillo and Moore sent off to Jamaica for bombshells, and mortars to throw them over the castillo walls into the defenders and the huddled refugees, and also to destroy the cattle sheltered in the moat.

> ". . .The enemy ceased cannonading, and I as well did not continue with the previous frequency . . . since I could not know how long the siege might last or if the enemy might receive reinforcements. . ."

In late November more houses were put to the torch, this time by the English, including the convent and nearby houses along St. Francis Street. As Christmas approached, Zúñiga tried to raise the low spirits of his crowded, restive guests with music for all and extra pay for the troops. Everyone's morale took a sharp turn for the better on the day after Christmas,

". . . for on the 26th, at 2 in the afternoon, there were
discovered 4 sails which the Governor of Havana had
sent me as a result of those letters, supplemented and
by means of Divine mercy, and my duplicate dispatches. . ."

The English too had seen the ships. Governor Moore had no
intention of being caught between the new arrivals and the
castillo. From the ramparts, the St. Augustinians watched the
enemy vessels turn their prows to the inlet. They hoped the
Spanish ships off-shore would face up to any challenge from the
English.

". . .At this time the enemy arranged to raise the siege
by setting fire to the city, the houses of which for the
most part were of thatch and boards . . . the naval
forces were already aboard their vessels, but seeing by
the 30th that their situation was hopeless, they set fire
early in the evening to the vessels near shore, and left
along the beach. . ."

Zúñiga urged the Cubans to follow, to capture the Carolinians,
perhaps at the mouth of the St. Johns, but he was successful only
in acquiring from them a few men and a sloop before they sailed
back to Havana.

The gates of the fort were opened. Those within could leave
to salvage what they could in the ashes of the town and
surrounding farms. St. Augustine, ravaged and burnt, was hard
put to it to survive. Only the little chapel of the hospital on what
is now St. George Street stood whole in the ruins. The church
and convent, the chapel at Nombre de Dios, the Governor's
House and all but a score of other houses had been destroyed.
Those twenty were badly damaged. While the townspeople
found shelter in huts and tents, a steady stream of appeals for
financial help went to the king, to the viceroy in Mexico, to the
governor of Cuba.

As Zúñiga worked on rebuilding his town, his old enemy
Moore, no longer governor but now colonel, worked to restore

his reputation tarnished by the failure before St. Augustine. With his own money he gathered a force of a thousand Indians and fifty white men, and embarked on a campaign of destruction to the southwest, throughout Apalache and into Apalachicola. In eighteen months he burned one mission after another, ranches and Indian villages, to such an extent that an official Spanish map identified the area between Apalache and St. Augustine as "wholly laid waste, being destroyed by the Carolinians, 1706."

One of the last outposts to be abandoned was *la Chua*, the ranch which had sent so many cattle, so much salted and dried beef to the presidio despite pirate raids from the Gulf coast. In the late summer of 1706, soldiers and ranchhands burned the blockhouse there on orders of the new governor, Francisco Córcoles y Martínez; with the remnants of the local Christian Indians, they withdrew to the presidio, leaving Timucua open to the English and raiding Creeks.

Drawn in upon itself, the garrison of St. Augustine still looked outward. Córcoles was intent on mounting attacks against Carolina, and in 1706 he supported a French-Spanish naval attack on Charles Town. The operation was a failure; the fleet was scattered, and hundreds of men were captured by the Carolinians.

The fortunes of the church fared little better. Ecclesiastical authorities in Spain were concerned that no bishop had visited Florida since Calderón in 1674-75, but the current bishop of Cuba was far from willing to make the trip himself, and was not eager to undertake the financing of any other solution. Eventually he had to act, however, when, with papal approval, the auxiliary bishopric of Florida was established. Dionisio Resino, the oldest priest in Cuba, was named to the post and reached St. Augustine on June 23, 1709. In three weeks he was on his way back to Cuba, unable to face up to the problems of the ruined town, no suitable living quarters, and only the chapel of the hospital as a parish church.

The Great Hunger came in 1712, when the subsidy ship was captured by the English. The town's population of horses, dogs and cats declined sharply in the interests of feeding their hungry owners. But supplies and money eventually arrived, and the very next year there could be elaborate festivities to mark the birth of the Prince of Navarre, son of Philip V and Maria Luisa of Savoy.

On the 28th of February, 1713, the "*Te Deum Laudamus* was sung with music and solemnity (together) with a general ringing of bells." The bells were joined by the firing of cannon at the castillo and of guns on the ships in the harbor. Afterwards, the assembled troops, men, women and children, and most of the local Indians, gathered in the plaza to swear allegiance to the child, and "His Excellency, from a large platter containing silver . . . threw various coins among the crowd."

More guns were fired, more bells were rung, and the special guests and the military walked across the plaza to the Governor's House where still more coins were flung from the balcony by His Excellency and his wife. The guests then had refreshments in the garden. For two nights candles lit up the windows and doors of the houses north and south of the plaza.

The formal end of Queen Anne's War in 1713 spurred authorities in Spain to consider some more advantageous use of the coastal holdings. A proposal to move the capital from St. Augustine to the richer land of Apalache was studied for a decade, then dropped. Development of Apalache proceeded, however, and in 1718 men from St. Augustine were planning a blockhouse not far from the site of the one purposely demolished in 1691.

Since 1702, building for St. Augustine's own defenses had used most of the funds sent from Spain to replace the church and convent; the newly arrived governor, Antonio de Benavides, continued the practise, defending his position with the argument that "dead men could not attend Mass, and his Floridians would surely perish if he did not attend to the defenses of his colony."

There was more trouble in the religious community and through Benavides' long term of sixteen years that trouble seethed and simmered.

It stemmed from the rivalry within the Franciscan order, between the floridanos and the friars sent out from Spain. With the loss of the missions, many of the latter chose to leave Florida for more challenging work. The floridanos had their roots in St. Augustine; they stayed on in makeshift quarters at the site of their old convent, moving into positions of control in the Franciscan hierarchy.

At the instigation of Philip V, almost twenty friars joined the Florida convent in 1719 and 1722. The floridano brothers were unwilling to surrender their control of the convent to the newcomers; between their active opposition and the difficulties of life in the presidio and in the few remaining missionary posts, by 1727 all but two of the Iberian friars had left.

The rivalry between native born and Spanish had relaxed on the military and civil side of St. Augustine life some decades before, when the need for able-bodied soldiers and officials eventually overrode the suspicions that floridanos were unreliable and untrained. Governor Márques Cabrera admitted that in the militia (where he did not have to pay them) they were capable and responsible. The royal accountant, a floridano himself, pointed out "the local men were acclimated to the country and knew every inch of it." They were not apt to desert because they had no intention of leaving their own homes.

Other practical arguments favored floridano soldiers: They knew the ways and languages of the Indians, they knew the countryside and as good horsemen made good time as messengers; too, they married, built houses, raised families and some food, a stabilizing factor in the small settlement.

Among the government officials floridanos of necessity predominated; if there was reluctance among Spaniards to leave Spain for military service in Florida, there was even less interest in making the dangerous voyage to become the accountant or treasurer of a colony so poor in resources. It became customary for those posts to be filled by local men, often by one generation after another of the same family.

In London, the Lords of Trade cited sure profits and the Privy Council dragged its heels, but by June 1721, in a faraway swamp, a twenty-six-foot square blockhouse was raised to set England's frontier less than a hundred miles from the castillo, at the mouth of the Altamaha in present-day Georgia. Benavides

protested to Carolina's governor, complained to the Council of
the Indies and sent his auditor as emissary to Charles Town to
discuss a treaty; across the ocean the Spanish ambassador to
London demanded the reduction of the fort.

Complaints and negotiations continued on the two levels and
the two continents, while the mosquito-plagued little fort with
the grand name of Fort King George barely survived. In 1727,
Yamassee and Creek raids, backed by Benavides, reached such a
pitch that the garrison was withdrawn to safer Charles Town.

But tensions, instead of lessening, increased, as did the raids.
In February 1728 a force of Carolinians under Colonel John
Palmer set out to deal with the Indians by destroying the
Yamassee settlements near St. Augustine. Palmer's attack on
March 9 at Nombre de Dios was a decisive victory for the
English, despite the fact that Nombre de Dios was then, as it is
today, in sight of the castillo. Benavides refused to be drawn out
of the fort and his guns could not reach the attackers. Palmer
burned the village, destroyed the chapel and with prisoners and
religious statues, returned to Charles Town.

The Carolinians argued that "Carolina must take St. Augustine,
or St. Augustine would take Carolina," and Benavides watched
with apprehension the signs of settlement at the Savannah River
led by General James Oglethorpe.

In 1734 the new governor, Francisco del Moral Sánchez, was
comparatively content with the defensive potentialities of the
castillo, but moved almost at once to protect the town's western
approaches. Two blockhouses were built where the trail to
Apalache crossed the St. Johns, Fort Picolata on the east bank
and Fort San Francisco de Pupo across the river.

If ever there was a time when St. Augustine needed a strong
government, it was in these days of the growing British presence
to the north. But after a few promising months, Moral's term,
1734-37, marked the nadir of Spanish Florida's governorship. He
managed to alienate every element of the town—he arrested
popular officers on pretexts, he supported one faction of the
Franciscans against the other, he profited from the illegal sales of
English goods at inflated prices when the town was in sore need
of supplies.

English General James Edward Oglethorpe founded Georgia, a buffer colony between British South Carolina and Spanish Florida, in 1733. He led two unsuccessful expeditions against St. Augustine, one in 1740 and a lesser attempt in 1743.

Moral believed that English expansion was still negotiable, and Oglethorpe's emissaries were courteously received in St. Augustine. In turn Moral sent a delegation to meet with the British general at Jekyll Island. Meanwhile, settlements, forts and defensive works were springing up on the barrier islands off Georgia.

While talks had been going on at Jekyll Island, St. Augustine's troubles with her governor had been mounting. Despite his attempts at censorship, frank letters and complaints from the presidio had reached former governor Benavides in Vera Cruz; others from friars got through to Cuban convents; still more went to the governor at Havana and thence to Madrid. In April 1736 Philip V ordered Juan Francisco de Güemes y Horcasitas, the Cuban governor, to remove Moral.

To learn more about the St. Augustine situation, and also to learn more about Oglethorpe, the man and his plans, Güemes used the second purpose to clothe the first. He dispatched the engineer Antonio de Arredondo to Florida, ostensibly to discuss with the English general in Georgia the ever-present border disputes.

At Frederica, Arredondo was met with elaborate hospitality. Although harsh words marred these talks, when Arredondo returned to St. Augustine in October, he brought to Moral the agreement that Oglethorpe would dismantle Fort St. George at the mouth of the St. Johns, that Spain would not then move to occupy the island, and that larger questions would be left to higher authorities across the Atlantic. Moral forwarded the document to Madrid, proud of the local diplomacy.

On Spain's part, those larger questions never came into consideration, for the Council of the Indies denounced the treaty out of hand. The governor of Florida had no authority to make agreements with another nation, it held, and that Moral had done so added emphasis to the need for his removal.

In the presidio, Arredondo was fulfilling the second part of his mission, gathering details of Moral's misuse of his position. The engineer's lengthy report went to Güemes in late November.

That worthy studied other firsthand reports, including one from the new auxiliary bishop for Florida, Francisco de San

Buenaventura, and in February 1737 ordered Josef de Justís to Florida as interim governor, with instructions for Moral's recall.

Then events moved rapidly. Justís sailed into Matanzas Bay on March 11, and next morning he presented his credentials and the order for Moral to return to Cuba. Moral refused to accept the papers, much less turn over the town and the castillo. Several days of maneuvering followed; Moral sought sanctuary in the Franciscan convent, Bishop Buenaventura went in after him, and eventually out came the governor to be put at once on a ship, destinations Havana, a cell at Morro Castle, and in a few months, another cell in a Cádiz prison while the ponderous Spanish legal system dealt with his case. After a decade of hearings and appeals, in July 1748 Moral was exonerated by the Council of the Indies.

Buenaventura, who had played so critical a part in Moral's ouster, had come to St. Augustine in July 1735 as the first auxiliary bishop to be seen there since Resino's three-week visit in 1709.

An ambitious, able Franciscan from Seville, Buenaventura found the church in shambles. Little morality, many scandals, a tumbledown, leaky chapel poorly furnished, and no living quarters for himself—these had been the conditions facing Resino twenty-six years before, but Buenaventura was of different stuff, and considerably younger.

The serious rift between the floridanos and the Spanish friars was a "deep abyss of enmity and dissension," the bishop discovered. He moved to strengthen the position of his fellow Iberians and generally accounted for a revival of religious strength in the town. The rivalries within the Franciscan order were reduced, and the secular clergy bolstered by added personnel.

By the time he reached St. Augustine in 1737, Manuel de Montiano, "late of the infantry of Aragon," had led grenadiers in Oran against the Moors, and had seen service in Central America. As governor now, he would use all he had learned and improvise as needed, for it was he who led the St. Augustinians at the time of their greatest threat, Oglethorpe's 1740 siege. He knew, and the engineer Arredondo agreed, that St. Augustine was ill-prepared for any effective defense and so Montiano wrote Governor Güemes in Havana, analyzing the weaknesses of his castillo. He warned, "We are as bare outside as we are without life inside, for there are no guns that could last 24 hours, and if there were, we have no artillerymen to serve them."

Güemes found soldiers, provisions and even hard cash for St. Augustine, along with a work force of convicts; all were put to use at once on their arrival in the spring of 1738.

A major enterprise was the construction of bombproofs, great coquina vaults which would line the four sides of the castillo's courtyard behind the thick walls. It took a year, from October to October, before the first eight, along the important east curtain, were completed.

After Moore's 1702 siege, earthwork defense lines had been built across the St. Augustine peninsula to bar an enemy approach to the town by land. In the years since the siege other earthworks were raised. Now the whole town was protected on this land side by walls and these barriers were further strengthened in hectic preparation for a confrontation with the British.

In the first weeks of 1740 the castillo's tall watch tower was completed, but Montiano figured that at the rate he was going it would take "at least eight years for the rehabilitation of the castillo."

He didn't have that much time. In the same month that the sentinels could first climb to the watch tower and look east for signs of trouble, Oglethorpe came down the St. Johns River, far to the west, to attack the twin forts of Pupo and Picolata and established his own garrison there while the Spanish forces retreated to St. Augustine.

From the St. Johns, Oglethorpe returned to Georgia, and proceeded to assemble a force of Carolinians, Indians and Georgians. In May he headed south again. He had organized a naval force also, under Commandant Vincent Pierse, and they would rendezvous at the mouth of the St. Johns.

In the weeks following his arrival there, the general's soldiers came to know only too well the palmettoes, sand, marshes, mosquitoes and heat of the coast south of the river. On the twenty-second they marched down to capture little Fort San

Diego, twenty miles to the north of St. Augustine, and returned to the St. Johns; five days later, off they went again to Fort Mose, within two miles of the castillo and then back to their river base.

While these king's men marched down the coast and marched back again, Montiano was desperately trying to keep communications open with Havana. He had twenty-four hundred people on his hands, and few supplies. "Unless help can come by June 20," he wrote Güemes, "it is the most natural thing in the world that this garrison perish."

Out in the bay at least, Montiano could move constructively. His six galliots, sheltering at times under the guns of the castillo, would be both an attack and a defense force. These maneuverable vessels, manned by thirty men and two officers (twenty men at the oars) were armed with a nine-pounder at the bow, and swivel guns fore and aft.

At the end of May, Oglethorpe moved his headquarters to Fort San Diego, temporarily putting an end to what his scornful Carolinians termed "fruitless marches" for mere "squirrel shooting." Some days later the general re-established a small force at Fort Mosa. In the following weeks, there were scattered encounters between Spanish and English in the palmetto scrub north of the town.

Artillery was landed at the northern edge of the St. Augustine inlet on June 23, under the command of Colonel Alexander Vander Dussen, and on the same day Oglethorpe set up his own guns on Anastasia Island, south of the inlet. Pierse's naval support, frigates and schooners, totally blocked the entrance to the harbor. Inside, the galliots harassed the English at all points.

The guns started to speak on June 24. Day in and day out, the English cannonballs and mortar shells dropped into the town, into the bay, and occasionally into the coquina walls of the fort.

> ". . .In this Affliction the Settlement and the Garrison took for their defense Most Holy Mary of the Rosary, ordering that at each shot from the Enemies no other thing was to be heard than AVE MARIA, the same with the balls and bombs. . ."

So Bishop Buenaventura described his contribution to the

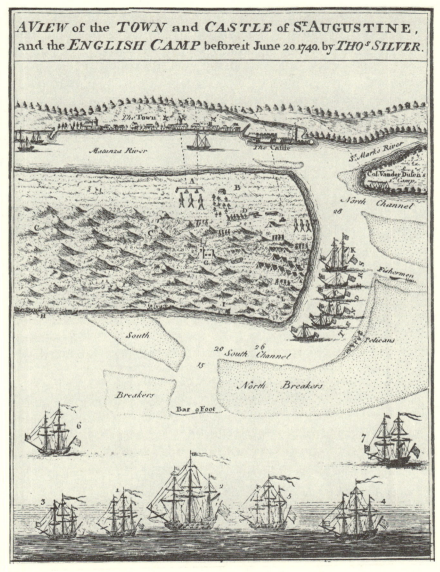

A VIEW of the TOWN and CASTLE of St. AUGUSTINE, and the ENGLISH CAMP before it June 20. 1740. by THOs SILVER.

Thomas Silver's map of the Oglethorpe siege of St. Augustine in 1740. The general's main force is shown in the center on Anastasia Island, firing at Castillo de San Marcos. A secondary force under Colonel Vander Dussen is north of the inlet at top right.

general welfare; such morale builders as these shouts of "Ave Maria" were of increasing importance as supplies dwindled and sleep was constantly interrupted by the shelling.

As a veteran soldier, Montiano was unwilling to accept a continued siege without striking back. On June 25 he gambled a goodly number of his able-bodied men in a midnight attack on Fort Mose. A few of the defending Highlanders escaped, vaulting (with painful results) over the sharp-pointed Spanish bayonets which surrounded the little fort, but most were killed or captured.

In the face of the subsequent upsurge of morale within the castillo at this success, Oglethorpe's next move was particularly inept. It was within that week he chose to send to Montiano a formal demand for surrender,

> ". . . in order to prevent the shedding of Christian blood and the evil consequences which may result from the unrestrained fury of the several [Indian] nations when they capture a plaza by force of arms. . ."

Two days later Montiano replied. The heart of his message:

> ". . . we respond that we are entirely prepared and resolved to shed Christian blood in defense of this fort and this plaza to the glory of the sacred name of God and the honour of the armed forces of the King of all Spains. . ."

For all his brave words, Montiano was worried. "My greatest anxiety is provisions," he wrote Güemes as before. "If these do not come, there is no doubt that we shall die in the hands of hunger."

Providentially, it was just as he wrote on July 6 that seven ships arrived off Mosquito Inlet some sixty miles to the south. From Cuba, they were loaded with all-important food and flour. Down the Matanzas River went assorted small craft, evading English gunfire on the way and back, their first return trip slowed by the welcome weight of two hundred barrels of flour.

Now, General Oglethorpe was faced with the castillo newly supplied, his men near to mutiny with their long weeks of duty at the sunbaked guns, battling mosquitoes rather than Spaniards. Vincent Pierse, commandant of the ships, was no help. He and his men had been infected by the fear of late summer storms, although in these weeks of July even the earliest severe weather was unlikely.

Oglethorpe set in motion plans to move out his forces and by July 20, some days after the general himself had left, Vander Dussen gathered the last British together, and headed north.

Montiano, while relieved, was baffled. In his interim report to Güemes the week after the English left, when the marshes and shores across the bay were quiet and deserted, he admitted "I cannot arrive at a comprehension of the conduct, or rules of this General. . ."

Several centuries later, a Carolinian was to write of Oglethorpe's venture: ". . . to take the castle in any event would have been difficult; but he rendered it hopeless by committing every possible blunder, the details of which have little value except for a military treatise on how not to do it."

Now Montiano was concerned about the condition of his fortifications, and he moved to repair damage to the castillo; to start work on a coquina fort at Matanzas Inlet, newly appreciated as a critical point of St. Augustine's defenses; and, as always, to try to feed and supply his garrison and the town.

Subsidies had failed to arrive in 1739 and 1740, and none came in 1741. Trade with the English colonies was forbidden by law, and while the law was often overlooked, even illegal trade cost money, and money was hard to come by.

One solution was the recognized field of privateering, when individuals financed ships and crews with the sole purpose of seizing other ships for their cargoes. English, French, Dutch and nationless freebooters roamed the shipping lanes.

Montiano adopted the practise without apologies. As 1741 opened, he reported to Governor Güemes: "after learning of the

Some twenty miles south of St. Augustine lies Matanzas Inlet. Too frequently, enemies used this "back door" to attack the town. In 1742 the Spanish finally plugged the route by building Fort Matanzas, today a part of the National Park system.

loss of the convoy of supplies sent by Your Excellency . . . I managed successfully to arm the Campeche sloop as a privateer. It went out the 17th of October. . ." With little delay, the St. Augustine vessel had captured a ship out of Charles Town, bound for Hamburg with a cargo of rice. Montiano wrote thankfully that such "has been the salvation of this city, because from the 28th of October when she came in, the troops and entire neighborhood have lived on it. . ."

He then bought and armed another sloop, "rigging it anew with captured tackle. . . She hoisted sail on Dec. 3 with a good wind." One prize came in on the nineteenth; but on the twenty-ninth the sloop came in herself "because the crew could not stand the rigors of the winter, which has been cruel."

The traffic was heavy in and out of St. Augustine's harbor.

Later in 1741, one could see at times thirteen English vessels anchored under the castillo's guns, all privateering prizes. In one three-week period, captured cargoes provided the town with Madeira wine, pork, beans, pitch and the always needed corn and flour. There was understandable disappointment when the cargo of one vessel, captured with the usual risk, was found to be principally flagstones.

The next two years saw a Spanish attack on St. Simons Island, followed by an English naval threat to St. Augustine, neither productive. In the spring of 1743, Oglethorpe went once more in arms into Florida, this time with a small force of Indians and English militia, sufficient only to destroy the fort newly rebuilt at his old headquarters, Fort San Diego. He ventured no farther, and St. Augustine breathed a little easier.

The town Oglethorpe repeatedly had hoped to capture was examined that year by an outsider, observant as befitted his trade of spy, and as anonymous.

". . . the place produces nothing but a few pomkings and Squashes & Small beans," he wrote. "They have no meat kind here but are suppl'd with Beef Pork & bread from Havana. . .it is a place of no Trade . . . they are all afraid of the Indians of the Country & seldom go off the Island."

He wandered among the townspeople and found them "of a Swarthy Complection. The men go much as they Do in England—Women go in black mostly & ware Vaile over their face as they do in Spain they are most of 'em tall & well Grown but very brown. . ."

In his little notebook he recorded the number of cannon on "the Castle," the routine of the guard and of the "5 Centries on ye lines at a time all night ye Man that is at the Bell Strieks it every 3, or 4, Minutes the Centry's calling from one to the other." The spy professionally judged it "a Very Good Watch."

After Oglethorpe's second venture into Florida, an unfamiliar peace came to the long disputed area. What was familiar were the presidio's economic difficulties, now somewhat alleviated by a limited commerce with New York and Charleston.

Despite Spanish regulations, independent merchants had come on the Florida scene as early as 1726, when New Yorker William Walton signed a contract with Governor Benavides for supplies. After the fact, Philip V granted the Florida governors the right to negotiate similar contracts for provisioning the garrison, and Walton's agents and captains were regularly seen in St. Augustine. There was commerce, too, with Charleston merchants, and vessels from both cities came and went across St. Augustine's treacherous bar, most of them sailing north loaded only with ballast.

Occasional "parcells of fruit" went north, and in October 1735 twenty-eight thousand oranges had made up a cargo for Charleston, to be followed by several other large shipments of fruit, but in the main there was no cargo out of St. Augustine.

Over the years, Governor Montiano strove to provide some economic foundation for the province. His efforts were varied: a revival of the Apalache naval stores trade, a debased currency for use only in Florida, a free port on Anastasia Island for English goods. In Madrid each plan met with no interest, no action, no funds.

Consistent as Madrid was in turning down Montiano's suggestions, the Council of the Indies approved of his record, and in 1749 ended his long term as governor with the prestigious appointment to the same post in Panama.

Succeeding governors served the more usual term of three years or so, all of them plagued by the familiar problems of inadequate funds, missing or lost supplies, and aging defenses.

The town was also aging; it had been burned and neglected, yet still survived, its appearance changing gradually. The narrow sandy streets were edged by the almost blank walls of the houses, now a good number of them of coquina, more of the less durable tabby which combined oyster shells, sand and lime.

Two rooms were about all most householders would claim, but whenever possible that core was added on to—another room, a loggia, preferably on the sunny south side, a second story when there was money enough to buy the increasingly scarce wood. An added balcony could mean still another room, for it served as a resting place, a storeroom, a place to dry clothes out of the rain.

The balcony of the Governor's House was put to more formal uses. It overlooked the plaza, and on state occasions officials appeared on it; from it there was a good view of the main wharf and the guardhouse on the bay.

The governor lived as comfortably as could be expected in St. Augustine. His house was large, with coquina walls on the first floor, and wood for the second, and its land covered the block from the plaza to the western wall of the town. There was a stable, a well and the usual separate kitchen, crowded together behind a wall, and there were fruit trees—oranges, of course, including the now native sour Seville variety, lemon and grapefruit, peach, pomegranate, cherry and quince, and eleven fig trees.

There were fruit trees at most houses and even the hospital had its plantings. Fruit from their trees, and fish from the bay and ocean were important in St. Augustine diets; the kitchen gardens helped too, but in the main, as in all the centuries before, many staples came from abroad.

In the mid-18th century, for a while, the town's fortunes improved. When the time came to honor Ferdinand VI as the new king of Spain and before Montiano left for Panama, there was money enough to provide a gala such as had never before been seen in St. Augustine.

Ferdinand's flag was raised over the castillo early on April 30, 1747, and from then until the last stumbling footsteps of tipsy troops were heard late on May 1, the hours brought new life to the town. There were speeches in the plaza, and private parties, a high mass for all and pardons for prisoners in the town jail. As always observant of class distinctions, Montiano entertained a certain element in the Governor's House while providing food and drink in the plaza for the rest of the townspeople.

There were horse races, and in the plaza dancing and plays. So successful was the celebration that some of the garrison, somewhat the worse for the free drinks, pushed their way into the governor's courtyard late in the evening, to declare loudly that this fiesta showed them "the advantages of service" in Florida.

Even with the expense of such occasions there were funds available with which to woo the newly interested Indians, propitiously just at the moment when the English were curtailing their policies of gifts. Montiano had reopened negotiations with the tribes in the late 1740's, and in 1751 his successor, Governor Melchor de Navarrete, played host to more than seven hundred Indians for three weeks of talk and festivities, and, importantly, gifts of guns, ammunition, clothing and jewelry.

In the new friendliness of these years, St. Augustinians felt safe in moving out to the hinterlands, and the naval store trade was given new impetus. A shipment of "10,000 ft plank" left the port in October of 1753, an indication of the financial merits of pacifying the local tribes and of what might become a degree of self-support for the province.

There could be optimism, too, on a wider front, with the adoption in 1753 by Ferdinand VI of the "New Law," based on recommendations from the viceroy of Mexico, the Conde de Revillagigedo. The viceroy had become familiar with Spanish colonial problems in his early assignment when, as Güemes y Horcasitas, he served as governor of Cuba. He was pragmatic in his recommendations for Florida.

Perhaps remembering his responsibilities for St. Augustine during the 1740 siege, he proposed a garrison of able-bodied soldiers for the presidio, to serve on rotation there and in Cuba. He outlined an improved pay system, and he went into other details: The crew of the official sloop should include a cook, a cooper and a caulker; the parish gravedigger should also sweep out the church; convicts and slaves were to be fed from a common mess rather than giving them money for food which all too often they spent for liquor, and an important morale point, there should be new red and blue uniforms, new swords and new epaulets for the garrison.

The castillo had fared well recently. Bombproof vaults now surrounded the courtyard on all four sides, and in 1756 Governor

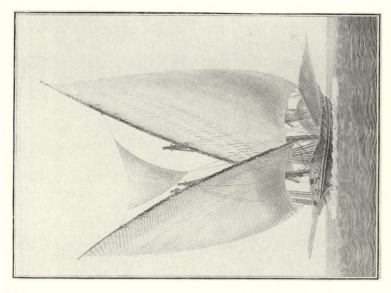

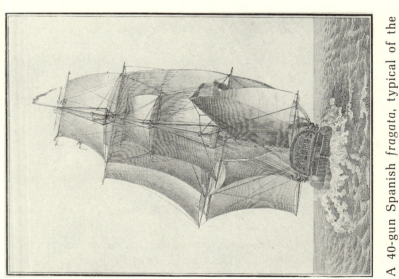

A Spanish *galeota* (or galliot), employing both oars and sails, was a shallow-draft, highly maneuverable warship.

A 40-gun Spanish *fragata*, typical of the warships that defended St. Augustine against pirates and the English.

Alonso Fernández de Heredia took it upon himself to declare that the fort was finished. The royal coat of arms installed over the entrance testified to that statement, but in no way brought the work on the fortification to an end. As long as there were funds, there were improvements to be made.

One brief threat to the unfamiliarly even temper of the times arose in 1756. There was war between France and England, a conflict which came to be known as the Seven Years' War, and the English established an embargo on exports to neutral ports, including St. Augustine, lest supplies reach the French through trans-shipment.

In New York William Walton moved to protect his longtime trade with Florida. The necessities he supplied the presidio, he told the authorities in New York, were vital to St. Augustine, nothing could, or would, be spared to reach the French, and moreover, the Spaniards paid him in silver, useful to bolster New York's paper money. In August 1757 Walton's arguments prevailed and the embargo was relaxed for St. Augustine, but only on assurances that no supplies were to reach the French.

The town may not have aided the French with supplies, but the presidio soon proved a thorn in English flesh in another manner. French privateers found its wide harbor a useful port for refitting on their voyages along the coast, once they came to terms with the difficult and ever-shifting channel. Not only did they sail from St. Augustine, but they brought their English prizes into the bay, on one occasion in the fall of 1758 shepherding in eleven such vessels.

With the declaration of war between Spain and England in January 1762, the castillo, which had saved Florida for Spain before, now faced another challenge, and needed improvement. Money arrived from Cuba, along with the engineer Pablo Castelló, only weeks before Havana itself came under siege by the English. With townspeople and soldiers as volunteers for the emergency, Castelló supervised an earthmoving enterprise unequalled since the first days of the castillo's construction. Bordering the moat, the parapet of the covered way was reconstructed of the always useful coquina. In an effort which produced St.

Augustine's first and only "hill," the glacis was redesigned so that, it has been said, "its upward slope would lift attackers right into the sights of the fort cannon."

While that slope slowly took shape, Castelló moved to enlarge the old ravelin, the outwork shielding the main gate from direct fire.

Ravelin, glacis and covered ways could not defend the town against its most serious threat. Starvation once more faced the inhabitants, for with the declaration of war, all trade between Spanish and English possessions had been suspended, and nothing could be expected from either New York or even Havana, which had now been captured by the English.

As in the 1740's, the governor turned to privateering for food. In the ten days between the fifth of September and the fifteenth, the *San Christoval* captured and sent to the presidio three vessels laden with rice and sugar, "a very seasonable supply to the garrison . . . almost starving when the privateer came out," according to the *South-Carolina Gazette*. What that newspaper did not know was that two of the three prizes were lost crossing the bar, and the badly needed food sank within sight of the garrison.

In January 1763 four privateers claimed St. Augustine as their home port, while they cruised north to New York and south off Havana; to balance the picture, that same month an English vessel retook four prizes which were being unloaded outside the St. Augustine harbor.

Such seesaws in St. Augustine's fortunes would not plague governor, garrison and people much longer, for in February 1763 England and Spain signed the Treaty of Paris, making Florida English by the stroke of a pen, where cannon, fire and sword had failed.

In the innumerable archives of Seville lie the inventories and reports which document the transfer of an entire population out of Florida to Cuba, some three thousand men, women and children, soldiers, slaves, Indians and priests, Germans and Catalans, floridanos, Canary Islanders, free blacks, the mix which had made up St. Augustine for so many decades. Documents list, too, inanimate objects: "all the royal property," from cannon to saddles to "boxes of old iron"; the religious articles, baptismal fonts, statues, bunches of dried flowers.

Nothing remains to tell of the personal traumas of the removal, the thoughts, resentments, expectations of the new life. The Crown would pay the costs of the move, and there would be for those not on the government payroll, some subsistence, and some land for settling in the Cuban countryside. But meanwhile the St. Augustine houses and land had to be disposed of by their owners, a virtually impossible task when the new inhabitants of Florida were few and, in the main, British soldiers scarcely able to afford an occasional glass of rum. When little was sold, agents were appointed to handle the matter in the months ahead.

The English put no great pressures on the Spanish to leave and, indeed, under the terms of the Treaty of Paris, would allow those who stayed to retain their Catholic faith. A Spanish official proudly wrote to Havana, "It is obvious that the British are surprised to witness the decision of all our people to emigrate, when they asserted there would not be enough evacuees to fill one vessel. . ."

Weeks of arrangements and scheduling followed the initial sailing on April 1, 1763 while Governor Melchor Feliú and Cuban officials put into action the detailed instructions sent from Spain. They were careful to arrange early shipment of the military, with arms and armament, and attended to the task of keeping together and sending out together, entire families and their possessions. There were some who could not bear to be separated even from their deceased loved ones; the remains of Governor Palacio went with his widow, and there were other similar instances.

Such arrangements take time. On July 21, when Governor Feliú met the ranking British officer, Captain John Hedges, at the castillo to see the British flag raised over the old fort, the town was still full of its Spanish inhabitants.

The new faces, new uniforms and new ways of the English were not accepted by these Spaniards, on the brink of their new life away from Florida. They particularly resented the presence of British officers in many of their homes.

In August the main exodus got under way. Schooners and sloops sailed every day or so during that month, carrying more than thirteen hundred people across the familiarly risky bar on their way to Cuba or to Campeche in Mexico.

Another thousand left in the remaining months of 1763 and more sailed early in the new year. Finally, on January 21 the governor, officials, some last townspeople and the parish priest with the church furnishings, boarded a convoy and sailed out of the harbor.

At the last moment Feliú had to detach a handful of soldiers to remain, "to attend to the final disposition of some horses that were running loose in the woods."

Feliú's official summary of events stated, and so perhaps he believed, that all Spaniards were out of St. Augustine. Later records show that three Spaniards did choose to stay on under British rule. Young Francisco Xavier Sanchez farmed on land west of town, and Manuel Solana, another farmer, was beyond, at Tocoi on the St. Johns. Luciano de Herrera, one of the militia assigned to find the horses, stayed, officially as an agent of the Crown, collecting monies from the sale of properties; within a few years he would be secretly transmitting information to the Havana authorities on British shipping and military matters.

Chapter Four

". . .not so gay a Town in America as this. . ."
1763 - 1784

by

Daniel L. Schafer

On July 20, 1763, when Captain John Hedges and four companies of the British First Regiment, later known as the "Royal Scots," anchored off St. Augustine in the *Renown*, they could hardly have been aware of the proud traditions of the Ancient City they were about to occupy. Still recuperating from the siege of Havana, the "Royals" were less concerned about the two centuries of Spanish rule that was about to end than with the promising new era at hand for the British. In addition to the Floridas, Canada had been acquired from France, giving Britain control of a vast seaboard empire. Safely snuggled near the southern end was St. Augustine, the sturdy walls of its castillo projecting defiance against enemy siege. Located conveniently adjacent to the Gulf Stream, St. Augustine promised a potential bonanza in the West Indies trade and a continual threat to the riches of Spanish shipping lanes.

Once ashore and after observing ceremonies in honor of the Spanish king and queen, Captain Hedges ordered the British flag raised over the castillo. Only ten days later, Major Francis Ogilvie of the Ninth Regiment replaced Hedges and incorporated many of the "Royals" into his command. Soldiers formerly under Hedges who chose civilian life were mustered out to become "pioneer" residents of British St. Augustine.

For the next thirteen months, until a governor arrived, Major Ogilvie directed both military and civil affairs in the new British colony. Finding adequate housing facilities for the men of the Ninth was an immediate problem, with common soldiers either consigned to depressing facilities in the castillo, renamed Fort St. Marks, or sent to the unfinished house of the Bishop of Cuba. As late as January 1766 a British officer complained that the fort was so hot in summer and cold and damp in winter that the men preferred sleeping in the available huts in the town.

Ogilvie ordered officers quartered amongst the town's nearly four hundred private homes, a move that aroused the ire of Spanish residents prior to their departure. Blind to local opinion as other English officials would be a dozen years later and farther north, visiting Lieutenant Colonel James Robertson commented with surprise that the Floridians, "disliking to have strangers in their familys, generally quitted the houses where officers were quarter'd." After arriving in Cuba, former Spanish Governor Melchor Feliú reported that the behavior of Captain Hedges and Major Ogilvie had originally been "such as to signify and establish the most perfect harmony among all." Problems over housing proved the exception, however, as Feliú remembered that "before my eyes (the troops) commenced to demolish houses, plundering whatever they could find in them easy to carry, and all combustible material on account of their scarcity of fire wood."

Although conflicts between the Floridians and the British had been few, Major Ogilvie had not been unhappy when reporting "The Spanish Governor and all the Spaniards inhabiting this town sail'd from this place the 21st (of January). . . It's no loss to His Majesty's Government of East Florida . . . as they were the least Industrious of any People I ever saw, having depended entirely on our Colonies in America for supplies of Provisions."

Lieutenant Colonel Robertson came to similar conclusions during his inspection tour of East and West Florida for General Jeffrey Amherst, commander-in-chief of British forces in North America. After a month of observations and interviews, a disappointed Robertson reported in October 1763 that, with the exception of abundant supplies of fish, St. Augustine was nearly devoid of food: ". . . not an herb, not a cabbage, all is overgrown with weeds."

When Colonel James Grant arrived on August 29, 1764 to begin his assignment as the first governor of British East Florida, he could hardly have been pleased with the largely abandoned town. After looking about St. Augustine and its countryside, Grant remarked that he found the colony ". . . in a State of Nature when I landed in Augustine 1764. Not an acre of land planted in this country and nobody to work or at work."

Fortunately, the climate appeared to be healthy as there were few sick soldiers among the tiny 197-man garrison.

Two days after reaching St. Augustine Grant wrote an urgent letter to James Moultrie of South Carolina, begging him to come immediately. Moultrie, a former attorney general in South Carolina, had been appointed chief justice of East Florida preceding the governor's departure from England. With Moultrie still in South Carolina and James Box, the designated attorney general, still in Georgia, Grant complained: "I cannot proceed to one act of government until you are on the Spot."

Even Grant's inauguration had to be delayed until enough people, preferably from aristocratic backgrounds, arrived in East Florida to form a governing council. He encouraged Moultrie to "prevail with some of your friends to come and live amongst us, tis a better climate, better soil, and better everything than Carolina."

It was during Grant's prior military career that he had made friends among the leading families of colonial American society, especially in South Carolina. Born at Ballindalloch Castle in the Highlands of Scotland, Grant had traded the study of law for a commission in the army at the age of twenty-one. After serving in the War of Austrian Succession, Grant was promoted and sent to North America. He soon saw action against the French and Indians in the Ohio country and in Canada before being given command of the 1760 campaign against the Cherokees in South Carolina. Greatly praised for this work, Grant was next sent to Cuba to participate in the siege of Havana before being named governor of East Florida.

Years later, at retirement, a much-decorated General James Grant would return to Ballindalloch Castle, carrying with him several cartons of letters and documents pertinent to his long career. The letters are still there in a small room at the top of the castle, many of them written by residents of St. Augustine. Rich in contemporary detail, the letters provide eyewitness accounts of life in British St. Augustine.

The Cherokee campaigns provided Grant the opportunity to build lasting friendships with the future leaders of South Carolina society, most of whom served in militia units under his com-

British Museum

Patrick Tonyn, the "intolerant and short-tempered" governor of East Florida in the troubled decade, 1774-1784, which ended with the return of the province to Spain.

National Galleries of Scotland

James Grant, "Captain General, Governor and the Commander-in-Chief in and over His Majesty's Province of East Florida" from 1764 to 1773, a period of growth and prosperity.

mand. Later, as governor of East Florida, he encouraged these friends to settle in his province, promising them government office, free land, and transportation for their slaves and equipment. Men like Francis Kinloch, William Drayton and John Moultrie (James' brother), already successful planters with experienced slave forces, could serve as beacons, the governor thought, attracting other settlers to East Florida and inducing the absentee landlords in Britain to invest in plantation development.

Governor Grant considered John Moultrie the most influential of the planters he recruited from the colonies to the north. Born in South Carolina of Scottish parents, with a degree in medicine from Edinburgh University in 1749, Moultrie was among the best educated gentlemen in the colonies. He also was one of the best planters in America, the governor thought, an "oracle" that all new planters would consult.

John Moultrie and his brother James were in St. Augustine on October 31, 1764, to participate in Grant's formal inauguration. The two Moultries were joined on the governor's council by others equally aristocratic, establishing a tone that Grant thought essential to good government.

In the absence of municipal institutions, St. Augustine was governed by the combination of Governor Grant, the council, and the courts of the province. Funding for the salaries and expenses of government came from an annual grant from Parliament. In 1764, £5,700 was appropriated, a sum that remained relatively constant in subsequent years. Approximately one-half was pegged for salaries for Governor Grant and his subordinates in the "civil establishment," a group which included clergy, teachers, provost marshal, harbor pilot and other minor officials. The remainder of the subsidy was divided into a contingent fund (used to pay unexpected expenses), an Indian gift fund and a £500 bonus to encourage cultivation of needed agricultural products.

Although Governor Grant's powers were extensive, they were primarily confined to the "civil establishment" so as not to conflict with the authority of the military commander. Largely a garrison town in the beginning, St. Augustine served as brigade headquarters for Brigadier General Frederick Haldimand for one year. Before the American Revolution, the town accommodated the Fourteenth Regiment and fluctuating numbers of additional troups. Grant's primary military authority as governor was limited to control of the militia. Overall, his relation with the military was excellent, enhanced in part by his weekly practice of hosting the entire officers' corps for dinner and drinks.

In the main, Grant headed a government similar in form to that of Governor George Johnstone in neighboring West Florida. Although the two new colonies shared a common boundary and faced similar problems, there was little interaction or even correspondence between the two governments.

In one area, Grant's government differed markedly from his West Florida neighbor—and from the governments of nearly every other British colony. Although Grant's instructions authorized him to ". . . summon and call General Assemblies of the Freeholders and Planters within the Province," no summons was issued during his tenure in office. Not until 1780, during the administration of Governor Patrick Tonyn, would an Assembly be called. While this created a potential constitutional dilemma, few complaints were made while the popular Grant remained in East Florida. After his departure, however, the absence of a General Assembly sparked a spirit of discord and led to the formation of a dissenting faction.

As settlers began arriving in St. Augustine in search of housing, they found one man in control of nearly two hundred buildings and lots, approximately one-half the entire housing. Unable to sell their property before departing, the former Spanish landowners had reached an agreement with Jesse Fish, agent for the New York merchant, William Walton, and a resident of the town since he was thirteen. Under terms of the confidential agreement, Fish agreed to sell the properties only after immigration increased and real estate prices recovered. Proceeds, minus fees, were to be paid through Juan Josef Elixio de la Puente in Cuba.

Whether or not Fish kept his promise is still debated. Critics charge that he failed to transmit some proceeds and that he charged excessive fees, taking advantage of the beleaguered Floridians for his own profit. Fish insisted that he acted honestly and charitably and that he in fact suffered great financial losses for his efforts. Several years ·later he argued that in 1763 "considerable sums of money were due from the Spanish inhabitants to Messrs. Walton, and to me, [but since] they were all ordered to embark in a precipitate manner . . . I took their debts on myself. . ."

Troubles began, however, shortly after the British soldiers arrived and burned and vandalized some of the houses, causing their resale prices to plummet. Some sale proceeds were transmitted to Havana but others were embezzled along the way. Through the intervention of his friend Luciano de Herrera, Fish eventually satisfied most of his creditors, but remained in debt until death.

There was a second clause in the Fish-Puente land agreement that Governor Grant viewed with alarm as a potential roadblock to plantation development. In partnership with Charleston merchant John Gordon and Lieutenant Colonel James Robertson, Fish had purchased ten million acres of land from the departing Spaniards, receiving land titles which he claimed were "executed in the most formal and solemn manner, according to the laws of Spain. . ."

The British Crown was adamantly opposed to the claims, instructing Governor Grant to refuse to recognize or record any of Fish's claims. Robertson withdrew from the scheme under pressure from Grant, but Fish and Gordon persisted. Gordon even initiated broadsides through the popular press in England and America, hoping to "at least strike a damp to the settling of this Province." The Crown remained unimpressed, and eventually disallowed the entire claim.

Even with the Fish and Gordon claims pending, the Crown had begun granting East Florida land, including numerous twenty-thousand-acre tracts, to influential Britons. Robertson and Gordon received grants and Fish acquired Anastasia Island, where he built a home and tended an orange grove, shipping juice to the northern colonies.

In addition to difficulties with land claims, Governor Grant was faced with an immediate problem of establishing peaceful relations with the Indians. Ironically, the man who had been

praised by General Amherst for burning Indian towns, destroying food crops and forcing the Cherokees to sue for peace or
starve, was an advocate of treating Indians justly and honestly
by negotiating rather than fighting. He also believed in generous
distribution of presents and strict control of Indian traders.

Accompanied by Indian Superintendent John Stuart, Grant
met with the Lower Creeks (soon to be known as Seminoles) at
Picolata on November 15, 1765. After lengthy negotiations, the
Indians agreed to cede all the coastal lands as far south as the
tidal waters flowed in the St. Johns River. Grant dispensed
presents liberally before returning to St. Augustine, convinced
that the treaty terms would permit the new colony to thrive.

The spirit of the meeting continued a few days later when the
headman of Alachua Creeks brought sixty Indians to visit
Governor Grant at St. Augustine. To win the friendship of Chief
Cow Keeper, who had been sick when the Picolata conference
was held, the governor entertained him lavishly and proclaimed
him a Great Medal Chief.

Throughout the British period Indians were a common sight in
St. Augustine, their numbers varying with circumstances, as
when food shortages drew them in. The Indian presence in town
was not without peril, as disputes with the residents could
explode into unexpected violence. David Yeats, physician and
council member, noted one such instance: "Some Indians being
in town got drunk and forced their way into a private house in
the night, raised a great riot, upon which the guard was called
for and one of the Indians [the Chehaw king's son] was wounded
and died two days after. Though the affair was purely accidental
it is not known what turn it may take in the nation."

To head off retaliatory violence when an Indian boy was
killed in December 1768, Grant swiftly apprehended two white
hunters. Comforting the father of the murdered boy in the
Governor's House, Grant had the hunters arrested, tried and
convicted, and with the father watching, had one of the men
executed. Such acts strengthened a friendship with the Indians
which would become extremely important during the American
Revolution, when border marauders from Georgia threatened
the safety of St. Augustine.

With the satisfactory conclusion of the Picolata conference Governor Grant was able to concentrate on transforming the virgin lands of East Florida into a productive agricultural colony. Soon after arriving in East Florida he had written to John Perceval, the second Earl of Egmont: "I consider the whole [province] as a great plantation put under my care, and in fact I am anxious about the success of every individual."

With great diligence the governor promoted plantation development, writing frequently to the influential grantees—absentee landlords like Egmont and the Earl of Hillsborough, Thomas Thoroton, Lord Cassillis, Peter Taylor and the Marquis of Hastings—imploring them to invest heavily during the start-up stages of their estates. Substantial initial sums were needed to acquire a labor force to clear the virgin lands, dam and dike the swamplands for rice fields, cut timber and construct shelter. But once established, the plantations would repay the investors through steady annual returns.

Each of the grantees received the same advice regarding the best labor force: White settlers could not be depended upon to make profits for absentee landlords. "Settlements in this warm climate," Grant wrote to one grantee, "must be formed by Negroes, our indented white people can hardly be prevailed upon to work for their own subsistence," much less the interests of investors.

Always ready to assist the planters, the governor ordered an official schooner for the province in 1764. Named the *East Florida*, it was built with a shallow draft to clear the hazardous sandbars at the river entrances. The *East Florida* became a familiar sight in St. Augustine harbor as Captain Adam Bachop piloted the schooner to and from ports to the north. Prospective planters, along with their labor forces and belongings, were provided free transportation to St. Augustine or to a river landing near their plantation sites, where the *East Florida* returned later to carry away indigo, rice and other export crops.

To set an example, Grant established his own plantation on the outskirts of St. Augustine in February 1765. Located to the north, between the city gate and the remains of Fort Mose, the three-hundred-acre plantation known as "Grant's Villa" became a successful indigo producer, employing between fifty and sixty slaves, with only one white overseer. For several years "the Villa" served as an agricultural "college" to train the overseers of the province.

The most promising settlement was the New Smyrna colony established by Dr. Andrew Turnbull on Mosquito Inlet. Turnbull recruited 1,403 laborers from Minorca, Greece and Italy to raise Mediterranean crops at New Smyrna, named after the birthplace of Mrs. Turnbull in Asia Minor. Expecting to operate under indenture labor contracts, the colonists left European waters in April 1768 and were at work at New Smryna by August. Troubled by sickness, high mortality rates and labor unrest amidst charges of cruel treatment and conditions akin to slavery, New Smyrna failed to fulfill the hopes of its founders.

By 1771 there had been a significant increase in the number of plantations in East Florida. Along most of the province's navigable waterways could be found cultivated fields, slave quarters and the dwellings of the planters or their agents and overseers. Since plantation crops were marketed and supplies purchased in St. Augustine, merchants there tended to prosper. Coasting vessels came primarily from Charleston and Savannah to supply the needs of over two dozen merchants and to provide clientele for the innkeepers, shipbuilders and ship carpenters. Prosperity helped attract new residents, bringing work for house carpenters, masons, joiners and bricklayers.

Although there was no local newspaper, residents of the town were able to find official notices posted at Payne's Corner on the plaza, outside the store of St. Augustine's leading merchant, Robert Payne. On more than one occasion, broadsides critical of the government were posted alongside official notices. News was also available at any one of the many taverns, at the town market, or the public slaughtering pen at the town gate. It was even possible to gossip at the public bathing house.

A somewhat unusual feature of life in St. Augustine was the existence of publicly supported education, something difficult to find in the colonies to the north or even in England at the time. The annual parliamentary subsidy included a salary for two schoolteachers. The first was Enoch Hawksworth, who arrived

Dr. Andrew Turnbull of Scotland and his wife, Gracia Dura Ben. New Smyrna, the colony established by Turnbull in 1768, was named for the Asia Minor birthplace of Mrs. Turnbull.

in 1765, to be followed by Jones Reed, the Reverend John Leadbeater and the Reverend John Kennedy. John Moultrie installed a private tutor at Bella Vista for his children, and for several years permitted the only son of Jesse Fish to take lessons at no cost to the debt-ridden father.

For the more prominent residents of the town there was a Masonic Lodge. Its founder was James Grant, who was appointed Grand Master by Masonic officials in Scotland. Other members of Grant Lodge were Lieutenant Governor John Moultrie, Chief Justice William Drayton, Reverend John Forbes and Lieutenant Frederick George Mulcaster, the latter reportedly an illegitimate half brother of King George III. The military establishment had its own lodge, a Regimental Lodge of the Fourteenth Regiment.

Originally a drab barracks town almost devoid of civilian residents, St. Augustine became, under the direction of an affable gourmet and "bon vivant," the bachelor governor James Grant, the unlikely seat of a glittering social life. Grant entertained often and lavishly, believing that social functions were necessary to counter disadvantages of life in an underpopulated frontier town in the colonies.

At the annual celebration of the king's birthday and on other holidays, Governor Grant hosted a dinner party for the town's leaders. Although the occasions were gregarious, deference to rank was insisted upon, to the point that Grant prevented Martin Jollie, agent for Lord Egmont's plantations and "rather a Low rank in Life—his Father is a Taylor in Edinburgh," from taking a seat on the Council for several years: "It would be very distressing if he was to take Rank of the others, they would not Submit to that, for going in at a Door or dancing first at a little Assembly are points among the Women which I cannot, and dare not interfere in."

Problems of rank were not mentioned in the lively St. Augustine of 1771 that Grant described to a friend in Scotland: "There is not so gay a Town in America as this is at present, the People Mason, Musick and Dancing mad. Major Small with the band of the 21st has turned all their Heads. His Colonel has not escaped the infection, he is as young as any of them, danced till twelve last night at the Weekly assembly, then carried the Ladys home to sup at his house and after they went away . . . got drunk with their partners till six in the morning." The governor's only regret was that he had been bothered by a stomach disorder that kept him from partaking; he did, however, invite twelve of the revelers to dine with him the following evening.

Governor Grant also nourished a small circle of intimate friends throughout his term in office. The regular "sharers of the wicked bottle" were fellow Masons, Yeats, Moultrie, Forbes and Mulcaster. When Grant returned to England these were the friends who wrote frequently, keeping him informed of events in East Florida.

Some indication of the frequency of entertainment can be found in the "State of the Governor's Cellars" inventories that were conducted on a regular basis. During Grant's first year in office, when the population of St. Augustine could only be classified as miniscule, there were "drunk from the Governor's Cellars" a prodigious quantity of alcoholic beverages. Consumed during these convivial months were 86 gallons of Jamaican rum, 150 gallons of common rum, 140 gallons of Madeira wine, 76 gallons of Teneriff, 1,200 bottles of claret, 519 bottles of port and similar amounts of champagne, sweet wine, porter, beer, ale, cider, arrack and "old hock."

To accompany the beverages, the governor and his guests consumed in the year four barrels of beef, two barrels of pork, four barrels of rice and twelve barrels of flour, as well as turtles, fish, venison, oysters, turkeys, chickens, ducks, capons, hams and bacon, and lamb. Fresh eggs were bought from Mrs. Young and Mrs. Payne, and milk from Mrs. Knowland.

Such fine victuals and drink were probably contributing factors in Grant's painful gout condition. Greatly overweight, he struggled with ill health while he tried to hold to his determination to stay in his province until it had become a successful indigo producer.

But he was forced to give up earlier. In hopes of recovery away from Florida, he sailed for England in May 1771, much to the distress of most of St. Augustine.

Lieutenant Governor Moultrie took over the administration of the province in his absence, which was assumed by all to be only temporary.

In London, Grant was an active and strong supporter of enterprises in East Florida. On the occasion of the arrival of twenty thousand weight of East Florida indigo, he took great pride in telling the Earl of Hillsborough that "I believe I may venture to say (East Florida) has done more in the time, than any Continental Province ever did since the first establishment of the British Empire in America."

Grant never returned to East Florida. Seizing an opportunity to become a Member of Parliament, he resigned his governorship in April 1773. The young colony lost an effective administrator and St. Augustine lost much of the glitter of its nightlife.

Until the replacement for Grant was named, John Moultrie presided. Under his direction St. Augustine's public buildings

The Governor's House, at the west side of the plaza, was one of the principal buildings in St. Augustine. It is shown here in a 1764 sketch.

In a companion sketch, the 1764 artist depicts the view to the east from the Governor's House, with the guardhouse, Matanzas River and, to the right, the Anastasia Island watchtower.

were renovated and a north-south network of roads was constructed. Planning for public works had begun early in Grant's administration, but work had been delayed until it could be financed through savings in the annual contingent fund.

In April 1772, Grant wrote from London that the time had arrived and urged Moultrie to act with urgency. Within a month the old Spanish hospital had been converted to a jail and it was agreed to transform radically the Spanish Bishop's house into a Town House containing Council chambers, an assembly room, and offices for Customs, the Land Surveyor, Secretary, Register and naval affairs.

Work on the Town House began in October, under the direction of carpenter John Hewitt and mason Thomas Hannah. Expecting it to be "the cheapest public building in America," Moultrie described the planning: "It cost me many days thought, and nights too, before I fixed on the plan. The old Spanish palace plagued me much. The walls were not square and many of them too thin and weak to build upon. I was therefore obliged to build the wings entirely new from the foundation and very strong to support the other parts. I intend to pave the lower story, where the offices will be kept, and the front and back piazzas with red tile, as it will be cheaper, look very well, and be less liable to accidents from fire."

News that St. Augustine would soon be beautified by church bells and a clock prompted Moultrie to write to Grant: "I am glad to find you have purchased a town clock. I hope it is a spring one, as it will be more commodious than one with weights for the top of the state house. I am also glad of the Church Bells. I see you begin to think of serving yourself a seat in heaven." The following year a wooden spire was added to Parson Forbes' church of St. Peter's and the clock and bells were installed.

Road construction was well under way by late June 1772, when the route south to the Matanzas Swamp was completed. "In the wettest season," Moultrie said, "a wagon or coach and six may goe full trot over it to the end." By October, Moultrie had contracted with Captain Robert Bisset to complete the southern road to Stobb's farm beyond New Smyrna, at a cost of £1,150.

In November 1772, Moultrie and Reverend Forbes "examined

the ground for the road to the Cowford [Jacksonville] and had it measured. It is thirty-five and one-fourth miles from the ferry to the town gate." That leg was built for £400. The remaining thirty-six-mile portion, from the Cowford to the St. Marys River, was not contracted out until June 1773, when Charles and Jeremyn Wright of Georgia signed to build the road for £600, a task they had not completed in late 1774 when the other routes were in use.

The roads between the Cowford and the Musketos were continually praised by residents of St. Augustine whose work required travel about the province. Reverend Forbes found that "Captain Bisset's road really may with propriety be called the King's Highway: it forms a wide beautiful avenue, not a stump of a tree to be found."

Luciano de Herrera made good use of that King's Highway, not always in the British king's interest. Knowing that Father Camps, priest for the Minorcans in Turnbull's colony, frequently wrote to the Bishop of Cuba by way of fishing boats out of Mosquito Inlet, Herrera used the highway, the priest and the boats to send his own reports to Havana.

Planters and their agents were other users of the road as they traveled between their St. Augustine houses and outlying estates. Lieutenant Governor Moultrie was one: "I go regularly once a month to Timoka, go through in a day, with great ease and pleasure to self and horses."

By the end of Moultrie's interim administration in March 1774 progress was visible wherever one looked in St. Augustine. Public buildings had been renovated, new houses were going up as the population increased, and improved transportation facilities padded the coffers of the growing merchant class as trade increased with the outlying plantations and with the colonies to the north.

A serious problem, however, remained unsolved. A spirit of discord had been growing since late in James Grant's tenure; it surfaced during Moultrie's time in office in the form of a dissenting faction.

The most prominent member of the opposition was Chief

Justice William Drayton, successor to Chief Justice James Moultrie. From a prominent South Carolina family, with a prestigious English education, Drayton was a scholarly advocate of English law and a somewhat pompous and contentious individual. Although Drayton had informed Governor Grant as early as 1768 that proclamations of the Council were potential violations of English law, their relationship had been harmonious and each man expressed admiration for the work and capabilities of the other.

That was not to be the relationship between Drayton and Moultrie. Although contemporary records tend to emphasize the haughty and vindictive behavior that was characteristic of the clashes between the two, there were significant issues at stake. Drayton and his compatriots, Dr. Andrew Turnbull, James Penman and others, were principled advocates of the rights of Englishmen in the colonies, and believed that their rights were being violated as long as East Florida was without an elected House of Assembly.

The trouble ahead was forecast by Reverend Forbes in June 1771: "Mr. Drayton declined being in any way connected" with a congratulatory note being sent to Moultrie when his promotion as Grant's stand-in was announced. Deeply distressed by the escalating factionalism, Forbes wrote to Governor Grant: "We were uninterruptedly quiet and happy under your guidance, at a time when all America was in a blaze," but there had been so many recent changes, Forbes lamented, that former friends "can scarce bear to look at one another." By acting "dogmatically, improperly and unpopularly," Moultrie was partly to blame, Forbes thought, but the true miscreant was Drayton, who was "disruptive, conceited and irascible."

Lieutenant Mulcaster was shocked when Drayton began discussing the possibility for freedom for East Florida's black slaves following the "Somerset Affair," a judicial decision which abolished slavery in Great Britain. Confessing that he was "astonished" by Drayton's utterances, Mulcaster wrote: "I suppose he will say as the laws of Great Britain are to be enforced in the colonies—he will therefore execute his duty by doing it effectually and therefore enfranchise the whole negro tribe! Don't you think he is mad. Don't you think he is paving the way for his own and his family's destruction?"

After a dispute with Moultrie over the right of the Council to examine and censure contingent fund expenditures, Drayton resigned his Council seat in October 1771, but was reinstated by officials in London. Confrontations continued until August 1773 when Moultrie suspended Drayton as a member of the Council for uttering "a Gross insult and Reflection" on the Council. However, Drayton continued to be a thorn in the lieutenant governor's imperious side, prompting Moultrie to denounce him as "a man destitute of worth, self-conceited, proud and envious."

Drayton held a different opinion, complaining that he was being persecuted and that "the inquisition never did worse." In early 1774 he asked James Grant to intercede, explaining that the recent controversies emanated from Moultrie's desire to suppress examinations of excess expenditures on public works. Drayton charged that Moultrie was trying to stifle all complaints against the government by falsely accusing that: "Every matter relative to them [government] may be supposed to partake of the general ferment which now unhappily prevails over this continent."

It was in this disharmonious atmosphere that Lieutenant Colonel Patrick Tonyn became governor of East Florida in March 1774. Forty-nine years old, Governor Tonyn was a career army man, a veteran of combat in Germany during the Seven Years' War, as well as the owner of an already established plantation in East Florida which he had never seen.

Tonyn's arrival had been keenly anticipated; many among the populace speculated that the new governor would restore the tranquility and gaiety of former days. Even former Governor Grant predicted that Tonyn would soon "bring all into good humour and drown anymosity in a Bottle of Claret."

Intently, Mulcaster scrutinized the new governor's actions and personality, noting that he "bows with a grace and drinks more water than wine" and "dines at home with his mistress and a Parson he brought out." After dining, the governor "walked arm in arm with his lady along the bay and so to the Fort." On the

evening of his inauguration, which included royal salutes and a
processional with beating drums as the party moved toward St.
Peter's to hear a sermon by Reverend Forbes, Tonyn again
walked with his lady along the bay, bowing before the ladies of
the town while they curtsied in return (for which Drayton
thought they were foolish).

Residents of St. Augustine soon learned that Governor Tonyn
lacked the sociability and tact necessary to promote social and
political harmony. Intolerant and short-tempered, Tonyn demanded strict deference to class and rank, and treated any
questioning of his authority with a rigid military disdain. Lower
Houses of Assembly, and all who advocated them, were viewed
by the new governor as seditious. Prone to over-reaction, Tonyn
assessed Chief Justice Drayton in a judgment unlikely to promote harmony: "I soon found his political principles were of the
levelling kind, and of a piece with the seditions and rebellions in
the other colonies, and to render himself popular and of consequence, he wished to degrade and reduce the authority of the
Governor and Council, and to establish that source of sedition,
the great bulwark of American liberty, a house of Assembly."

Basing his reactions on reports of disloyalty in the northern
colonies, Tonyn seemed unaware that East Florida residents had
not formed chapters of the Sons of Liberty nor of Committees of
Correspondence. The opposition in St. Augustine remained loyal
to the Crown, and were willing to pay taxes on glass, lead,
paper—even tea. Rather than oppose a British Court of Admiralty, as colonials had done with a vigor in New England,
residents supported the one located in St. Augustine.

What Drayton and the others in the opposition wanted was
protection of their basic rights as Englishmen, including the right
to representation in an elective House of Assembly. As officials
of the colonial government or recipients of Parliament's largesse,
they were hardly radicals intent on inflaming mobs into rebellion. By sensing "jarring flames" in St. Augustine when he
arrived, the new governor misread the actual situation and
exacerbated the tensions.

Town residents' initial impressions of the new governor were
hardly flattering. Lieutenant Mulcaster was startled by the large

entourage that Tonyn brought with him: "about Twenty White servants as dirty a sett of fellows as [you] would wish to look at—they got all hands drunk the second night after they landed." No one was safe from Mulcaster's caustic judgments. He even attacked the governor's lady: "The whore he has brought is handsome enough, she has three children with her and is big with a fourth. She takes great State and I hear is called Mrs. Tonyn."

It was six weeks before Tonyn entertained the town's dignitaries. Thirty dined and afterwards there were reports of "bad port, bad madeira and bad sherry." A few days later, after "a very bad dinner and a tawdry dessert," a depressed Mulcaster lamented: "this is a pleasant prospect for us who drank out of wicker bottles. . ." To Grant he wrote, "I assure you Baptiste (Grant's cook) is much missed here. The Parson cries, 'Ah, woe is me. I wonder when we shall see any more good dinners. I think if the Governor had returned, Jossey [Grant's house servant] would have often called upon us.' To which I answer, 'Parson, it's better for us as it is—we live temperate, you often preach it— and now necessity compels you to exercise what you recommend. There is nothing like following a good example.' For Grant, read Tonyn, for bon soup and old Madeira, read bad broth and fresh water. In this manner we sometimes laugh on the wrong side of our mouth."

Reminding James Grant of his prediction that Tonyn would restore tranquility, Mulcaster countered: "You are quite mistaken in your man—he neither drinks nor gives Claret—he has no wine of any kind, at least that is good for anything, and he has not seen Company six times since he has been in the Province. He hangs at home miserably, no method, bad servants and a dirty table cloth . . . [are] all the comfort he seems to have, except the comfort of a more dirty whore."

By November, even Parson Forbes was moved to comment that "hopes have failed with Tonyn." In St. Augustine, "invariable gloom prevails, the reverse of what it was," with the new governor exercising "little management in his family, [and] is expensive in horses and servants, of whom he makes little use."

After months of observation, Mulcaster finally concluded that Tonyn was "not very alert at his pen" and "not very wise," but overall "a good-meaning man . . . [who] will never bring fire to the pan."

Harsh criticism was also penned against Tonyn for laxity in paying for furniture he agreed to buy from former Governor Grant and for cruel treatment of slaves and servants. It took six years of repeated requests before Tonyn paid for the furniture, and then several pieces had been lost. Several witnesses blamed the governor's lady and directed their invectives against her. In January 1775 David Yeats considered she "in general rules the roost," and later said: "There is a female in the family who without either understanding or knowledge has a great deal to say."

The unhappiest commerce between the two governors concerned Tonyn's rental of three of Grant's domestic slaves. Yeats, who was Grant's business manager as well as a medical doctor, planter and government official, became alarmed about the treatment of the slaves. "I have not received a shilling since they have been there," he informed his employer, "and [Alexander, Peg and Sue] are greatly complaining about bad usage, which indeed is no fault of his, but the WOMAN'S, who appears to be of a cruel hard-headed disposition, at least to the servants."

Reverend Forbes investigated and concluded it would be cruel to sell the slaves to Tonyn. "They plead hard," he informed Grant, "and the town says [they] have Iron Caps . . . Alexander complains that Madam is the devil, he told me the governor was well enough, but since I saw him he has had the cap above mentioned and been flogged." Two days later Forbes sent another urgent letter: "Your Negroes, from the mismanagement and a capricious cruelty of a fine lady, are considered as being in a state of the most abject slavery. Alexander has got an iron cap with which he walks the streets."

This news infuriated Grant. He sent an unequivocal order to Dr. Yeats: "If Alexander and Peg are still in the woods [they had run away], which I wish them to be, you are publickly to make it known that Governor Tonyn has nothing to do with them, that they have nothing to fear, and are to live in the future at Grant's Villa."

Although discord persisted throughout Tonyn's tenure as governor (and it should be tempered by comparison to the violence in cities to the north), the repercussions tended to diminish as war engulfed the American colonies. A portent of the months ahead came in August 1775 when the *Betsy*, under Captain Lofthouse, was attacked off the St. Augustine bar by a rebel vessel out of South Carolina. Loaded with gunpowder, the *Betsy* had anchored overnight off the bar to await favorable winds and tide. Sailing north from Matanzas Inlet at daybreak, the rebel privateer surprised and sacked her without a shot being fired in return.

The plight of the *Betsy* prompted a review of the town's defenses. Fewer than two hundred men of the Fourteenth Regiment were on station, with the numbers often fluctuating drastically downward. After conducting a census of the province's white inhabitants fit to bear arms and the loyal slaves who could be trusted with weapons, Tonyn ordered that seven white and four black militia companies be formed.

Under threat of an attack from Georgia, life in St. Augustine took on dismal tones. Moultrie complained in October 1775 that rebels in Georgia and South Carolina were trying to starve the town residents; fortunately, there had been bumper crops in East Florida. Sickness had become prevalent in the town following an unusually wet summer and fall. Dr. Yeats, who had a flourishing medical practice, said the sickness "fell chiefly on the lower sort of people, the grog drinkers, no person of any note died except Mr. [Witter] Cuming a month ago."

In February 1776 William Drayton was suspended as Chief Justice, largely for political reasons, as Governor Tonyn still felt that Drayton's political principles were in total agreement with the "factious leaders" in the northern colonies. Yeats felt that Drayton "certainly drew it upon himself," but worried about the repercussions, since "this town may literally be said to be divided against itself."

The town was indeed divided. At Wood's Tavern the day following Drayton's suspension, his supporters held a meeting chaired by Dr. Andrew Turnbull. Drayton was backed by respected citizens such as Francis Philip Fatio, Spencer Man, Robert Bisset and James Penman; seventy-four signed a petition to the Crown which Governor Tonyn refused to forward.

After defending himself before the Board of Trade in London, Drayton was reinstated. He returned to St. Augustine only to be suspended again by the governor in December of 1777. This time Drayton made another trip to London but resigned from office before his case was discussed. Returning to East Florida for the final time, Drayton continued as a part-time planter until 1780, when he moved to Charleston.

Throughout this period of tension and gloom Parson Forbes retained an optimistic attitude. He was now a member of the Council, the sole judge of the Court of Vice Admiralty and assistant judge of the Courts of Common Law. Always anxious to increase his income, Forbes asked James Grant to advocate in London that he become the next chief justice, citing in his own behalf that the "study of divinity is laying a good foundation for law."

As the Revolution grew in the north, John Moultrie resumed an old military career as a colonel of the East Florida militia, commanding a regiment which mustered three hundred men. In August 1776 he reminisced: "When we left the Cherokees I pleased myself with the thought of beating my sword into a plow share and that I should never arm again, but I begin to think I flattered myself."

Moultrie noted the paradox that would continue throughout the war: St. Augustine remained safe from attack, even flourished in trade and population, while the northern portion of the colony, between the St. Johns and St. Marys rivers, became a frontier battle zone of raid and counter raid conducted primarily for plunder of cattle and slaves. "This town is full of people who have fled for safety," Moultrie wrote. "Our planting thrives finely, good indigo, plenty of provisions; every plantation has enough and some to spare, but the consumption of the town at present is great." There were in August 1776 between twenty and thirty vessels anchored in the bay awaiting loads of lumber which was then bringing "such an amazing price."

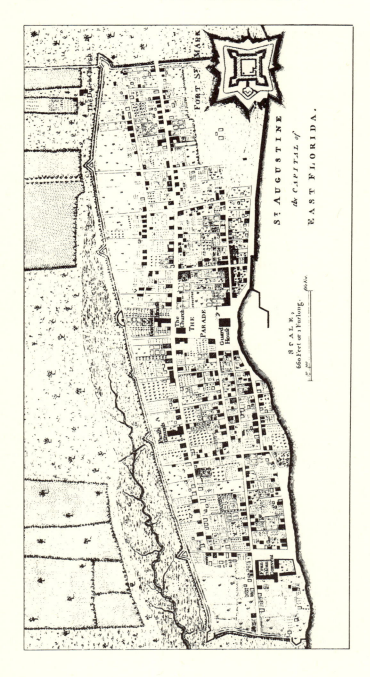

Thomas Jefferys' plan of British St. Augustine clearly shows the long narrow geography of the town, with the Matanzas River in the foreground, Maria Sanchez Creek above left, at the north the familar angles of Fort St. Mark (Castillo de San Marcos) and in the center, the Parade or plaza. These and the easily identifiable streets are all present in today's St. Augustine.

Away from the town rebel attacks had broken up some plantations north of the St. Johns River, which Forbes thought could not be protected from "this lawless banditti." Yeats complained: "We have been pestered here by the Rebels from Georgia driving away our cattle and stealing our Negroes. They have lately carried away between thirty and forty Negroes on the west side of the St. Johns River under the management of Mr. Gray." Even south and east of the river James Penman, Martin Jollie and Francis Fatio were talking of breaking up their estates and moving toward town. More alarming was talk of capitulation if a rumored attack on St. Augustine by two thousand rebels materialized.

With border war raging even Reverend Forbes condoned the East Florida forces engaged in plunder. English officers had "70 men and 25 crackers," and Chief Cow Keeper and his Seminole Indian warriors on the St. Marys to drive cattle from Georgia. Forbes thought the Indians "will be the best guard to the settlement," and was especially pleased that Thomas Brown, a refugee who had been tarred, feathered and scalped in Augusta, Georgia for supporting the Crown, was with the Indians "and will seek revenge."

Late in October 1776 the ever optimistic John Moultrie summed up the year of hostilities: "Georgia began to plunder us, we retaliated, the common frontier quite abandoned on both sides, horses and crops destroyed, people and cattle moved away; numbers of refugees from Virginia, Carolina and Georgia have fled to us; they almost eat up our provision, but providence has favoured us." An abundant supply of flour and rice had come into St. Augustine and "we drive off as many cattle from the Georgians as have hitherto supplied our market, and I hope we shall continue to do so."

When Lieutenant Colonel Thomas Brown and the East Florida Rangers were in St. Augustine, along with their Indian allies, the town's streets and markets presented a kaleidoscope of activity. The Rangers were a mixed corps of white and black men dressed in frontier garb of hunting shirt, breeches and leggings appropriate for border marauders. In addition to the Rangers, St. Augustine was for months the training site for raw Swiss and

German recruits of the Sixtieth Regiment under command of General Augustine Prevost. Later, three hundred plantation slaves were drafted to work with a hundred soldiers repairing the fort and exterior defenses.

Such troop movements did not go unnoticed by Luciano de Herrera. As a respected, though Spanish, St. Augustinian, he could and did gather not only local military news, but also, from seamen and other travelers, rumors and reports of English activities elsewhere, all of which he secretly sent on to Havana.

In February of 1777 East Florida forces captured Fort McIntosh on the Satilla River in Georgia, returning to St. Augustine with two thousand head of cattle and sixty-eight prisoners. In May a Georgia invasion force struck back but was totally defeated at Thomas Creek (in today's Duval County). An American naval force was turned back by Captain Mowbray in the *Rebecca*.

In March 1778 the Rangers again crossed the Georgia border to capture and burn Fort Barrington on the Altamaha River. An American force of three thousand counterattacked across the St. Marys River in June, captured Fort Tonyn and moved south toward the St. Johns, until turned back at the Alligator Creek bridge on the Nassau River. The American forces retreated to Georgia, ending what was to be the last invasion attempt of the war.

Reinforcements, eventually two thousand strong, began pouring into St. Augustine late in the summer of 1778 to participate in a major invasion of Georgia. In November and December, British forces under General Prevost pushed all the way to Savannah, securing the northern frontier and shielding East Florida from further incursions.

"Sometimes alarmed, never much afraid and not hurt," was John Moultrie's memory of St. Augustine in 1778. If anything, mercantile activity had been greatly stimulated by the war; Moultrie noted that "pitch, tar, turpentine and lumber in abundance," were available to "vessels loading from all ports." Merchants were, however, short of fresh provisions, caused primarily by a decline in the beef supply at market: "The Georgia stocks of cattle lately have supplied us well, they now fail us, the large stocks of their frontier pretty well expended."

The war had certainly not hurt Moultrie or his prosperous plantations. He looked forward to the completion of his "handsome stone house at Bella Vista, near finished, which I shall retire to. . . It will last forever, a good country house with ten rooms, plows and carts going in the fields since March, more rice than I can beat out. . . . Fine stock of cattle and hogs and plenty of beef, fish, butter and cream cheese, everything. . ."

With a great deal of pride, Moultrie described his latest patriotic contribution to the defense of St. Augustine and the province: "I have become a prodigious manufacturer of gallies. Many of the knowing ones laughed me to scorn; my but I was right. My *Thunder* gally with two 24 pounders that draws only 18 inches water has done more than all the fleet at Savannah. She took the famous rebel gally, the *Congress*, beside several other vessels. . . . We have four of the Thunderars for the defense of St. Johns, St. Augustine and Musquito inlets. Nothing can oppose them, their metal so Heavy and their draw of water so small and they are so active and it costs so little money."

With food crops bringing all-time high prices, David Yeats too was enthusiastic about the future of East Florida. The only problem he encountered was purchasing clothing and supplies for the slaves under his care, with clothing selling in 1780 for six times its value in England, and flour bringing between £7 and £9 Sterling per barrel. For the refugees flocking to St. Augustine, many sick and destitute, such prices meant severe hardship.

The refugees sometimes brought severe problems for the town. In May of 1780 a smallpox contagion prompted Dr. Yeats to institute an inoculation program. In six weeks he inoculated two hundred persons with no patients lost.

For the merchants, laborers, artisans, butchers, bakers, shopkeepers and tavern operators the influx of soldiers, sailors and loyalist refugees meant unprecedented opportunities for work and profit. Equipping and feeding the armies and ships of the Royal Navy kept crews working overtime. To house the burgeoning population, carpenters and stonemasons worked feverishly renovating buildings, and soon were throwing up structures outside the town walls.

Among the refugees seeking shelter in 1777 was a group of six hundred Minorcans who had marched along the King's Road from Dr. Andrew Turnbull's colony at New Smyrna. After complaining of cruel treatment to Governor Tonyn in March and May of 1777 they were released from their indentures by Turnbull's attorneys. Joined in November by their parish priest, Father Pedro Camps, they reconstituted their church of San Pedro on St. George Street and joined the town's labor force.

Three years later, in December 1780, Yeats complained that the town was becoming crowded, accentuated by the recent arrival of sixty-three principal Carolina rebels who had been captured and sent to St. Augustine for confinement. Following his customary policy with rebel prisoners, Tonyn paroled all those who pledged not to try to escape and gave them freedom of the town. Only Christopher Gadsden refused and was confined to the fort.

Alexander Moultrie, the younger brother of the lieutenant governor, was among those paroled; he went to live with his family at Bella Vista. Although few prisoners could expect such congenial accommodations, they were all able to arrange for housing, to write home for money and to obtain a sufficient daily diet at the fort.

"The malignant spirit has almost subsided," Governor Tonyn declared in 1779, responding at last to the long-standing request for an elective assembly for East Florida. For years Tonyn had opposed an assembly, but migration to East Florida after 1776 included such men as Henry Yonge, William Panton, Jeremyn and Charles Wright, James Hume and Thomas Brown, conspicuously loyal to the Crown, which convinced Tonyn that a lower house could prove beneficial to governing the colony. For fear of potential danger from the American prisoners in town, Tonyn delayed the elections until February 1781 by which time the rebels had been released to return north.

From March 27, 1781 until March 25, 1784 two legislative bodies met in the Town House chambers in St. Augustine, the Council, with Lieutenant Governor Moultrie presiding and the

Commons, with William Brown as Speaker. Legislation of importance for the town approved by both houses included a slave code and a police act, the latter calling for regulations in sanitation, building codes, fire prevention, weights and measures, and other municipal matters.

While the two houses were in session, news reached St. Augustine that West Florida had fallen to the Spanish after the capture of Pensacola in May 1781. In October the news was even more distressing. At Yorktown, Virginia, Lord Cornwallis surrendered his entire seven-thousand-man army to George Washington and the American forces. St. Augustine residents again lived in fear of attack.

One St. Augustinian had more reason to fear, for Tonyn had finally become aware of Herrera's sub-rosa activities. Alerted to his danger, the spy fled to Havana.

At this late date, however, the greatest threat was the active disinterest of British diplomats in protecting the interests of East Florida residents in the peace negotiations. In May 1782, well before terms had been reached, Sir Guy Carleton, the British commander, ordered the evacuation of Savannah and St. Augustine. To the residents of St. Augustine this was crushing news. After years of struggle to establish businesses, plantations and homes, the province had only recently become prosperous; sacrifices had been made on behalf of the Crown during the recent war, and loyal residents felt that they were being betrayed. Dr. Yeats was thrown into the "utmost consternation" when he heard the news: "I am totally ruined and see nothing but want and misery before me."

A reprieve came in late July 1782 when Carleton changed the order, designating East Florida as a haven for refugees from Savannah and Charleston. During the ensuing year over seventy-five hundred refugees reached East Florida, inflating the total population to more than seventeen thousand. Yeats noted in September 1782 that "thousands of Refugees and Negroes arrived here from Georgia upon the evacuation of that province," many of them "sick and destitute."

Land, tools and rations were provided for the refugees, now forced to start anew in a strange land of rugged pioneering conditions. Much uncultivated land, still held in huge tracts by absentee landlords, was cleared and planted, and new towns grew to serve the expanding trade and production of the province. St. Johns Town, at Hester's Bluff (where French Fort Caroline is recreated), grew overnight to over three hundred houses, with numerous businesses and warehouses. Hillsborough, on the St. Marys River, also grew, prompted by the upsurge in exports of lumber and naval stores.

At the State House in St. Augustine, the town's first theater gave its initial performance on March 3, 1783 with proceeds pledged to assist needy refugees. Further evidence of progress came with the town's first printing press and first newspaper, *The East-Florida Gazette*, which was published weekly from February 1, 1783 through March 23, 1784. Charles Wright was the printer for John Wells, Jr., a refugee editor from Charleston.

It was amidst such signs of hope and progress that Governor Tonyn received notice that the province had been returned to Spain. In June 1783, Moultrie related the tragic news to James Grant: "I may probably once more join company with you. We have often parted without a prospect of meeting again, but the chapter of accidents has brought us together; tis the only good chapter." After finally achieving a life of "real plenty, ease and elegance" in a province that had recently shown an astonishing productivity in agriculture, lumber and naval stores, Moultrie was about "to be turned adrift, and again seek a resting place."

Terribly disturbed about the fate of his slaves, especially "a number of faithful servants brought up for several generations in our family," Moultrie contemplated freeing them all, burning his houses and becoming "a real philosopher." For the future, "England, I think, will bring me up. My feelings, principles, everything prevents me having any idea of remaining in America."

The decision was final, however, and Moultrie and others began to prepare for evacuation. It was a hectic and chaotic transition period, lasting for more than two years and marred by cruel raids by "lawless banditti" left over from the war.

The "banditti" were a mixed group of refugees and Florida residents, veterans of the cattle and slave raids that had traumatized both sides of the Florida-Georgia border during the war. Led by Daniel McGirtt, a former East Florida Ranger, the "banditti" raided plantations north of St. Augustine for cattle, horses and slaves, paying little attention to whether their victims had been rebels or loyalists. Acting as highwaymen, they robbed and kidnapped travellers on the King's Road, ambushed British troops sent against them and retreated to hideaways in the Diego Plains.

While turmoil reigned in the countryside, tensions ran high in St. Augustine as well. In 1783 Captain Robert Bisset learned of a terrifying conspiracy only narrowly averted: "A few nights ago several [British soldiers] were killed, their plan was to burn the barracks, plunder the Town, and take Possession of the Fort, to arm all the Negroes, and to put every white Man to Death that opposed them keeping the Country to themselves as they will rather die than be Carried to Halifax to be discharged."

In May 1784 Governor Tonyn notified British residents that they had to apply for space on the evacuation vessels. Dr. Yeats, like nearly all the British settlers, made plans to depart: "The idea of keeping possession of Estates in this Province, under the Spanish government is now I suppose vanished, we being told that such as choose to remain must publickly profess the Catholic religion or absolutely quit their Estates."

In July, Yeats reported that "two troops of Light Horse" had recently subdued the "banditti," permitting him to keep Grant's slaves working at a plantation they had just opened on the Guano River. Within six weeks he expected them to harvest corn and pack it in barrels to ship along to the Bahamas. Also aboard would be the disassembled houses from the plantation.

Yeats reported that Spanish Governor Zéspedes had arrived from Havana on June 27 with a five-hundred-man garrison: "The Spanish Colours are now dayly displayed on Fort St. Marks, a new and distressing sight to British subjects." Fortunately, Yeats wrote, "everything has gone very smoothly—indeed, Governor Zéspedes appears to be a polite, well bred gentleman, and shows every disposition to make matters as easy and agreeable to the British inhabitants as possible."

Governor Tonyn would not have agreed, as he and Zéspedes

quarreled for months. Since other British officials praised the Spanish governor, it seems safe to conclude that Tonyn's prickly nature was as evident at the end of his time in East Florida as it was when he arrived.

One disagreeable matter that neither Zéspedes nor Tonyn could alleviate was the depressed market for houses in St. Augustine. Selling prices had plummeted to approximately ten percent of construction costs. As Yeats found, the market for country plantations was even more depressed, with "not the smallest prospect of a shilling being offered for them." Since only the Spanish military was coming to St. Augustine initially, Yeats concluded that in a "few months we must abandon our property here without money and without price to His Catholic Majesty's subjects to the utter and inevitable ruin of many."

Yeats and Tonyn moved to the St. Marys River on June 1, 1785 to help supervise the final departures. A tent city had sprung up there, with planters living alongside their slaves, threatened by plunderers as they awaited transport to the Bahamas or other British colonies.

Tonyn had already informed Lieutenant Governor Powell in the Bahamas: "I have sent the boards that were the frames of the Pews of the Church of St. Augustine to be erected in the Church intended to be built by the Loyalists in the Island of Providence. By another opportunity I shall send likewise the Bells of this City, and the fire Engine for the use of the above cited Town intended to be raised by the Loyal Emigrants. . . ." Tonyn dolefully predicted that "a few Minorcans professing the roman catholic Religion excepted; there will not be more than three or four British that will become Residenters with the Spaniards in the Province."

In mid-November, Governor Tonyn and the last of the evacuees sailed from the mouth of the St. Marys River, arriving in Portsmouth, England on January 11, 1786. Without even church bells to sound the demise, British East Florida had expired.

The streets of St. Augustine were once again nearly deserted. The town had received a face-lift under the British, but it remained essentially the same as when Spanish homeowners had departed two decades before. Some would return from Cuba to their old dwellings and try to pick up the pieces of their previous lives. On hand to greet them would be a few old friends: Jesse Fish, Francisco Xavier Sanchez and Manuel Solana. There would be new faces, British subjects like John Leslie and Francis Philip Fatio who chose to remain on their estates and make a new life under the Spanish. And there were six hundred Minorcans in the vicinity of St. Augustine; Catholic and Spain-oriented already, they stayed on to become a vital and enduring part of the town's history.

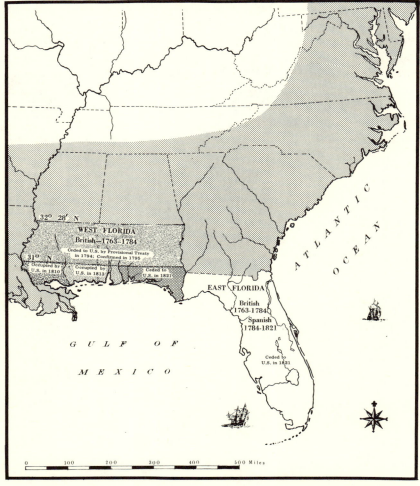

WEST FLORIDA
British—1763-1784
Ceded to U.S. by Provisional Treaty
in 1794; Confirmed in 1795

32° 28' N

31° N

Occupied by
U.S. in 1810

Occupied by
U.S. in 1813

Ceded to
U.S. in 1821

EAST FLORIDA

British
1763-1784
Spanish
1784-1821

Ceded to
U.S. in 1821

ATLANTIC OCEAN

GULF OF MEXICO

0   100   200   300   400   500 Miles

Map by Charles S. Coomes

From the 16th century the land called Florida has had a variety of
shapes and boundaries. *La Florida* of the Spanish explorers
included not only the territory indicated on this map, but also all of
present-day Louisiana, Arkansas and much of Oklahoma and
Texas. Treaties, annexations, purchases and accessions over the
years have reduced Florida to its present size.

Chapter Five

The Spanish Return: The People-Mix Period
1784 - 1821

by

Patricia C. Griffin

For nearly a year and a half two governments existed side by side in St. Augustine as the British engaged in a reluctant withdrawal, and the Spanish regime reinstated itself. Governor Vizente Manuel de Zéspedes, newly arrived, wrote terse communiques to be translated by his able assistant, Captain Carlos Howard, and taken a few doors away to Governor Tonyn whose responses bristled with chilly British formality. The problems were many. Besides the tedious job of expediting the departure of some seventeen thousand British from the province, difficulties with slaves, Indians and the local populace, as well as the menacing wave of land-hungry Americans on the northern border, demanded attention.

The "banditti" were still roaming the countryside under the leadership of Dan McGirtt whose name had become synonymous with lawlessness in the province. McGirtt and his associates played off one government against the other. Zéspedes and Tonyn alternately vied with each other to curry the favor of the bandits, and then each in turn attempted to round up the outlaws to make a show of bringing peace to the province. This inglorious round of two cats and one mouse finally ended when Zéspedes ordered the arrest of McGirtt and other ringleaders and bundled them off to jail in Havana.

The departure of McGirtt did not solve the problems of slave stealing. When Spain regained East Florida about five or six thousand Negroes were in the area. They fell into four groups— slaves of British subjects, slaves plundered from the American colonies, runaway slaves, and free Negroes. Slaves were a large part of the wealth of the colony and, unlike landholdings, portable. Departing Britishers concealed extra blacks on board ship as they left, often sailing without port clearance. Slave raids took place back and forth across the Georgia-Florida border with recovery of stolen property the justification, an activity which continued to harass both the American and Spanish governments throughout the second Spanish period. Indians frequently harbored runaway slaves, and even some of the free Negroes dealt in slave marketing. The inaugural ball given by the English for incoming Spanish officials was marred by word that eight slaves belonging to Samuel Farley, one of the ball's sponsors, had been stolen.

The difficulty of determining the actual status of many of the blacks led Zéspedes to issue a proclamation requiring slave owners to show proof of ownership or have their slaves seized as Crown property. Free blacks were to register in twenty days to receive work permits.

The British authorities, still in town, promptly protested that under British law slave owners held such chattel without written deed. Zéspedes for his own reasons backed down and did not enforce the decree.

Blacks who could show some claim to freedom soon found their rights assiduously respected by the new government. Their dignity as humans was recognized under Spanish law and culture, and blacks in the province were astonished to see members of their race in the regiments newly arrived in town, some holding officer rank.

Notwithstanding the general benevolence toward Negroes, some individual Spaniards were unable to withstand the temptation of trafficking in "black gold." In a celebrated case, an English woman named Louisa Waldron was accused of harboring Lucy, a runaway slave belonging to a Spaniard who had recently bought her from a departing British woman. Although the slave was not found on her premises, Louisa Waldron was put under guard along with a female slave whom she rightfully owned. She remained in confinement at the home of John Thomas, the gaoler who had served in British times. Louisa's horse was confiscated and several of her friends watched as her house was ransacked by Spanish soldiers and all of her valuables carried away.

Louisa was threatened with imprisonment at the castillo unless she turned over the "wench" with her in exchange for the missing

Lucy. Maintaining innocence, she refused, becoming more and more distraught until, at the end of twenty-seven days, she attempted to kill herself with a penknife. Several days later Lucy was found at a nearby plantation, and Louisa returned to the shambles of her home with a scant four shillings in her pocket as reparation for her stolen horse. In spite of a drawn-out court case and Tonyn's appeals to Zéspedes on "that miserable womans sufferings," attempts to recoup the other losses failed.

If the two governors readily used the banditti and slaves as pawns in their power struggle, they were in uneasy agreement on the subject of the Indians. For some years the English firm, Panton, Leslie & Company, had been an important element in maintaining peaceful relations with the tribes through their highly skilled trading practices.

Taking advantage of the government changeover, enter-prising groups in the United States began a campaign to win over the Indians by trading with them on terms more advanta-geous to the tribes. Any such change in Indian loyalty spelled ruin for the Spanish rule in East and West Florida. Zéspedes and his counterpart in West Florida saw no other solution except continuance of the exclusive franchise as requested by the British. Tonyn found himself in the ridiculous position of plead-ing the case of the returning Spaniards with the Indians, "a very unpleasant task," he wrote to his superior in England, Lord Sydney, after years of convincing the Indians of the perfidy of all those of Spanish descent.

The American menace took other forms. All along the Spanish borderlands, citizens of the infant United States were eyeing lands across the frontier, jockeying into position, ready to jump for land claims when, not if, the Spanish territories were annexed by the growing nation. Georgians massed along the flexible line between the Floridas and the United States rubbed elbows with British royalists. These Tories, mostly near Fernandina, still hoped that England would reclaim the peninsula.

Meanwhile, in April 1785 Zéspedes was the surprised host of a distinguished American, Nathaniel Greene, the major general who had commanded the victorious Continental forces in the southern colonies during the American Revolution. Greene's purpose in visiting St. Augustine was unclear, so Zéspedes, who was told only that his guest was on "private business," decided to entertain him with lavish hospitality. The stranger was escorted into town by a lieutenant general's guard and an elegant dinner arranged. The entertainment was the first the new governor had given since his arrival and served to annoy further Governor Tonyn and his aides who had feasted the Spanish governor several times with no return of the compliment.

In a letter to his wife Greene described the banquet as "truly elegant and I believe in my soul there was from one hundred and fifty to two hundred dishes of different kinds served up in seven courses." The American visitor was impressed with the French cookery and with Zéspedes's vivacious wife and two unmarried daughters whom he found "not hansome, their complexion is rather tawny but they have got sweet, languishing eyes."

Greene added, "they look as if they could love with great violence," a statement which proved to be prophetic. Scarcely two months later, one of the daughters, Dominga, ran away with a sublieutenant of the Hibernian regiment.

Lieutenant Juan O'Donovan previously had the effrontery to ask for Dominga's hand and had been told by her father that nobility of birth was an indispensible prerequisite, as were adequate resources to maintain a proper station in life. After all, Dominga's mother was the sister of the then Viceroy of Mexico and Zéspedes himself was of gentle birth. A hurried request was put in for O'Donovan's transfer and the worried father set a "careful watch" over his daughter.

During the festive farewell party for the departing British in late May, Dominga sneaked away to meet her love at the home of Angela Huet, the English wife of the chief engineer, Mariano de la Rocque. In an elaborate ruse a Minorcan servant of doña Angela's was sent to beseech Father Miguel O'Reilly to come at once to attend her sick mistress at her house on St. Francis Street near the barracks. When the priest entered the house he saw the engineer's wife in rosy good health and heard, to his consternation, the young couple reciting the marriage vows, an action which, taking place before a man of the cloth, constituted a clandestine marriage in the eyes of the Catholic Church.

Captain Mariano de la Rocque, Spanish military engineer, designed the entrance of the chapel in Castillo de San Marcos.

To save the honor of his daughter, the governor allowed a somewhat more proper marriage to take place that same night at the English woman's house. Then O'Donovan was promptly put under arrest and sent to Havana for confinement until Church and king gave their blessing to the marriage. Eventually the two lovers were reunited in St. Augustine; yet a third marriage ceremony took place in the parish church, and the young couple moved into a house facing the bay on what is now the corner of Marine and St. Francis streets.

O'Donovan was an Irishman, serving the Spanish king as many of his countrymen had done before him, a part of the garrison which had come to the province with Zéspedes. He and other Hibernian soldiers hardly stood out as foreign in a town where one could hear in the course of a day as many as six or seven languages and multiple dialects.

Even after the departure of the last English officials in June 1785, St. Augustine retained its lively mixture of peoples. Possibly no small town on the North American continent has ever had such a diverse population. In the span of the thirty-eight years of the second Spanish period, Spaniards, Englishmen, Americans, Minorcans, Italians, Greeks, Swiss, Germans, French, Canary Islanders, Scots and Irish, along with the sizable number of blacks and visiting Indians rendered the little town cosmopolitan. The seven censuses taken during the period present conflicting pictures, sometimes including the garrison as part of the count and in one case lumping the town population with that of the province. The population of the town itself appears to have varied from 900 to 1600, and the garrison commonly comprised an additional 450 to 500.

But numbers tell only part of the story. People came and went, the garrison was changed periodically, persons were absent from town temporarily, shipping out as seamen or visiting Havana or the colonies. Census takers had difficulty counting heads because of the number who shifted back and forth between hinterland and town, some owning both a town house and a plantation house. Others had no permanent residence at all.

In the 1786 census the Minorcan group numbered 469, over 50 percent of the town population. In the nine years since they had trudged overland from New Smyrna to St. Augustine they had become an integral part of the town. Most of the families lived in the northwest section of town which became known as the Minorcan quarter. They and their few slaves raised food crops on small garden plots outside of the town boundary and fished in season, while a few were seafarers. Many worked at two or even three occupations to support themselves, a pattern remembered from their homelands.

As Spanish rule returned to St. Augustine a concerted effort was made to repatriate the previous Florida inhabitants (and their descendents) of the first Spanish period. These expatriots had been settled by the Spanish government in a rural area near Matanzas, Cuba, where they nostalgically named their little settlement *San Agustín de la Nueva Florida*. The twenty years of their exile covered a substantial portion of their lives; many had died and few of the living were willing to return to the place of their birth. By 1786 only 132 of these floridanos had returned to St. Augustine. Eager to have Spanish-speaking settlers take up the land rather than those of suspect nationalities, inducements were added. Returnees were promised extra land, stipends, long-term loans of slaves and farm implements, and compensation for their former estates which had fallen into other hands in the interim. Still only a trickle responded, numbering less than five hundred, and some of these now found Florida a disappointment and returned to Cuba.

However, a few Spanish nationals immigrated directly to the colony from Spain. One was Gerónimo Alvarez, a twenty-five-year-old baker, who took up residence with a Minorcan family and later married one of the stepdaughters.

Also, a group of Canary Islanders, originally sent to Pensacola, were transferred to East Florida. They were to be peasant farmers in the reconstituted settlement, but a year after their arrival Zéspedes complained in a letter to the Viceroy that "their sloth compels me to inform your excellency that they are nothing but a source of useless expense to the royal treasury."

If Spanish-speaking citizens were hard to come by, others filled the gap. Surprisingly, about three hundred of the English elected to stay even though required to swear allegiance to the Spanish Crown and to convert to Catholicism. Most owned land outside the town and having sunk their fortunes in the Florida enterprise, found change of loyalty more to their liking than poverty. They were joined as time went on by colonists from the newly formed United States as well as by opportunists from other parts of the world.

Of the British holdovers, several played a significant role in the new regime. John Leslie, a native of Scotland and a bachelor, remained in town to manage the trading interests of his firm, Panton, Leslie & Company. Bilingual and of an adaptable disposition, he was much in demand as an interpreter and arbitrator, and his relationship with Zéspedes and later Spanish governors was amiable although detractors thought this a possible result of his ability to secure furniture in the latest mode for Government House.

Francis Philip Fatio, of Swiss origin, remained to oversee his extensive plantation holdings on the St. Johns River. He had an Italian wife, and as a gentleman and scholar, spoke six languages. Much of his time was spent in his house in town, and, like Leslie, he was often called into service as a lay judge to settle claims such as that of Louisa Waldron.

A few, very few, St. Augustinians had lived under the two previous regimes. One was Jesse Fish, New York born, who had lived with the Herrera family and later represented Walton & Company, merchants in the first Spanish period. When Florida was ceded to England the bilingual, bicultural Fish stayed and sold property and slaves to the incoming British. Then once again when the Spanish returned he reversed that procedure. In his late maturity he married a young wife, a disastrous union. Because of her "madcap" qualities he eventually separated from her and their two children to live as a recluse on his plantation on Anastasia Island, making the additional mistake of trusting his business dealings to an inept relative. Although he continued to raise and ship oranges whose quality was highly regarded as far away as London, his estate was in financial ruin by the time of his death in 1790.

Francisco Xavier Sanchez was about seventeen when the British flag was raised in 1763. He became a successful planter in the English era, skillfully withstanding Tonyn's attempt to implicate him in the banditti conspiracies. By the time of the

Spanish return he had a mulatto mistress whose progeny he recognized as his legal heirs. Later he, like Fish, took a young wife, although a more respected one, and by the time of his death in 1807 was one of the most venerated citizens in town.

Manuel Solana too had prospered through the British years. In 1783 he was living on the San Sebastian River, where not much later the Solana ferry crossed over from what is now Bridge Street. By his death in November 1821 he had acquired several houses, one of which is the large two-story one on the corner of present Charlotte and Cadiz streets.

Luciano de Herrera, who had escaped from St. Augustine just three years before, was one of those who returned in the summer of 1784. Rewarded for the years when he reported to Cuba on events in British St. Augustine, now he was Zéspedes's Overseer of Public Works and an intermediary for the governor in his relations with the Indians.

The call for settlers did not always attract the right sort. John Hudson, a young Irish Catholic, came from Havana on the earliest boat. By 1786 he had married a rich fifty-six-year-old English widow, Mary Evans (Peavett), who owned a thriving inn on St. Francis Street across from the barracks, as well as several plantations. This May-December marriage led to disaster, for John gambled away most of Mary's fortune, and as matters grew worse was clapped into the guardhouse for making the indecent gesture of wiping his backside with one of the governor's edicts. In 1791 he was banished to live twenty miles from the city gate at their only remaining plantation, New Waterford, where he died a year later. By that time Gerónimo Alvarez had prospered and was able to buy at auction the house on St. Francis Street (known now as "The Oldest House").

The motley population had scrambled for housing in the wake of the departing British. And a difficult search it was, for at least 40 percent of the existing structures were uninhabitable. The repair problem was compounded by lack of money in the colony. In spite of pleas by Zéspedes and his successors, the Spanish authorities in Cuba appeared to have better things to worry about than a poor frontier outpost.

Notwithstanding the poverty, poor housing and shortage of

The González-Alvarez House ("The Oldest House") on St. Francis Street. In the first Spanish period the home of artilleryman González, during the British period it was expanded and became the home and later the inn of Mary Evans Peavett. Some time after the return of the Spanish, Gerónimo Alvarez acquired the house; he and his family lived here for almost a century (1790-1882). A series of owners followed, until in 1918 the St. Augustine Historical Society purchased it, today presenting to the public as an example of St. Augustine's domestic architecture. In 1970 it was designated a National Historic Landmark.

food, a certain note of optimism prevailed. Governor Zéspedes dreamed of a self-supporting economy, for he had caught the spirit of modern times. Though Florida was again to be a military station and buffer zone for Spain, a new attitude toward empire also prevailed. The first Spanish period had its roots in medieval times, but by the late 18th century the Enlightenment and the Industrial Revolution had affected the whole western world. Emphasis was on efficient colonies able to make a contribution to the Crown by farming, trade and commerce.

It was Zéspedes's hope to expand and to continue the plantation complex of the British period. One of his first moves was a trip to the outlying areas in the company of Father Hassett to inventory the populace, their holdings, and their plans for the future. On their grand tour Hassett carried a portable altar and succeeded in bringing some settlers to the faith.

At this time the governor set about distributing small plots to the Minorcans and granting lands to the returning floridanos. In the early days floridanos, Spanish nationals and Irish Catholics were deemed desirable recruits for the colonial settlement. By 1786 some of these attempts had failed, so a royal order was promulgated permitting Protestant British subjects to stay providing they took an oath of loyalty to Spain. In 1787 Zéspedes wrote a long letter to his superiors outlining the possibilities for development of the province.

The tenor of this missive is confidence, but a plaintive note creeps in. The want of proper immigrants is the problem, and Zéspedes suggests that European nationals who had homesteaded in the new United States within the past five years and had become dissatisfied would make good Florida settlers. "Such Europeans," he explains, "are the most suitable immigrants for this country, for, since they are poor and destitute in America and separated from their respective fatherlands by the Atlantic Ocean, it is presumed they will settle in good faith and with grateful loyalty upon the lands that may be assigned to them for their own by the king's generosity."

This letter with its request for expanded immigration as well as free trade for ten years until the colony was on its feet evidently caused some furor in Spain. It prompted a "discourse" written by José Salcedo, a Spanish official, who refuted the positive points made by Zéspedes one by one and suggested in no uncertain terms that the Crown would do well to divest itself with all possible haste of such a miserable colony. He recommended return of Florida to England; Spain would not be harmed by any ownership other than American.

However, that same year a royal order opened the gates of Louisiana and the Floridas to "aliens and heretics," prompting Thomas Jefferson to write gleefully to George Washington that it raised the possibility of peaceful conquest of the Spanish territories by the United States. This had not been Zéspedes's intent, but he was forced to allow Americans along the border to take up lands or allow others to take advantage of the relaxation in rules to add to their holdings.

In spite of all the problems, Zéspedes felt a certain sense of satisfaction in launching the colony. The English officers had finally departed, all government and religious officials were now on hand, although he could have used a legal officer. Barracks had been built for the soldiers and Zéspedes believed that the bandits, Indians and ever present Americans were under control.

During the early period several priests had arrived to join Hassett and to supplement the ministry of Father Camps who had come to Florida with his Minorcan flock in 1768 and continued to administer to their needs. A school was founded by one of the priests, probably the first free public school on the North American continent. It was located at the southeast corner of present Bridge and St. George streets, on land still used for Catholic school purposes.

All of the white boys in town were required to attend; Negro boys could do so if they wished but must sit aside from the others. All of the lessons were conducted in Spanish, and Minorcan boys were severely punished for speaking in their own dialect. The rules promulgated for the school have a surprisingly modern ring. Classes were graded, progress monitored by the ranking priest in town, and a procedure outlined for truants. A ruler was kept on the teacher's desk to be carried by boys in turn as they needed to be excused to attend to the calls of nature. A pendulum was set in motion and should still be swinging when the boy returned. The hours were long, from roughly sunup to sunset with several hours off in the middle of the day for the boys to return home for dinner and siesta. Moderation in punishment was urged on the teachers. Facing the sad realities of those days, instructions were given for proper funerals for those pupils not living to maturity.

Given the benign rigors of their school life, the boys looked forward to festivals and holy days where, although certain duties of a religious nature were required of them, they still could enjoy the novelty and excitement. On ordinary days "on leaving school" they were supposed to "go directly home without loitering, or shouting, or committing mischievous pranks in the streets."

The long series of festival activities in December 1789 provided an extended outlet for their high spirits. Zéspedes in typical flamboyant Spanish style planned a grand commemoration of the ascension of Charles IV to the throne of Spain, an event being celebrated all over the empire. Zéspedes, who had asked to be removed to another station because of his failing health, also hoped to end his regime on a positive note.

The three-day event was an impressive spectacle with public processions passing down decorated streets, the unveiling of the royal portraits, the noise of cannon salutes, rifle volleys and church bells, parties all over town and theatrical entertainments lit by bonfires in the evening. The celebration ended with the parade of a triumphal float drawn by six magnificent horses. The elaborate contraption had been constructed by the Minorcan carpenter guild, all of whom, red cockades stuck jauntily in their broad hats, rode therein, flaming torches in their hands. At every corner they stopped to lead the bystanders in huzzahs for the new rulers of Spain.

Two days later the annual two-day celebration of the Immaculate Conception of Holy Mary took place with the traditional festive illumination of the windows of the town.

This barely ended when word was received of the birth of a girl child to the king and queen, so two more days were set aside during that December, which had miraculously continued as balmy as May, to rejoice in the happy birth of the royal Infanta.

Then finally, on December 14, the wineshops were quiet and the candles in the house windows put to mundane use.

This jubilant fête was a one-time addition to the customary yearly holiday round. To the Mediterranean, then as now, the days of toil and dreary stretches of life were punctuated with feasts and holidays. In spite of English disapproval, the Minorcans had continued their religious processions and traditional holidays. Under the sunny beneficence of Spain's reign, their merrymaking and carnival engaged the whole town.

Carnival, just before the austere Lenten period, was a rollicking, sometimes riotous time. A traveler of the day describes how "Masks, dominoes, Harlequins, Punchinelloes, and a great variety of grotesque disguises, on horseback, in cars, gigs, and on foot, paraded the streets with guitars, violins, and other instruments." In the evenings parties of maskers visited in the houses, often putting on mini-theatrical productions.

Posey dances, a custom of the day, were kept up by the Minorcan ladies for eleven nights prior to Ash Wednesday. A flower-garlanded altar lit by tapers was constructed in a home, usually of a family with marriageable daughters. After an evening of graceful Spanish dances the Posey Queen of the evening presented one of the gentlemen present with two bouquets. He was thus named Posey King for the next night and must pay for the entertainment and present one of the nosegays to his choice for the new Posey Queen.

With the beginning of Lent the excitement died down, only to commence again as Easter weekend approached. On Good Friday a man representing St. Peter dressed in rags delighted groups of boys lying in wait around town by throwing his mullet net to capture them.

Holy Saturday found the girls about the town during the daylight hours presenting bouquets to young men of their choice. Of all of the activities, the *formatjada* serenade on Easter Eve was the most unusual. In this early "trick or treat" event, gangs of young men went about singing the *formatjada* song at the houses of the town. The air ended with a request for the little pastries containing nuggets of cheese, threatening a malediction on the house if the cakes were not forthcoming. Even in the poorest times the women had spent days baking for the Easter feast, and the minstrels were rewarded with goodies dropped from the balconies into their waiting bags; if they were lucky, the man of the house poured them noggins of wine as well. Easter itself was given over to religious celebration and feasting.

Of all of the yearly holidays, St. John's Eve, June 23, was, as one observer described it, "the great drama of this light-hearted people," a time of general merrymaking based on the ancient summer solstice celebration. Maskers delighted in dressing up as highborn persons of the opposite sex—the women representing the ancient chivalry on gaily comparisoned steeds, and the men wearing the trappings of the ancient dames. This small carnival, which sometimes stretched to three days, featured posey dances, parades and heavily decorated altars set up all over town where young dark-eyed girls offered bouquets to male passersby who took their fancy.

Dancing and serenades spiced up life between the regular holidays. *Chivarées*, loud raucous serenades conducted outside the house of a newly married couple if one of the pair had been married before, caricatured the soft serenades of a swain at the window of his innocent ladylove. Given the death and re-marriage rates of those times, occasions calling for *chivarée* were far from rare.

The thing that most impressed a man who had come to Spanish St. Augustine as a young slave was, as he told it many years later, the festive atmosphere: "The people were the gayest I can imagine. Serenades, processions, balls, picnics, masquer-ades came the year round in constant succession."

The revelries of the era served to mask the hard realities of everyday living. When Juan Nepomuceno Quesada, the new governor, together with his young family sailed into the estuary on the ship, *La Terrible*, he was appalled at the squalor and chaos he discovered at this remote outpost. He had asked to be relieved of his station on the swampy mosquito-infested coast of Honduras where his health had been undermined only to come to this!

He found scant comfort in the fact that his children had a school to attend in St. Augustine, when over half of the government buildings were falling down, and he and his family could not occupy Government House because one side had caved in.

Morale was low. Employees, officers and day laborers who had received no pay for nineteen months had little enthusiasm for working on public projects. Quesada complained that "the condition of the army, the vicious habits and perverse inclinations of theft, drunkenness, desertion causes all my ingenuity to be directed to maintaining [the province] in some degree of subordination." He discovered that St. Augustine was used as a dumping ground for an undesirable element. Criminals in Havana were given the choice of jail in Cuba or army service in St. Augustine. Most who chose the latter deserted promptly on arrival; casements of the castillo were constantly full of such rabble. One night engineer Mariano de la Rocque heard a terrific, clanging, crunching sound as he passed the castillo, which upon investigation turned out to be some condemned men trying to dig their way out, using their chains as clumsy shovels.

Adequate and good food was a problem. Minorcan gardeners grew scarcely enough for their own tables, although they were able to supply the town with fresh fish. Even when the market stalls in the plaza contained produce, there was little currency for purchases. A complicated system of barter, trade and debt incurrment ensued.

The regiment was fed from the commissary, the frequently tainted flour blamed for illnesses of soldiers arriving at the presidio. In the summer of 1792 the warehouse where supplies were stored caught fire. To make an already bad situation worse, the storm season came early that year delaying the supply ships. The flour and ham bound for the colony were ruined. The creative solution was to vary good bread one day with hardtack made from spoiled flour on the next.

Aside from minor debilities, the population stayed healthy and epidemic-free. Nevertheless, the temporary hospital in the barracks had outgrown its quarters. In 1793 a new structure was built just south of the plaza near the bay where it caught the fresh sea breezes.

Other projects were undertaken. The barracks were rebuilt, a new school building was constructed on the site of the old one and badly needed repairs were made to the castillo, including an attractive neoclassic doorway designed by Mariano de la Rocque for the chapel.

As a symbol of Spanish Catholicism an elaborate new parish church was begun on the north side of the plaza. By this time the priest of the Minorcans, Father Camps, beloved by all who knew him, had died, and his parish-within-a-parish was no more.

Governor Quesada, like his visionary predecessor, had come with grand plans for the increased settlement and economic prosperity of the colony. In 1790, soon after his arrival, he had Luis Fatio prepare an account of the agricultural land and commercial potentialities of the province. Fatio spoke of the cash crops of cotton, rice and corn which could be much expanded by the introduction of additional "industrious settlers" who might also prosper by growing rye, wheat, tobacco, hemp, flax, indigo, oranges, olives and sugar cane (with its by-product rum). Lumber and naval stores were largely untapped resources while bee culture and silkworms could be developed. Ambitious residents might raise cattle and catch fish, some of which could be exported if trading policies were advantageous.

Regardless of the glowing opportunities which Fatio and others saw, the population in the town and in the countryside did not increase greatly. Citizens blamed the sluggish growth on the restrictive trading practices imposed by the Crown. Quesada, who agreed, sent futile pleas to Havana and eventually went over the heads of his superiors in Cuba and wrote directly to the king. In 1792 a group of prominent citizens also petitioned the king.

When trade regulations established by a new royal order in 1793 proved to be not much of an improvement on the one in effect since June 1782, fifteen irate settlers sent a petition to the Crown complaining that the rules were being enforced too strictly. They also turned on Quesada, charging him with mismanagement and with favoring Panton, Leslie & Co. The letter asked for an investigation, declaring that grievances could be verified by the "whole town."

But these problems of governorship faded from the foreground as rumblings of possible rebellion on the northern border

In 1797 a new Catholic parish church was completed on the north side of the plaza. This 1875 sketch shows the substantial facade, broken pediment, Doric columns and four bells at the apex, as designed by Mariano de la Rocque.

of East Florida became increasingly audible. Plots and counter-plots to annex Florida to the United States, or even to set it up as an independent nation, had existed ever since the English withdrawal, but the serious eruption known as the East Florida Rebellion did not occur until 1795.

Along the Florida-Georgia border an insurgent force began to gather, in part recruited by a former Revolutionary War general, Elijah Clarke, who promised his recruits rich lands when the Spaniards were driven out of Florida. Ready adherents were found within Florida, particularly among the English-speaking planters between the St. Johns and St. Marys rivers.

In November 1794, officials in St. Augustine had learned to their horror that the Havana courts had ordered freed for lack of evidence a number of persons charged with treasonous activities in Florida and held in the cells of El Morro in Havana and the castillo in St. Augustine. John McIntosh and Richard Lang, former landholders and minor officials in Spanish Florida, were among the former prisoners who headed north to join the increasing force on the St. Marys River. Even Dan McGirtt, breaking his exile in the Bahamas, turned up in the middle of the ruckus to cast his lot with the revolutionaries.

It was late June 1795 before the insurgent force was ready to move. Fort Juana and Fort San Nicolas, both near present-day Jacksonville, fell, and Amelia Island was occupied. The taste of victory was short-lived for the rebels. Spanish troops, supported by English and Spanish brigantines, retook the captured positions, and put the insurgents to flight. Known and suspected conspirators who were apprehended were clapped in irons in the castillo. Some were held there for more than two years, and several died in captivity, before sentences were handed down. Each ringleader was to be dragged to the gallows by a rope tied to a horse and, after hanging, was to be quartered with the body parts set up near the Florida-Georgia frontier as a warning. However, there is no record that these severe sentences were ever carried out.

By this time Quesada had left the province. His old illness had flared up under the stress of his stint in East Florida and he implored his superiors to transfer him to a place where he could serve the Crown with "zeal and credit", but "with less anguish" than the hardships of Florida afforded.

The new governor, Enrique White, who arrived in 1796, was

another of the many Irish officers serving the Spanish Crown, a crusty old bachelor with a record of success in Pensacola as governor of West Florida. Knowledgeable in colonial warfare and in the politics of the borderland, he was competent, well-liked and completely dedicated to Spain's interests. He was a wise choice in a period when it had become obvious that the grand colonial schemes must be set aside and the province held as well and as long as possible against the tide of American pressures. Officials in the United States knew him as stubborn and incorruptible.

In St. Augustine the ties to things Spanish were weakening. Expanding trade brought 42 ships into the harbor in 1806, but only five came from Havana. The other 37 hailed from ports in the United States.

Too, the Church was moving away from zealous conversion of Protestant citizens and worrying more about the question of clandestine marriages, those between Catholic and Protestant, or between two Protestants. Catholic doctrine held that marriages recognized by the Church could be the only ones recognized by civil authorities, but as intermarriage increased, and the proportion of Catholics to Protestants in the province declined, it was difficult to enforce the 1792 ruling that couples should appear before a priest to legitimize their marriage.

The physical appearance of the town changed also as time went on. New, more substantial houses were built and a distinctive domestic style developed, an architecture which still gives the old part of the city a certain Spanish colonial charm.

The better houses were built of coquina, still quarried on Anastasia Island, and many had a second floor reached by a stairway leading from the loggia, with a balcony on the street side.

Wood-shingled roofs contrasted with the rustling palm fronds which covered some poorer houses and outbuildings. Kitchens were usually separate, removing the heat and danger of fire from the main house. Wells lined with cut coquina penetrated to the level of underlying fresh water, and, as in the past, the yards themselves supported a number of fruit trees, small kitchen gardens and occasional chicken coops. The Spanish pink was a particularly favored flower, grown always in pots and used on balconies and in patios.

The center of community life was the new church, completed in 1797. Inside, near the door, was displayed a crucifix recovered from ruined Nombre de Dios after the Palmer raid of 1728, reminding the parishioners of an earlier period of Catholicism in the city. For church services, the women spread their rugs to sit upon the floor while the men sat in a double row of benches along the walls. The black congregation occupied the first balcony and *Te Deums* rang out from the choir in the second balcony.

Some of the boys had the privilege of standing outside on the wooden platform behind the belfry, high on the facade, to ring the bells which hung in the four niches. Holidays or a bishop's visit called forth a joyous peal, while at other times their sad measured beat could be heard tolling the number of years of life of the recently deceased. Every night at nine o'clock they rang out, halting the faithful wherever they were for a silent prayer. After this curfew the town was quiet and until sunrise the guard challenged any person abroad without proper business.

Time was kept by the sentry in the plaza who minded an hourglass during the day. At each hour he clanged the bell raised at the west end of the market house near the bay.

In the protected angle of the market and another small building, facing south and east, was the open-air meat and vegetable market. On market days beef and pork were the common meats. Fish, more plentiful and much cheaper, was sold on little four-foot-square tables. Farmers placed their baskets of vegetables on the ground nearby and poultry lay tied beside them. Tomatoes, sweet peppers, yams, chayote, squash and melons were frequent local products. Hawkers milled about, baskets on their heads, offering shrimp, or oysters, or fruit. Figs, grapes, peaches and bananas were among the seasonal fruits. In spring the perfume of orange blossoms from the rows of trees planted along the sides of the plaza and from those in the patios of the houses, drifted on the light breeze, promising the golden harvest of the fall.

The appearance of the inhabitants as they sold and bought

The distinctive architectural style of St. Augustine's finer residences usually included an arched loggia.

produce and wares was as different as their languages. The average man wore a hunting shirt of checked cotton, with "common breeches" and an intricately braided palmetto hat. He might be barefoot or wearing moccasins if the weather were cooler. Soldiers were dressed in the uniforms of their units, and the Franciscan friars were garbed in brilliant blue robes, sandals and picturesque flat-crowned broad-brimmed hats.

The women wore petticoats of cotton, linen, or silk, depending on their station, and home-fashioned fabric shoes, some even made of satin. Kerchiefs or lace veils controlled their hair, and were tucked into the open fronts of their bodices, assuring modesty in public.

The elite of the community were less likely to be at the market, but when they did appear in public they wore the latest and highest fashions that they could afford and secure through the uncertainties of import.

Slaves were dressed fitting the rank of their owners, and freedmen according to their affluence. But the Indian visitors on market days were the most eye-catching. The men wore ill-fashioned dirty linen jackets or torn blankets above their loincloths. Their ears were resplendent with rings of silver and brass and the pungent odor of bear grease rose from their pomaded hair. Slung across their shoulders were haunches of deer and other products of the hunt. They also brought ponies, hogs, wild honey, beeswax, snakeroot, bears' oil, raw and dressed deerskins and sometimes even a slave for exchange. Before they left town with their purchases of powder, lead, cotton homespun clothes and shrouds, beads, combs, looking glasses and carmine to paint their faces, they hunkered down in small groups, passing around bottles of *aguardiente*, the drinkers later sleeping it off under the town balconies.

Occasionally in the market one could see beautiful cardinals and nonpareils in large palmetto cages, or hear the *trinzonetti* (mockingbirds) which had been taught to mimic Spanish airs. The birds were caught from the nest, cared for and trained and were much valued for decoration and song no matter how humble the home. They also provided a lucrative export to Havana.

By early summer only the peppers had survived the hot sun in the gardens and the beef carts did not creak along the streets as often because meat could spoil when the summer rains began. The youths enjoyed marbles, tops and kites, and after St. John's Day found sea bathing a cooling pastime. Picnics, or *convités*, were a common form of entertainment, and a favorite spot for large Sunday afternoon oyster roasts was the site of old Fort Mosa north of town.

But in March 1812 the picnic site at Mose was not available to the citizens of St. Augustine. Instead the area was occupied by enemy forces calling themselves "Patriots," who were demanding the surrender of the city.

It was all part of yet another plan to wrest the control of Florida from Spain, and it had the blessing of the president of the United States, James Madison. A revolutionary government was to be organized in Florida, whose ranks were to be swelled by volunteers from the United States. The captured territory would then be offered to the United States, which would thus be free to move its troops into the area. As the plan was put into action, Fernandina and lands near the St. Johns River were rapidly occupied. The Patriots marched unopposed to the outskirts of St. Augustine. Acting Governor Juan José de Estrada emphatically refused to surrender and St. Augustine prepared to withstand attack, protected by the mighty castillo and the newly strengthened Cubo Line, which stretched from the fort west to the banks of the San Sebastian River.

On April 12 a hundred United States soldiers reinforced the Patriots, but already the situation had become so blatant and embarrassing that President Madison had to repudiate the actions which had been taken. The American troops and the Patriots withdrew.

A little over two years later the Treaty of Ghent, which ended the War of 1812, provided that portions of West Florida seized by the Americans would remain in their hands. This, and the general deterioration of Spain's relations with its other trans-atlantic colonies, made it evident that the annexation of Florida was but a matter of time. Secretary of State John Quincy Adams and the Spanish ambassador, Luis de Onís, began negotiations, but years would pass before a treaty became a reality.

Local government grew in the period following the Patriot War. Governor Sebastián Kindelán set up districts in the outlying areas dominated by English-speaking residents, appointing commissioners and magistrates from among them, and provided for local militia. Fernandina boomed as a base for smuggling into the United States, but did not officially become a municipality. St. Augustine, however, under the liberal Spanish constitution of 1811, was provided with a city government and Gerónimo Alvarez became the *alcalde*. Alvarez tried to claim the same privilege of office for Fernandina since in Spanish practice the bounds of a town spread outward, and St. Augustine was the only municipality in the entire province.

Alvarez lost his battle to "capture" Fernandina, but a Scottish adventurer, Sir Gregor McGregor, took it in 1817 in the name of the republics of Venezuela, New Granada, Mexico, and Rio de la Plata. To the great frustration of Governor José Coppinger two military expeditions dispatched from St. Augustine were thrown back by the intruders. They eventually were driven out by forces of the United States in December 1817.

More important was the early 1818 incursion farther to the west by General Andrew Jackson, with orders to bring the raiding Seminoles under control. Spain was as important as the Seminoles in Jackson's war plans, and his soldiers' rallying cry was "To storm the walls of St. Augustine." In this First Seminole War, Jackson came nowhere near St. Augustine, but by the time he withdrew in the late spring he had shown once again that the Spanish Floridas were indefensible. He was roundly criticized in Congress, in part because his actions came as negotiations leading to the annexation of Florida by the United States were well under way. The end of Spanish Florida was very near. But the diverse population that formed the "people-mix" of the second Spanish period became the town's stable base which continues to the present day.

Three members of St. Augustine's Smith family sat for their portraits in 1819, Master Buckingham Smith, his sister Anita and his mother Hannah. Buckingham Smith went on to become an outstanding historical scholar, a diplomat in the American embassies of Mexico and Spain, and a benefactor of St. Augustine's black citizens through the Buckingham Smith Benevolent Association.

Chapter Six

The Americanization of St. Augustine
1821 - 1865

by

George E. Buker

"Florida, sir, is not worth buying, It is a land of swamps, of quagmires, of frogs and alligators and mosquitoes! A man, sir, would not immigrate into Florida. No, sir! No man would immigrate into Florida—no, not from hell itself!"

John Randolph was speaking in the House of Representatives, voicing the opinion of many in the long arguments surrounding the proposed acquisition of Florida. For two years the representatives of Spain and the United States had worked over the treaty by which the provinces of East and West Florida became American.

President James Monroe outlined his support for the acquisition at his March 1821 inauguration. While Florida was important in itself, he said, as a part of the United States it would provide neighboring states access to the ocean, its Gulf coast harbors could berth warships "of the largest size," and he was certain the step would bring security against warring Indian tribes.

Within a month of taking office, Monroe appointed General Andrew Jackson as the military governor of the new Territory of Florida, joining under one rule the long separated East and West provinces. The last individual acts of those provinces were their transfers to the United States at the capitals of Pensacola and St. Augustine.

In St. Augustine, José Coppinger, the Spanish governor, was punctilious in his duties at the transfer, as was Jackson's representative, Colonel Robert Butler. On July 10, 1821, the familiar Spanish flag, which had for so many centuries flown over Castillo de San Marcos, was lowered, the Stars and Stripes rose in its place, salutes were fired, Spanish and American troops marched and countermarched, and the Americanization of St. Augustine could commence.

Inevitably, American St. Augustine on July 10 was what Spanish St. Augustine had been on July 9. About three-quarters of a mile long and a quarter of a mile wide, it centered on what the newcomers called a parade (to the natives it was and would later be the plaza.)

Around that open area clustered the principal buildings. Americans replaced Spanish officials in the dilapidated Government House, natives worked in the market place to the east and on the north was the Roman Catholic church. Houses bordered the sandy narrow streets across the peninsula.

What happens when territory changes sovereignty through peaceful means? Generally there is great anxiety on the part of the inhabitants. Some, whose roots are deep in the territory, will elect to remain, changing their allegiance. Some, with stronger ties to the motherland, will prepare to sell out and leave. Others, undecided, will swing one way one day and another the next. It is a time of indecision. The inhabitants' wavering is detrimental to the town as people refrain from making necessary repairs and doing upkeep during the unsettled period. Even the dwellings of those determined to remain will suffer until the uncertainty ends.

Foremost among the buildings neglected would be the public structures. Two of the more run-down buildings in town dated from the English period. The British had not completed the State House before they departed, and the Spanish did nothing to the building, which was crumbling when the Americans arrived. Another building in ruins was the British barracks, near the Franciscan convent. Castillo de San Marcos still dominated the town, but now that it was American, it would become Fort Marion, named after General Francis Marion of Revolutionary War fame.

A surprising number of former Spanish subjects remained in St. Augustine. Surnames such as Alvarez, Hernandez, Sanchez and Ximénez appeared in official documents with the newer Anglo names of Rogers, Davis, Coathwaite and Harrison. The townspeople spoke Spanish, French and English, and of necessity, some of the American administrators learned and used Spanish until, with Americanization, the English language gained ascendency in town.

Towers of various kinds have stood on Anastasia Island for centuries, looking out to sea. The early Spanish wooden watchtowers were replaced in the 1700's by the coquina tower at left. Added to by the British, it served through the second Spanish period and was finally converted into a lighthouse by the Americans in 1823. By the time the sea undercut and demolished the structure in 1874, the new lighthouse (right) was completed; it continues to operate today.

Old St. Augustine's first American challenge was political. Jackson's civil appointee, Acting Governor William Worthington, was willing to work with the city council elected in the Spanish days, but each member of that body, save one, refused to take the oath of allegiance to the United States, and Worthington was forced to replace them from the small band of American civilians at hand. James Grant Forbes was named mayor; he had acted for Monroe in the preceding months, when he brought from Cuba to Jackson in Pensacola the authoritative Spanish papers concerning the transfer. Now he was back in St. Augustine, where he had been born fifty-two years before, the son of the Anglican minister who served during the British period.

Worthington appointed a judge, a city clerk and the council members in accordance with Jackson's orders, and after a festive ball celebrating the establishment of the new city government, it was assumed that matters might proceed smoothly.

But there were to be no easy days ahead. In a matter of weeks, yellow fever came to the old town, probably carried by the crews of three American schooners which had stopped in Havana before sailing to St. Augustine. Within days of his appointment as judge, Thomas Fitch died of the fever, his wife and children followed soon after, and the epidemic was in full swing.

Citizens met to face the immediate needs of a burying ground, and at the same time voted to form a Protestant church, establish a school and found a library.

William Hayne Simmons of Charleston, South Carolina, a litterateur and poet, had anxiously awaited the acquisition of Florida, for he was also a land speculator. Arriving in St. Augustine right after the transfer, he laid the blame for the epidemic on the departed Spaniards who "had neglected most of the precautions of cleanliness which they usually adopt, so that great accumulations of filth were formed in the streets, and different yards and lots."

Simmons had not practiced medicine since his graduation in 1806 from the University of Pennsylvania Medical School, but when the army surgeon in town died during the epidemic, he took charge of the military hospital. Other newcomers served where needed until, with the arrival of cold weather in December, the epidemic slowed, and disappeared.

Simmons tried to allay the fears generated by the yellow fever. In his book, *Notices of East Florida,* published in 1822, he wrote that once the town was cleaned up it would regain its reputation as a salubrious, enjoyable place to live, and the population would increase. He was wrong, for St. Augustine's population in 1830 was 1,708, a little less than it had been before the transfer.

In these days of change there were some St. Augustinians who in themselves provided a strong continuity with the past. Joseph M. Hernandez was native-born; his parents had been among those who had fled from Andrew Turnbull's colony in New Smyrna, and found refuge in St. Augustine. Hernandez took the oath of allegiance, served on the city council, and in 1822 was appointed the first Territorial delegate to Congress where, although he had no vote, he spoke eloquently and effectively on behalf of Florida. Next he represented St. Augustine in the Legislative Council of the Territory and later served as brigadier general in the militia.

Pedro Benet, known familiarly as the "king of the Minorcans," was another native; he would later be a power among Catholic laymen, was already an influential landowner and taxpayer, and would be the antecedent of Florida's first West Point graduate, Stephen Vincent Benet, who in turn was the progenitor of the writers Stephen Vincent, William Rose and Laura Benet.

Antonio Proctor represents another ethnic group which remained after the Spanish departed. Born in Jamaica about 1743, this mulatto slave, servant of a British army officer, arrived in East Florida some time during the American Revolution. He may have received his freedom under British Governor Patrick Tonyn's proclamation in March 1781 when slaves who had shown courage in battle were emancipated. When the Spanish returned in 1783, Proctor remained and was present to greet the Americans forty years later.

He had prospered during those years, serving as an interpreter to the Seminole Indians for the English trading firm of Panton, Leslie and Company, and for the Spanish governor. Governor

Coppinger rewarded the trilingual Proctor with a gift of 185 acres of rich land five miles west of town, and his English employers may have been the ones who freed him, if indeed it had not been done in 1781.

When the Americans took over, Antonio Proctor was living with his family on St. Francis Street. He again offered his services and assisted Indian Agent Gad Humphries during the 1820's, "taking presents to the Indians, carrying letters between agencies of government, standing as interpreter in dealing with the Seminoles and conducting them to land assigned by treaty."

Another of the longtime residents who had seen more than one change of flag was Manuel Solana. In 1821 he was well along in years, and although he lived on only a few months under American rule (he died in November 1821) his very presence in those four months was indicative of how short a time it had taken for Florida to be Spanish, then British, Spanish again and now American.

The change in sovereignty meant that Florida would no longer be almost wholly Catholic, for the majority of the incoming Americans were Protestants of one sect or another. Few of them had lived in as mixed a religious society as they found in St. Augustine, and most were ill-at-ease in a community which had supported an official religion.

To the northern Protestants, many Catholic customs bordered on the sacrilegious. Carnival, with masked townspeople crowding the streets in the days and nights preceding Lent, was "gross and vulgar" to the newcomers. That the market stayed open on Sundays offended them also. On this latter point, the new city council reached an early compromise, ordering a strict "cessation from worldly occupations on Sundays until noon," after which time "the national habits of this newly acquired territory" should be recognized, permitting an open market and "innocent mirth and bodily exercise" for the balance of the Sabbath.

The new government assumed that Catholic properties had belonged to the Spanish crown, and as such, by the terms of the treaty, should automatically become the property of the United

John James Audubon, famed artist, visited St. Augustine in 1832. He had little good to say of the town, despite his use of Castillo de San Marcos as the background for his "Greenshank."

States. To see their church and burying ground, the barracks which had been the Franciscan convent and even the site of the old Mission of Nombre de Dios claimed by the Americans shook the Catholic community. A greater loss came in 1823 with the death of the second of the two priests who had served the three or four hundred faithful for years.

Technically under the jurisdiction of the Bishop of Charleston, John England, St. Augustine now had to compete for church support with the rest of England's diocese, Georgia and South Carolina. Despite the bishop's concern (St. Augustine is "overrun with Methodists and Presbyterians," he wrote in June 1823) he had no priests to send south at the moment. Nor would the church on the plaza be served with any continuity over the next five years.

The Protestants, on the other hand, had been, as England said, moving in in strength. When the yellow fever epidemic began, and the newcomers met to organize a congregation and find the vitally needed burying ground, the majority voted to seek a minister from the Episcopal Young Men's Missionary Society. In response, the Reverend Andrew Fowler came down from Charleston, arriving in October at the height of the epidemic. In the two months of his stay he presided over more burials than baptisms, and held services where he could, in Government House and in private homes. After a short stay back in Charleston, he returned to St. Augustine the following spring, and continued his Episcopal services for another year before again leaving for South Carolina.

Methodism, strong as a frontier religion, also moved into the new territory. In 1823 when the Reverend Joshua Nichols Glenn arrived, he found only one other Methodist in town. Within the year, Glenn's congregation had ten members. The young minister was sure of his calling and on one occasion faced down one of the Catholic priests in an encounter which appears in most accounts of the time. Glenn's preaching distressed the priest, and he remonstrated against that and the tracts Glenn was wont to give out freely. Mr. Glenn's only reply was to point to the American flag flying nearby.

For a time Glenn preached to Presbyterians as well as to

Methodists in a united congregation; eventually the former were numerous and strong enough to establish their own church in mid-1824.

Some time after Episcopalian Mr. Fowler left St. Augustine, his congregation acquired a regular minister, the Reverend Edward Phillips, who in 1825 laid the cornerstone for Trinity Church on the plaza. When the coquina church was consecrated eight years later, the congregation, now led by the Reverend Raymond Henderson, included a hundred sixty souls, the largest Protestant denomination in the Territory.

By 1828 Bishop England could spare a priest for regular service in St. Augustine, and Father Edward Mayne arrived from Charleston that November. His was not an easy position, for in the years without continued clerical guidance the lay Board of Wardens had come to feel they were the authorities in all things Catholic. Pedro Benet and Gerónimo Alvarez managed the church properties and to the priest, and to the bishop, it seemed they intended to manage ecclesiastical matters as well.

Four years of altercation followed. Mayne was dismissed by the wardens (1829), other priests supplied by England served briefly (1829), Mayne was sent back to St. Augustine by the bishop (1830) only to find the church doors locked by the wardens. In 1832 Bishop England came on the scene in person, the church was opened to Mayne, the congregation could worship in peace again and the wardens admitted that "the opposition to Father Mayne was upon caprice and dislike for which they could not account."

The first meeting of the Territorial Legislative Council took place in June 1822 at Pensacola. The four members from St. Augustine had their choice of overland travel along poorly marked forest trails or a hazardous sea voyage around the peninsula subject to violent storms and the pirates who still cruised the Gulf of Mexico.

The delegates chose the sea route and embarked upon the *Lady Washington* in late May. On the forty-ninth day out, they were on deck, looking at the entrance to Pensacola Harbor, when the wind arose. Before their ship could cross the bar into port, it was blown out into the Gulf. The tempest lasted three days, buffeting the *Lady Washington* in open waters. It took another seven days after the storm for the ship to beat its way back to Pensacola. The delegates had had an arduous voyage of more than eight weeks.

When St. Augustine was the site of the second meeting in May 1823, the Pensacola delegates, traveling overland, spent twenty-eight days on the trail. One of the first orders of business for the Council was to select a more central location for the territorial capital. The members appointed John Lee Williams of Pensacola and William Simmons of St. Augustine to be the site selection committee, and delineated the area between the Suwannee and the Ochlockonee rivers as suitable for the capital.

Simmons and Williams met at St. Marks, on the Gulf, in the fall. They set out traveling northward, and were impressed by Old Tallahassee, a former Indian campground. It had fine fields, peach orchards and a few huts. Simmons insisted on viewing the land along the Suwannee also, because he knew St. Augustinians would prefer their new capital to be as near as possible. But, after examining both regions, he had to agree with Williams that the Tallahassee site was the better place.

Once the location had been determined, Governor William P. Duval requested that the next Legislative Council meet there. In the following spring a U.S. naval ship arrived in St. Augustine to carry the public documents, books and furniture of the Council to St. Marks, the port for Tallahassee. On November 8, 1824, the third meeting of the Legislative Council, with Joseph M. Hernandez as elected president, began in a crude log hut in the new capital. After two and a half centuries, St. Augustine was no longer the seat of government.

In late 1822 President Monroe had to swallow his optimistic words of 1821 regarding "a new degree of security" for Indian affairs in Florida. Now he urged Congress to establish limits for Indian country or else to get the tribes out of the Territory, for there had been no peace between them and the Americans spreading over the peninsula. Settlements were raided, inevitably Americans were killed, and the Americanization of the Territory was in jeopardy.

Hernandez used his position as Territorial delegate in preparing the way for a conference of Seminole leaders to discuss the new approach. Indians and Americans met in September 1823 on the shores of Moultrie Creek, a few miles south of St. Augustine, near enough so that townspeople organized an excursion and went down by water to observe the opening days of the meeting.

Under the terms of the Treaty of Moultrie Creek, the Seminoles agreed to exchange all claims to Florida in return for a reservation of some four million acres in the center of the peninsula. The Americans were to provide cash, livestock, transportation, food, a school and skilled artisans to ease the move to the reservation. A point of earlier conflict, and one which would increase in importance in the years to come, was the Indians' retention of runaway slaves; now the Negroes were to be returned to white authorities.

The move onto the reservation was accompanied by constant troubles. When supplies failed to appear, the Seminoles ranged beyond their new limits, raiding and stealing. In the coming years, raids and reprisals flared through the Territory until there was little left of the Treaty of Moultrie Creek.

In St. Augustine, where for so long the town had relied on the Spanish crown for its economic life, the newcomers were determined to create their own wealth. East Florida seemed to offer unlimited opportunities for financial advancement: Land speculation, sugar and citrus production, transportation development and banking were foremost adventures. John M. Hanson had a flourishing sugar plantation just west of the San Sebastian River on the Tocoi Road. Williams Simmons acquired eighteen hundred acres on the St. Johns, nine or ten miles below Picolata, which he devoted to oranges. In 1829 Dr. Andrew Anderson of New York City moved his family to St. Augustine, set up a medical practise, began speculating in land, and developed his own groves. Later he ventured a planting of a hundred thousand mulberry trees for silkworm cultivation.

A typical bedroom of a pre-Civil War St. Augustine boarding house can be seen today in the Ximénez/Fatio House, restored by The National Society of Colonial Dames in Florida.

In 1831 Simmons was a member of the Planters and Citizens Company, organized to build a canal south from the Matanzas River to the Halifax River. In 1836 Simmons, Anderson and Peter Sken Smith, another transplanted New Yorker, helped form the St. Augustine and Picolata Rail Road Company. A year earlier Smith and Anderson had become directors of the Southern Life Insurance and Trust Company of St. Augustine, a banking company.

These exciting days of economic development were in sharp contrast to the decade 1835-1845. On February 7, 1835, the town suffered a freeze during which the temperature plummeted to the unheard-of low of seven degrees above zero. As low temperatures continued day after day, orange trees died in substantial numbers. Within weeks many growers were ruined. Those who could afford to do so replanted, but their new groves could not be in production for several years.

The transportation schemes did not materialize because the federal government did not provide the expected financial aid. Then President Andrew Jackson's fight with the Bank of the United States led to the great Panic of 1837. The Southern Life Insurance and Trust Company had to suspend specie payments. Dr. Anderson assumed the presidency of the bank in an attempt to save the tottering institution, but by 1843 the bank was finished. Four years before, the silk boom had collapsed.

While the economy rose and fell, the Seminoles had continued their attacks on settlements and lone travelers, ranches and farms. The whites determined to rid Florida of the Indians by moving them to western reservations. The Seminoles were less than amenable, and their opposition increased.

By October 1835, Joseph Hernandez, now a militia brigadier general, believed that the strain of Indian-white relations was increasing. He thought that mounted volunteers should be called out as a show of force to deter desertions by slaves and violence by Indians. In St. Augustine, Hernandez, on his own authority, called out part of his command as Indian depredations increased throughout the Territory. In the waning months of 1835, despite General Hernandez's efforts, the East Florida orange groves and sugar plantations were especially hard hit. On Christmas Day

Chief Philip led his Miccosukee warriors on the warpath, destroying five plantations south of St. Augustine. The Second
Seminole War had begun, and the population of St. Augustine
became swollen with white refugees and their slaves, flocking to
the town for safety.

As the war continued, regular troops were added to the
garrison in town, officered in many instances by young gradu-
ates from West Point. Indian campaigns in the west and in
Florida would provide many of them with their first active
service before they went on to the larger conflicts of the Mexican
War and the maelstrom of the Civil War. Now they gathered in
St. Augustine, many on leave, many recovering from wounds,
but more often from malaria and fevers, and more on duty.

The Second Seminole War was unique for many reasons: It
was the United States' longest and most costly Indian war, it was
the only Indian conflict in which the United States Navy was an
active participant (principally at the southern end of Florida),
and it was an Indian war intimately connected to the nation's
most serious domestic problem—slavery. A disturbing issue
leading up to the war, and a factor during the conflict was the
plight of the Indian-Negroes. Were they to be shipped west as
the Seminoles insisted? Or kept in Florida to be turned over to
white owners as the Floridians desired?

For decades Florida and its Indians had been a haven for
slaves escaping from states to the north. Efforts of their white
owners to reclaim them were in the main unsuccessful and the
blacks joined with the Seminoles, sometimes willingly, and at
other times exchanging slavery under white masters for the same
state under Seminoles. Some became warriors and fought even
more fiercely than their Indian counterparts, fearing the ven-
geance of whites if they were captured.

Other blacks came to the forefront as interpreters between the
white and red men, for few whites could speak the Indians'
tongue and even fewer Seminoles spoke English. Abraham
served the Seminoles for years, from the time he interpreted for
a group of chiefs visiting Washington, D.C. in 1826. Through
Chief Micanopy, the nominal leader of the Seminoles, Abraham
was a leader among the black men of influence. John Caesar

similarly rose to prominence under Chief Philip. John Cavalo interpreted and counseled Philip's son, Coacoochee.

From the first, Major General Thomas S. Jesup, who commanded the military forces in Florida from December 1836 to May 1838, recognized the blacks' importance in the conflict. As his limited forces were attacked here, there and everywhere by the roaming Seminoles and their Indian-Negro cohorts, he called on neighboring governors for reinforcements, using an appeal certain to be effective in those slaveholding states. "This is a Negro, not an Indian war," he wrote.

On January 17, 1836, Hernandez's militiamen overtook a band of raiders at John M. Hanson's plantation only two miles out of town on the road to Tocoi. The engagement provoked sobering thought for not only had the enemy been daring enough to strike so close to St. Augustine, but many of the warriors were blacks who only a few months earlier had been plantation slaves. Much of the band's provisions had come from St. Augustine; two free Negroes were later indicted for supplying the Seminoles.

In September 1837 General Hernandez had a stroke of good luck when a group of former slaves defected from their Indian allies and returned to St. Augustine. Among them was John Philip, a slave of Chief Philip who volunteered to lead Hernandez to the camp of his former master. Under the Negro's guidance, Hernandez led a force to the ruined Dunlawton Plantation about thirty miles south of St. Augustine, where Philip had set up his camp.

At dawn the Americans charged the camp, catching the Seminoles completely by surprise. Roused from their sleep, the naked or half-clad Indians were rounded up before they could organize any resistance. Army Surgeon Jacob Motte later reported: "We soon found ourselves unexpectedly in the presence of royalty, for there stood King Philip . . . naked as he was born, except the breechcloth; and covered with most unkingly dirt." (He had been knocked down during the mounted charge.)

Among Hernandez's prisoners was an Indian named Tomoka John who offered to lead the general to another camp five or six

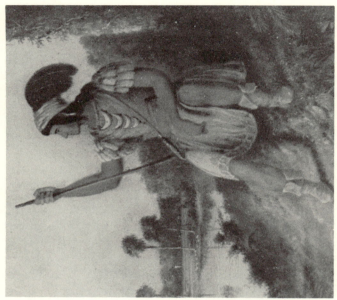

By permission of the portrait's owner

John Rogers Vinton, a captain in the U.S. Army, met and sketched Osceola when the two men were at Fort Mellon (present-day Sanford) some months before the Seminole's capture.

Brigadier General Joseph M. Hernandez, planter and territorial delegate, mayor of St. Augustine and captor of Osceola under orders of Major General Thomas J. Jesup.

A drawing by H. S. Wyllie of the capture of Osceola by Americans at Moultrie Creek, just south of St. Augustine.

miles away in a swamp. This time the troops went in on foot; as before, they surrounded the camp and waited for daylight. At the charge, only a few shots were fired by the surprised Indians. Among the captured were two more Indian leaders, Yuchi Billy and his brother Yuchi Jack.

The next important Indians to be captured were Coacoochee and Blue Snake. King Philip had sent for the former, his son, under the instructions of General Jesup, who decided the capture of the two was more important to the war effort than respect for one of the most honored rules of war; he ignored the flag of truce and detained both men. Now there were five major Indians in custody.

Despite that treacherous act, in October the important leaders, Osceola and Coa Hadjo, agreed to meet with representatives of the army, and a parley was set for later that month at Moultrie Creek, near the site where the 1823 treaty had been signed. Convinced that his tactics were successful, if less than honorable, Jesup directed General Hernandez to meet the Seminoles with a sufficient force to capture them despite their flag of truce.

At the parley, Coa Hadjo stated firmly that they had not come in to surrender, but that they wanted to make peace. Hernandez, however, was on no peaceful mission, and on orders, his troops surrounded the Seminoles, who offered no resistance. That was not surprising, in view of the numbers—71 Indian warriors, the two leaders, six women and four Indian-Negroes faced 250 soldiers.

Without delay, Hernandez and his captives marched the few miles north to St. Augustine and Fort Marion, where the band was imprisoned.

The events of that day at Moultrie Creek would dog Jesup through the years ahead as he repeatedly defended his actions. Another participant, Captain John Masters of St. Augustine, could not forget the day, "nor the sad, disappointed face of Chief Osceola and the other Indians." Masters returned to Moultrie Creek fifty-nine years later, when, at the age of ninety, he led members of the St. Augustine Historical Society to the site of the capture, where a marker was later placed.

As for the Seminole prisoners, some would not long suffer

Fort Marion's damp autumn chill. Coacoochee was the first to leave. His route to freedom was up his prison wall to an aperture fifteen feet above the floor. Here a narrow slit cut through the six-foot walls of the fort. Two iron bars blocked this opening; outside was the moat, twenty-one feet below. Thought to be escape-proof, this section of the fort was not guarded. Somehow Coacoochee managed to remove one of the bars and to tie a rope to the other. On the night of November 29, 1837, Coacoochee, John Cavalo and eighteen of his band (two of them women) made their exit.

Osceola, in failing health, was moved in late December to Fort Moultrie at Charleston, South Carolina, where doctors tried in vain to save his life. On January 31, 1838, Osceola died.

Around 1839 the main theater of the war shifted south to the Everglades. While this action diminished the number of soldiers stationed in and passing through St. Augustine, there was an increase in the local activity of the naval forces, many risking the difficulties of the harbor's bar to stop off at the old city. One such was the *U. S. S. Poinsett*, which arrived in July 1839.

According to the editor of the *Florida Herald and Southern Democrat*, her black hull and white ports looked as sleek as a sloop of war, but her superstructure resembled a load of hay. He questioned the usefulness of a steamer in the Florida Keys, with hot boilers, a tropical sun overhead, smoke, cinders and mangrove-key mosquitoes. He felt the crew would suffer long before they saw any action. The steamer *Poinsett* did prove ineffective, not for the reasons listed by the editor, but because of her deep draft and her constant need for firewood. A day's cruise consumed wood that would take several days to cut. Just five months after her arrival in St. Augustine, she was withdrawn from service in Florida.

Although there was greater action to the south as the 1840's opened, St. Augustine and its environs continued to be harassed by bands of Seminoles. In May 1840 Coacoochee attacked an unescorted carriage and baggage wagon of a theatrical troupe on the Picolata Road headed towards St. Augustine. He killed three of the actors; the other three and their driver escaped. Coacoochee acquired a treasure of colorful theatrical costumes styled beyond his most vivid imagination.

St. Augustine's newspaper, the *Florida Herald*, reported in December 1840 that the area's two largest sugar growers, each employing about seventy slaves, had been forced to leave their plantations and move into town because of Indian deprivations.

Hard pressed by Indians, crowded with refugees and uncertain of the future, St. Augustine still smarted from its loss of position as the seat of government. In 1838 Congress had acceded to the demands of the Territory and replaced the Legislative Council with a bicameral legislative body. Tallahassee's growth as the political center of the Territory was viewed with alarm by many in East Florida. St. Augustine had been the capital under Spanish rule and the development of other towns and regions could only detract from that position of prestige. In 1840 the *Pensacola Gazette* noted that "St. Augustine sighs for the return of those days when she was all of Florida, and all of Florida was comprised in her," and indeed there was active promotion for a separation of East Florida from the rest of the Territory.

Florida's new life as a territory did not come to a halt in the years of the Seminole war despite ruined sugar plantations and burned orange groves. The peninsula, and St. Augustine in particular, survived and to a degree prospered. The war was not all negative in its impact upon the economy. The conflict abetted a land and building boom in the crowded town. In 1835 the Florida House joined the Union Hotel as a part of the town's growing hostelry. Later as the military forces gathered to build up supplies for future combat operations, St. Augustine had nearly three thousand people living within its limits. Owners of lots, especially of lots with buildings upon them, demanded high prices. Real estate operators planned to expand the town, designing new residential areas beyond the city limits to the north and west. Speculators, not settlers, became the purveyors of wealth, and the future looked bright.

In 1841, just as the new orange groves were reaching maturity, the industry was jolted by an infestation of the orange coccus, an insect which destroys the fruit. By the time the local growers cleared their groves of the pest, the citrus industry was flourishing farther south.

The war was winding down, as one Seminole leader after another was captured or killed. Coacoochee made a dramatic appearance in March 1841 at Fort Cummings in mid-peninsula when he appeared at a parley dressed in finery he had taken from the hapless actors at Picolata the year before. Hamlet's costume was his choice; his aides appeared as Horatio and Richard III. Less well dressed, Coacoochee attended another meeting in June of the same year; at this one, through the familiar ruse of parleying, he was captured and some months later shipped west.

Sending the Seminoles west, considered from the early days of Seminole-American confrontations, became the final solution to the threat their presence meant to Floridians. Orders came in May 1842 to Colonel William Worth, the field commander, to put an end to the war as soon as possible. There was no dramatic end to the long conflict, but gradually the soldiers were no longer seen on the streets of St. Augustine, farmers and ranchers could return to the outlying areas, and St. Augustine could again become a haven for travelers seeking the unusual, and invalids seeking a healthy climate.

The tourist trade picked up even as the war was coming to an end. The old fort was a must item on every itinerary, a monument out of the past evoking a sense of history in all who viewed its impressive walls. It was a structure to be saved, but soon after Florida changed hands, some officials allowed stones from a nearby section of the seawall to be removed to build a wharf near the barracks. This unthinking act soon presented a threat to the fort as the tides began to flow in behind the seawall and the fort's foundation began to erode.

In December 1832 the town's leading citizens sent a memorial to Congress requesting money to restore the seawall and to repair Fort Marion. Two months later the Florida Legislative Council adopted a resolution requesting Congressional funds.

These pleas were heard, and Lieutenant Stephen Tuttle of the Corps of Engineers arrived to repair the seawall. Unfortunately for the fort, Tuttle interpreted his instructions as being limited to rebuilding the seawall and making only basic repairs to the fort.

In the fall of 1834 severe northeast gales brought high water into Matanzas Bay and erosion was rampant at the fort. Lieutenant Francis L. Dancy had replaced Lieutenant Tuttle by this time, and it was to Dancy that the town fathers appealed for action. Dancy wrote to the chief engineer of the Corps that "should the government cause a few thousand dollars to be judiciously expended on it [the fort] it would remain for ages a monument, and not an unworthy one, of the Spanish Nation, by whom it was erected, and a memento of events more memorable in the history of our country." Dancy's eloquent plea succeeded; funds were made available and Fort Marion was saved.

St. Augustine could feel justified in appealing to the national legislature, for by the mid-1830's there was already a strong move to promote Florida from territorial status to statehood. The framing of a constitution was begun by a convention which convened in December 1838 and which concluded its work at the end of January 1839.

David Levy of St. Augustine was one of the champions of unity and statehood for Florida. Elected as the Territory's Congressional delegate in 1841 and re-elected in 1843, Levy saw the advantages of a unified state and he steadfastly worked to that end, despite petitions from friends, constituents and neighbors in St. Augustine encouraging separation of East Florida from the rest of the Territory.

In 1845, after Florida became a state, Levy was honored by being elected one of Florida's first United States senators, and the nation's first Jewish senator. Always an advocate of the Americanization of St. Augustine, at the same time Levy adopted the Old World family name of his paternal grandfather, Yulee, and became David L. Yulee.

David Levy Yulee, territorial delegate to Congress and later senator from Florida, studied law in the St. Augustine office of Robert R. Reid, territorial governor. Margarita Yulee, his wife and the daughter of Kentucky Governor Wickliffe, was called "the Wickliffe Madonna" because of her "beauty and goodness."

In spite of the changes wrought by growing Americanization, most visitors to St. Augustine were impressed by elements from the past, its old-world charm, its Spanish heritage and its fort. In countless diaries, journals, magazines and books these visitors recorded their impressions of the ancient city, some general, some particular.

Ellen Call Long wrote of the Spanish dance she observed: "It is a gliding swinging movement, particularly adapted to display the graceful actions, but very intricate. . . There is more latitude at a ball than (at) other entertainments, more freedom for flirtations, which ladies married and single comprehend."

In 1843 when William Cullen Bryant visited St. Augustine, he witnessed the old Minorcan custom of serenading. Late in the night before Easter Sunday, a group of young men strolled through the streets with their musical instruments. Tradition called for them to tap upon the shutter of a house. If a return tap was heard the men gathered to sing. If their signal was not answered, they would go on to the next house.

Another visitor, Robert Carter, thought St. Augustine resembled the old towns of Spain and Italy. He was especially taken by the narrow streets. He noted that one, nearly a mile long, was but fifteen feet wide. The principal hotel in town during his stay was on a street only twelve feet wide. Carter explained the purpose of narrow streets in this warm climate was to provide strollers with shade, and in addition, the narrow ways acted as flues increasing the draught of air flowing down them.

Change was inevitable. Bryant noted that the children seldom spoke Minorcan or Spanish. He predicted that "in another generation the last traces of the majestic speech of Castile will have been effaced from a country which the Spaniards held for more than two hundred years."

The influx of northerners to St. Augustine caused the town's leading merchant, Burroughs E. Carr, to build the Magnolia Hotel, which soon became the benchmark by which all other hotels were to be judged. By 1853 Carr had expanded his hotel to forty-five rooms, and still there were so many visitors that often private homes in town took in boarders.

In the 1850's St. Augustine passed through a decade of the

doldrums, although there was a mild building boom after 1856. Orange groves and sugar plantations no longer flourished. The political center of Florida now was in Tallahassee. The transportation center for east Florida was in Jacksonville. Life in the ancient city moved at a slower pace.

St. Augustine underwent its final act of Americanization during the national tragedy of civil war.

Colonel Stephen Vincent Benet, Florida's first West Point appointee, elected to remain with the Union. His sister, Isabel, was an outspoken secessionist in St. Augustine. Young Andrew Anderson, son of Dr. Anderson, sought to remain neutral by going north to medical school in New York City. William Wing Loring, Edmund Kirby Smith and William J. Hardee, all St. Augustinians, became Confederate generals. Truly the town was divided.

In the early confused days after the outbreak of hostilities in April 1861 and when Florida had joined the Confederacy, the east coast lighthouses continued operating. Captain George Couper Gibbs, CSA, in command of Fort Marion, ordered the lights extinguished. Mayor Paul Arnau immediately acted, leading a group of men to dismantle the St. Augustine light on Anastasia Island. Then they moved down the coast, putting out the other lights.

The following spring, shortly after capturing Fernandina, Union forces sent gunboats south to occupy St. Augustine. The change of command was quiet. On March 11, 1862 Commander C. R. P. Rodgers, USN, anchored in the mouth of the harbor. The day before, Confederate soldiers, accompanied by many of the town's civilians, had departed for the interior. Boarding a small boat, Rodgers was rowed into St. Augustine without benefit of any protecting troops. Acting Mayor Christobal Bravo raised the white flag upon Fort Marion. Everything was peaceful and proper. When Rodgers landed at the town's wharf, he was met by Bravo and the two went to the town hall where the council waited in session for the formal ceremony of surrender.

Union troops drawn up in the plaza during the Civil War, as shown in *Frank Leslie's Illustrated Newspaper*, December 13, 1862.

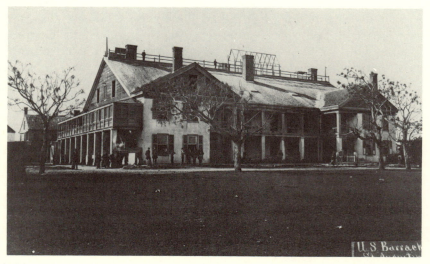

The U.S. Army barracks in St. Augustine during the Civil War. The original building was ravaged by fire in 1915 but was restored to its former design in 1922. Since then it has served as state headquarters for the Florida National Guard.

Rodgers reported that "there are many citizens who are earnestly attached to the Union and a large number who care very little about the matter." But Rodgers found more belligerent actions among the ladies, who had cut down the town's flagpole to keep the Stars and Stripes from flying over St. Augustine. One woman later declared that "the men had behaved like cowards, but there were stout hearts in other bosoms." There was no mistaking she meant her own among those others. Rodgers commented that the women "seem to mistake treason for courage, and have a theatrical desire to figure as heroines."

Not long after the surrender, Lieutenant J. W. A. Nicholson, USN, brought Paul Arnau aboard his ship and demanded the missing government lighthouse machinery. Under threat of permanent confinement, Arnau sent some carts into the countryside to retrieve the St. Augustine and Cape Canaveral gear, all of it carefully packed and preserved. Once Nicholson had his equipment, Arnau was released.

The years just ahead saw townspeople and Union troops coping together with wartime shortages, red tape and the long wait for peace. Confederate control of the areas to the west led Union sympathizers caught there into lengthy maneuvers for passes through the lines. One family, the William Burr Joneses, hoping to reach relatives in the north, succeeded in getting from Orange Springs as far as St. Augustine; Jones was fortunate in obtaining a paying job with the army commissary.

The commissary served more than the army's needs, and in these difficult times was open to civilian St. Augustine. According to a reporter for the *St. Augustine Examiner*, one local woman, irate because she was refused permission to buy flour and sugar from the quartermaster, was reminded that commissary privileges were available to all who took the oath of allegiance to the United States. Surely not an unreasonable requirement, wrote the reporter. "Why not take the oath and obtain your supplies?" the woman was asked. "Never," she replied. She would send to New York and get her supplies there. The reporter's conclusion: "She did not act with the strictest consistency."

Lincoln's Emancipation Proclamation of January 1, 1863,

meant freedom for St. Augustine's slaves and they gathered in an empty lot on St. George Street to hear the official words. For years to come, January 1, "Emancipation Day," was their special occasion for celebration.

Strategically St. Augustine was a backwater in the national conflict. Its military events might best be expressed in the words of a military visitor. In September 1862 the Seventh Regiment, New Hampshire Volunteers, arrived at St. Augustine for duty. Nineteen-year-old Private Onville Upton, Company D, from Hopkinton, New Hampshire, wrote letters home about life in St. Augustine.

Toward the end of the month, he wrote, his company had completed its section of the Union entrenchments thrown up around the town. He helped dig a half-mile-long, ten-foot-wide trench, and he also had to chop a large section of woods in front of the entrenchment. His colonel wanted the area cleared so the guns of the fort could shoot at any rebel snipers and raiders.

In December Private Upton wrote his sister that the army was recruiting a black company in St. Augustine. He said that other black companies were being formed at Fernandina, Hilton Head and Beaufort. Some of the privates from his regiment were being commissioned to officer these new companies, but Upton was not interested. According to him, this black regiment would be primarily a labor construction unit working on fortifications and woodcutting.

It was a quiet period for Upton. He told his mother his company practised battalion drills; his letter was filled with trivia about the company, and he ended with a request for a photograph of his parents.

Upton's last letter from St. Augustine told of action at last. Three companies had gone out into the countryside in search of sugar, with skirmishers moving ahead of the battalion. Suddenly a hidden rebel cavalry group, led by Captain J. J. Dickison, opened fire. Private Upton said, "It sat us all on tip-toe." Immediately the New Hampshire soldiers advanced in line of battle and, according to Upton, everyone appeared eager to get ahead of the next man to get a shot at the rebels. However, as the firing continued, the scouts on the wings began to fall back for fear of being taken. Upton said that though they drove the rebels back, they lost five men captured by the enemy. He wrote exuberantly: "I have not enjoyed myself so much since I have bin in the Service."

When the war ended St. Augustine had completed its process of Americanization. The institution of slavery had ended; the belief in the indivisibility of the United States had been forged in battle, and the Spanish heritage had changed from a living culture to an historic concept. St. Augustine, and the rest of the nation, stood poised on the threshold of the Gilded Era of American history.

Chapter Seven

The Flagler Era
1865 - 1913

by

Thomas Graham

Whitelaw Reid squinted out from beneath the brim of his hat, and from the top of the fort's grey battlements surveyed the countryside. Close by lay the graveyard, bleaching in the summer glare; beyond stretched a wasteland whose only promise appeared as still standing patches of green trees. Turning to the south, he contemplated the town of St. Augustine—"a collection of curious little antique houses . . . a paltry two thousand inhabitants." His disdain for this outpost of the defeated rebels was evident. The war had been over for only a few months, and Yankees like this noted Ohio newspaperman were still accustomed to thinking of southerners as the enemy.

Reid and Chief Justice Salmon P. Chase were touring the states of the former Confederacy as representatives of President Andrew Johnson, investigating and reporting on conditions they encountered. All down the Atlantic coast they had found a beaten, embittered population inhabiting a devastated land. St. Augustine, while it had escaped armed conflict, had suffered economic collapse from the disruptions of the war and particularly from the absence of winter visitors. Nearly fifty of the town's men had died on distant battlefields in Virginia, Tennessee and elsewhere. Reid found wives and families still waiting for their surviving menfolk to make their way home from the front lines or northern prisons.

Others venturing to St. Augustine immediately after the war similarly reported a sullen, hopeless attitude among the natives which seemed to preclude a rapid recovery. Northerners were warned that those immigrating into the area would face hostility and resentment. Newcomers purchasing land might find their titles challenged by ex-rebels who had lost their property during the rebellion. Yet some northern settlers had already established themselves in town. Even as the war raged the United States had encouraged loyal citizens to move to St. Augustine and other places in east Florida as a way of solidifying control over the region. George Greeno exemplified these early arrivals, coming with the Fourth New Hampshire in 1864 and remaining to start a grocery business and eventually to win acceptance as one of the town's leading men and politicians.

That emotion which was perceived by northerners as resentment was felt by the defeated locals as just and righteous indignation against an alien government which had overturned their society, confiscated their property, killed their sons, revolutionized the "natural" relationship between the races and now threatened to establish itself in power in the town. The newly freed blacks were accused of insolence toward white men and were feared a threat to white women.

The historian George R. Fairbanks was among those who cultivated the romantic memory of a humane Old South society which had been vanquished by the brute force of a ruthless, aggressive North. Fairbanks would remain an exile from his old home after the war, as did several other leading St. Augustine men, including the generals Loring and Kirby Smith. Those who stayed saw a new class of wealthy newcomers buying up land, driving up prices in local markets and seizing for themselves the places of preference in society. Judge Benjamin A. Putnam and other old-timers fought back, vowing that the wartime tax sales of land were "illegal and void," and that they would go to court to defend title to their property.

Clearly St. Augustine did not escape the enmity which prevailed in the south during the Reconstruction period between northern immigrants and native southerners—"carpetbaggers" and "unreconstructed rebels"—but overall, despite the bitterness permeating its society, St. Augustine fared better than many areas. Evidence of animosity can be balanced by testimonies of good will, or at least of benign indifference between diverse elements in the town. This comparatively moderate adjustment can be partly explained by the fact that St. Augustine had a long tradition of encounters between local residents and visiting strangers. Partly, the observance of peaceful order can be attributed to the presence of the United States Army.

Colonel John T. Sprague, the former Seminole fighter and an old acquaintance of the town's, made St. Augustine the head-quarters of the military forces occupying Florida. By the standards of local white society, Sprague was a good commander: while firm in enforcing the war's verdict, he was familiar with the state and moderate in his political opinions. He would not use force to make great changes in long-established customs. On the question of race, he insisted that the freedmen be unobstructed in exercising their new right to vote, and he encouraged education for blacks, but he did not envision Negroes rising very much in the social hierarchy.

The military presence rested lightly on the town. There were some incidents between townspeople and soldiers, but perhaps only a few more than might be expected in a garrison town in normal times. Sprague courted amity by sending the army band to play in the plaza for the benefit of townspeople and winter visitors. A more basic contribution to the community were the greenbacks which the soldiers spent in town. The army represented an important source of income for a destitute population. During the first few years after the war St. Augustine almost reverted to its old Spanish empire status as a garrison outpost.

Although Sprague favored a policy of standing aside from local politics, the military did intervene occasionally in the sometimes turbulent struggles over the town government. At first the conservative Democratic leaders who had long dominated town offices continued to hold power, but increasingly their hegemony faced challenges from blacks and northern immigrants, both of whom usually voted Republican. The resultant struggle for dominance created bitterness and sometimes violence. Fortunately for St. Augustine the military presence kept violence from rising to the high levels that distressed some areas of the South during Reconstruction.

Following the surrender of the South, Democrats hoped that the victorious North would insist on few alterations in the political and social status quo. President Andrew Johnson's "moderate" plan of reconstruction was praised, and differences with northerners were minimized in Democratic party rhetoric. However, by the fall of 1866 it was becoming evident that the federal government would insist on voting rights for freedmen and that the Republican Party would try to establish itself in the South. These developments, and Congress's imposition of military rule under a "radical Reconstruction" plan, inaugurated a period of intense political hostility in 1867 and 1868.

In St. Augustine an attempt was made to form a Union Conservative Party as a coalition of anti-Republican elements. One token black was given a prominent place in the party's organization, and the freedmen were invited to join forces with their professed "true friends"—the conservative whites—rather than be misled by the "delusive promises" of the Republicans, who allegedly only wanted the votes of the freedmen. However, the freedmen chose to ally themselves with the party of Lincoln, rather than the party of their former masters. Blacks organized a local chapter of the Republican Party's Loyal League and wore a star on their lapels to show their membership in this organization. In the fall elections of 1867 the Republicans, drawing the votes of the freedmen and white Republican immigrants from the North, swept the district. St. Augustine's Democrats, many of whom had temporarily lost their voting rights as ex-traitors, boycotted the election rather than face certain defeat.

The following year violence was injected into politics as both sides resorted to force. In August a Democratic rally was broken up by a group of blacks who fired into the gathering and wounded one white man in the leg. Colonel Sprague called out the troops. In succeeding weeks whites intimidated freedmen with threats of violence; blacks struck back through acts of vandalism. Municipal offices were swept by the resurgent Democrats since, this fall, the Republicans refused to offer opposition at the ballot box.

In 1869 moderates from both parties engineered a Citizens Party slate of candidates for local offices which carried the town government. Frank H. Palmer, a Republican newcomer from Massachusetts, took office as mayor, while Andrew Anderson, a prominent native-born Republican, served on the city council with leading Democrats. This harmony movement represented an attempt to leave sectional animosities in the past and concentrate on bringing prosperity to the town. However, local politics remained unsettled for the next two decades because of Republican-Democratic rivalry, accentuated by the fact that most Republicans were black and almost all Democrats were white.

Although the Democrats held a voting majority in St. Augustine, blacks continued to win election to various offices in the town government through four decades following the Civil War. The end of the national government's reconstruction program in 1877 did not end black participation in politics. A new state constitution adopted by conservative Democrats in 1885 provided for a poll tax as a means of limiting black voting, but St. Augustine's blacks refused to give up political power without a fight and attempted to register even if they had not paid the tax. In 1888 when the great yellow fever epidemic caused many of the town's white inhabitants to flee from their homes, St. Augustine's blacks comprised a temporary voting majority. As late as the 1890's the town still employed black policemen and one black served on the town council, but shortly after the turn of the century the attempt to insure civil and political rights for the freedmen had been stifled by the solid opposition of the white South.

Despite the economic decay and political tumult of the 1860's and 1870's, St. Augustine did see some genuine progress in the aftermath of the war. Education received unprecedented support. The town began a public school system in 1868 when an agent of the Peabody Fund helped organize a free school committee among leaders of the town's major churches. The town government contributed money to the support of the Peabody School, which at first held classes in the City Hall.

Two years earlier Bishop Augustin Verot had brought eight Sisters of St. Joseph from Le Puy, France to open a school for freedmen. Soon the Catholic sisters were also teaching classes for the white boys and girls of the town and were receiving financial support from the town council on an equal footing with the Peabody School.

The Freedmen's Bureau had opened a school for black children even before the conclusion of the war. This school was partly supported by a tax levied on the black citizens of the town. When the Freedmen's Bureau was abolished, the education of black children was assumed by a second Peabody School.

While all these schools were modest undertakings, they represented a broad commitment to community education which had been lacking in the prewar society.

Improvements in transportation came slowly, but they were crucial if St. Augustine was to avoid becoming a stagnant backwater, isolated from the growth enjoyed elsewhere in the state. The danger was real, for while Florida experienced a one-third increase in population in the 1860's, St. Augustine actually lost inhabitants. This was the golden age of steamboating on the St. Johns River and the beginning of the state's railroad building boom. Unless St. Augustine could link up with the major transportation arteries, its demise was certain.

Since few ships dared to enter the town's sandbar-choked harbor, the town's major link with the world was the rutted trail to Picolata on the St. Johns River, fifteen miles away. After the war the stage line resumed traffic between the St. Johns and a depot on the west bank of the San Sebastian River. The bridge across the San Sebastian had fallen victim to the war and had been replaced by a ferry. Following every heavy rain the ferryboat could have replaced the stage over much of the road since the lowlands west of town would be covered by a foot or more of water.

The telegraph line reached town in December 1867, permitting communication with the broad world more often than had been possible by the thrice-weekly mail from Jacksonville. Shortly thereafter the town established a rail link to the St. Johns. Dr. John Westcott had completed his St. Johns Railroad back at the start of the Civil War, but the turmoil of the conflict ended its use. The road which resumed operating after the war consisted of wooden stringers along which a small car was pulled by mules. In the 1870's William Astor of New York put new capital into the corporation, purchasing iron tracks and two wood-burning locomotives. The trip from the railhead at Tocoi to West Augustine, however, still remained a primitive adventure.

A hopeful sign for the local economy was the revival of the orange groves, which thirty years earlier had been the town's

Two free non-sectarian schools, financed chiefly by the Peabody Fund, opened in St. Augustine in the late 1860's. The one for white children occupied the former City Hall quarters on what is now Aviles Street, at a rent of one cent a year. The location of the one for black children is presently unknown.

money crop. The orange scale which had decimated the groves in the 1830's disappeared about the time of the war just as mysteriously as it had originated. One of the first northerners to invest in the revived industry was John Hay, who had bought an orange grove at a tax sale during the war when he was in town as Lincoln's representative trying to organize a pro-Union government. Soon a regular boom in orange grove property was under way all along the Florida frontier. St. Augustine's groves received much of the attention because they were the oldest and because their fragrant blossoms were right under the noses of the winter visitors. A favorite pastime among the guests in the hotels was to take a carriage ride or stroll through the groves just outside the town. Orange enthusiasts, calculating that a mature tree could produce a yearly profit of forty dollars, multiplied that times trees per acre and determined that, on paper, fortunes were available for the taking.

However, most growers of the golden fruit found real profits much more modest. While St. Augustine did enjoy a period of genuine prosperity via oranges during the 1870's, the citrus industry eventually gravitated away from the town toward more southerly parts of the peninsula. A new uncontrollable orange blight disease and periodic killing freezes would finally doom commercial citrus culture in St. Augustine.

In the late 1860's another sign of returning prosperity was the development of new residential areas outside the walls of the old Spanish settlement. A small number of northerners were coming to Florida to settle permanently, many of them attracted by claims of the area's healthfulness. John F. Whitney migrated from New Jersey, bought a large tract of land west of the San Sebastian which he named Ravenswood and began selling small lots to other newcomers. The road running north from the city gate was paved with oyster shells and along its route through North City trim new cottages appeared.

The new suburb which revealed another aspect of changed social conditions in town was Lincolnville, which originated as a collection of black squatters' cabins called Africa. When the slaves were freed they could do little to improve their status because of their ignorance and poverty; however, they could put some distance between themselves and the physical reminders of their slavery by moving out of town. The settlers who moved into the Africa district, south of town between Maria Sanchez Creek and the San Sebastian, began farming for themselves and created their own separate social institutions, most notably their own churches. The resulting social and economic independence was very limited, but of great psychological importance to the black community.

The surest sign of renewed life in town was the erection of the St. Augustine Hotel in 1869 on the block just north of the plaza's old market. This was the first major hotel to open since the Magnolia began taking in winter visitors back in the 1840's. Wooden and barn-like, except for its carpenter gothic trim and the piazzas on its south front, this new hotel continued a tradition of conventional ordinariness in architecture. The new hotel could accommodate the increasing flow of seasonal visitors coming to town. Local promoters had expressed concern that St. Augustine might lose out in the competition for winter patronage to rising resort centers such as Jacksonville and the towns along the St. Johns. Travelers on the river were being warned that accommodations in St. Augustine were overcrowded and prices outrageous.

The promise suggested by the erection of the new hotel failed to materialize largely because no additional big new hotels followed. The economy rose to a slightly higher level and then stagnated for most of the decade of the 1870's. The town continued in the tradition of offering a quiet, quaint setting in which the aged and infirm could spend the winter months while during the summer, weeds grew in the streets as the "dull season" dragged on. The poet Sidney Lanier visited St. Augustine during the slack period of 1875 and mused that it was a time to lie on one's back on the seawall, staring at the heavens, feet dangling over the edge—and yawn.

The melancholy poet found the romantic old fort inhabited by noble savages from the western deserts: "The Cheyennes, the Kiowas, the Comanches, the Caddoes, and the Arapahoes, with their shuffling chains, and strange tongues and barbaric gestures." These men were prisoners of the United States govern-

Overland travel to St. Augustine took various forms in the past. Mules pulled the "train" between Tocoi on the St. Johns River and St. Augustine in the 1870's (above). Not many years later, the Jacksonville, St. Augustine and Halifax Railroad boasted wood-burning engines for excursions such as that pictured below.

ment, "troublemakers" who had been separated from their tribes
in an effort to pacify the western frontier. Lanier saw nothing
romantic and something tragic in the way that the Indians
accommodated to their new home by making souvenir trinkets
for the tourists. The Indians' jailer and mentor, Captain Richard
Pratt, encouraged money-making enterprises as a means of
earning spending money and raising funds to provide educa-
tional scholarships for some of the red youths. During the winter
season the captives staged shows on the fort green or in hotel
dining rooms, demonstrating their skills with the bow and arrow,
traditional songs and dances, sign language and "war whoops."

Captain Pratt sympathized with his charges and in accordance
with that day's enlightened thought labored to uplift and civilize
the Indians by teaching them the English language and the skills
of an industrial economy. Several of the town's ladies opened a
school in the fort's chapel, and Pratt arranged for some Indians
to find employment with local businesses. However, he realized
that St. Augustine presented few opportunities for on-the-job
training, and he began exploring other possibilities which included study at Hampton Institute in Virginia, and which would
later lead to the founding of the Carlisle Indian School in
Pennsylvania.

When the Indians were allowed to return home in the spring of
1878, Pratt accompanied them as far as Virginia. As their steamer
churned out of the harbor many St. Augustine townspeople lined
the seawall to wave farewell.

For several months in 1886 and 1887 the fort would again hold
Indian prisoners—Apaches from Arizona and New Mexico,
including all three of Geronimo's wives. The Apaches lived in
teepee-like Sibley army tents pitched atop the fort's terreplein.
Again the local whites opened a school, and the tourists flocked
to the fort in such numbers to view the captives that the army
had to lock out visitors. Captain Pratt returned to recruit
students for his new Carlisle School.

In the late 1870's a tide began to run in the affairs of the town,
but at first its current was barely perceptible. It could be seen in
the new houses being constructed in and around town, and it
could be measured in the lengthening tax rolls and the increased

population recorded in the 1880 census. More people were living in town permanently, and more winter visitors were coming during the December-to-March season. The new railroads and steamship lines were making it easier to escape the cold north, bringing a new class of affluent guests who came simply for pleasure and comfort rather than as a necessity dictated by frail health. To celebrate the town's rising fortunes, as well as to induce more winter visitors into local hotels, a grand Ponce de Leon Celebration was staged periodically in the spring. Houses were festooned with bunting and banners hung across the streets welcoming Juan Ponce de León and his Spanish troopers, who landed at the seawall and marched to the fort. Joining the parade were units of state militia, ladies of social clubs riding in carriages, fire engines and a throng of people caught up in the spirit of the occasion. The evening concluded with a bay-front band concert, followed the next day by yacht races and fireworks.

Among St. Augustine's winter guests in 1884 was a grey-haired, stony-faced representative of the new class of wealthy visitors to Florida: Henry M. Flagler. He was, in fact, one of the richest, most powerful men in America, a founder with John D. Rockefeller of Standard Oil Company. Flagler and his second wife, Alice Shourds Flagler, were spending their honeymoon in Florida, away from the winter cold of New York. He would not remain long in St. Augustine, but the seed of a grand design had been planted in his imagination.

A year later, Flagler returned to St. Augustine and stayed in the town's newest and most ambitious hotel, the San Marco, whose ornate towers rose just west of the fort. While at the San Marco, Flagler perfected a plan which would transform America's oldest city and ultimately alter the course of Florida history. He proposed to build a resort hotel of his own, surpassing anything ever seen in Florida and rivaling the best hotels in the world. Having achieved the pinnacle of success in the business world with Standard Oil, Flagler essayed the challenge of a second career as a resort developer. He planned for St. Augustine to become the winter refuge of the country's economic and social elite: the American Riviera.

O. D. Seavey, manager of the San Marco and an experienced hotel man, was drawn into the planning at the beginning, resigning his position with the San Marco to work for Flagler. The builders of the San Marco, James McGuire and Joseph McDonald, were employed to build the new hotel. One of St. Augustine's winter residents, Franklin W. Smith of Boston, provided part of the concept for Flagler's project. Smith was a connoisseur of exotic architecture and had just completed a whimsical Moorish palace on King Street which served as his home for the season. The Villa Zorayda was one of the first all-concrete buildings constructed in America, and its grey walls suggested a means of liberating Florida hotel architecture from the tyranny of pitch-pine lumber. Finally, Flagler enlisted Dr. Andrew Anderson to use his lifelong experience and connections in St. Augustine to facilitate acquisition of the property needed for the hotel.

Sensitive to St. Augustine's European heritage and unique architecture, Flagler desired a building which would blend with and accentuate the antique charm of the community. His choice of architects was providential. The selection of Thomas Hastings, twenty-five-year-old son of an old friend of the family, turned out to be a stroke of genius. Hastings and his business partner John M. Carrère, together with their associate Bernard Maybeck, would rise to the top rank of American architects in the early 20th century. Their first work, the Hotel Ponce de Leon, would be their most extravagant and among their best. Its opening in January 1888 was an epoch-making event in the history of Florida tourism.

Carrère and Hastings called the style Spanish Renaissance, but it echoed the motifs of Rome, medieval castles and cathedrals, the Near East and its own late Victorian times. Built on the filled bed of Maria Sanchez Creek, the spreading, four-story structure rose from amid orange, palm and live oak trees. Open balconies and a large courtyard served to unite the building with its tropical surroundings. There were even potted citrus trees on the roof. Embedded in the rough concrete of the building's walls were the same coquina shells found in the fort, the old stone houses on St. George Street and on the beaches of Anastasia

Island. Two soaring spires decorated with orange terra-cotta ornamentation flanked the hotel's central dome, adding a final touch of lofty majesty to the whole creation.

Magnificent though it was, the Hotel Ponce de Leon was only the centerpiece of a whole program of additions and alterations Flagler planned for St. Augustine. Across the way from the Ponce de Leon, also on filled land, he built the Alcazar, a smaller hotel which offered slightly more modest accommodations for the overflow from his major hotel. The Alcazar also contained an arcade of shops for the hotel's guests, and to the rear there was an elaborate health and entertainment casino. The Casino contained a large indoor swimming pool, several types of therapeutic baths, steam rooms, a gymnasium, bowling alley and dance floor. The Alcazar continued Carrère and Hastings' Spanish Renaissance architecture, making it a fitting complement to the Ponce de Leon.

Franklin W. Smith entered into the spirit of the moment by erecting the Casa Monica Hotel just across Cordova Street from Flagler's hotels. The walls of Smith's exuberant medieval Moorish castle were of the same cast concrete as the Ponce de Leon and Alcazar and his own Villa Zorayda. Inside was a large, glassed-over patio, the Sun Room, where winter chills were completely banished. The effort to complete the hotel, however, proved too much for Smith's finances, and he sold out to Flagler, who renamed the hotel the Cordova and added it to his enterprises.

To insure that guests could reach his hotels, which were, after all, on the edge of the Florida frontier, Flagler purchased the railroad running north from St. Augustine to the St. Johns River and built the first bridge across the river to connect with the rail lines from the north. Henceforth, a traveler could step out of the dismal, frigid weather of New York City into a Pullman "palace" car and thirty-five hours later step out into the warm sunshine and blossoming flowers at Flagler's new railroad station in St. Augustine. The magic of changing winter into spring overnight captured the imagination of the winter-bound north and set the Florida tourist industry booming.

From the rail depot travelers went to the hotels in brightly

The Spanish Renaissance Hotel Ponce de Leon (top) was the first
built by Henry M. Flagler, opening in 1888. A year later, across King
Street, the Alcazar (lower right) welcomed guests. The Cordova, of
Moorish architecture (lower left) completed the luxurious
triumvirate.

painted omnibuses of the St. Augustine Transfer Company, whose stables were built by Flagler, over asphalt streets paved by Flagler. On the way they would pass the Flagler-built baseball field, Flagler's laundry building and the dairy which supplied milk for Flagler's hotels. The city streets were kept clean by Flagler's maintenance crew. On Sunday worshipers might attend Memorial Presbyterian Church or Grace Methodist Church (both designed by Carrère and Hastings and financed by Flagler), or Ancient City Baptist Church (built on land donated by Flagler) or the Catholic Cathedral, whose new campanile was designed by James Renwick, Jr. of St. Patrick's Cathedral fame and donated by Flagler. In the event of illness one could repair to Alicia Hospital, named for Alice Flagler, wife of the hospital's benefactor. The business of government was conducted in the City Building, built and owned by Flagler and rented to the city for a pittance. The new town market and fire station were incorporated in this buiding. Waste from the hotels was carried far out into the bay, away from the Flagler-built wharf, through a modern sewer pipe laid by Flagler. If a visitor desired to purchase a home in St. Augustine, it was available through the Model Land Company, the real estate arm of Flagler, in a new subdivision which Flagler opened up north and west of his hotels.

Flagler's munificence was overwhelming. His gifts were so extraordinary that he was hailed as the city's benefactor. Yet, from another perspective, Flagler created grave problems for St. Augustine. It was as if the old and tattered fabric of society was unable to bear the great weight of Flagler's presence. The town's population doubled in the span of less than a year. A village that had been a sleepy enclave on the seashore was forced overnight to shoulder the burdens of a modern, urban municipality. As the crime rate went up, a larger professional police force became a requirement. Streets had to be paved, the fire department expanded, a new water system developed, gas lines laid and a host of new public responsibilities shouldered. Pressed to make these improvements, the city went into debt, defaulted on its creditors and sometimes resorted to paying its employees in script. When taxes were increased the city council was besieged by irate citizens demanding reductions; many of them benefited only marginally from Flagler's enterprises. The council reduced taxes for everyone—except Flagler.

Old-timers were divided in their sentiments toward Flagler. Some were in complete sympathy with his dream of a winter Newport and criticized their fellow citizens for their unprogressive foot-dragging. Others felt that they were losing control of their own town to an outsider who demanded that everything be done his way. Indeed, Flagler was accustomed to getting his way, and he resented what he felt was the stubborn backwardness of the old guard element in town. Alternately posing as a philanthropist whose highest aim was the improvement of the community, or offering thinly veiled threats to withdraw his patronage, Flagler cajoled the town fathers into following his lead.

The trauma of Flagler's advent was worsened by two back-to-back disasters which devastated the town. For months during 1886 the city council had debated purchase of a new fire engine, and had postponed action due to lack of funds. The unwisdom of this decision suddenly became apparent early in the dark hours of morning, April 12, 1887. The town awoke to the clanging of the fire bell. The four-story St. Augustine Hotel on the plaza was sheeted with towering flames, against which the puny stream of water from the town's only fire engine was impotent. Soon the flames spread to adjacent buildings, sending occupants streaming into the streets. Furniture and valuables were tossed out windows and carried to jumbled piles near the seawall or in the plaza. Building after building in the block north of the plaza burst into flame; even the roof of the old public market took fire. Finally the cathedral's turn came; its interior glowed red, then its wooden roof burned and collapsed into the shell of the church's old stone walls.

By dawn the fire had been contained, and the St. Augustine Guards were out patrolling the streets to prevent looting. Both schools and saloons were closed that day. Miraculously only one person, a woman employed in the hotel, died. Shortly thereafter the city council placed an order for another fire engine.

In the fall of 1887 there was a yellow fever scare. Rumors

drifted into town that several people in Tampa had been stricken with "yellow jack," and just to be on the safe side the city council placed inspectors at the railroad station and on the main roads to watch for anyone who might be carrying the disease. Even at this late date, no one knew the cause of yellow fever, but it was supposed that it spread through contagion. Therefore any town stricken by an epidemic would become a pariah among its neighbors—isolated from the rest of the world by strict quarantines. Being quarantined was a disaster to any town's economy, so naturally local authorities treated any suspected cases of yellow fever with quiet circumspection, or sometimes openly lied about the existence of verified cases. On the other hand, sometimes towns were unjustly accused of harboring yellow fever by rival towns intent upon stealing away tourist patronage. Evaluating rumors of epidemics was an uncertain science.

By the late summer of the following year there was no longer any doubt that yellow fever was rampant in south Florida. Numbers of St. Augustine residents, described by a Jacksonville observer as "a panic stricken crowd," hastily departed for cooler refuges in states to the north where there was no threat of fever. Those left in town, hoping to keep the epidemic out, drew a cordon around St. Augustine and turned back at the point of a shotgun anyone attempting to cross. Crews went around town clearing up debris and burning rubbish in the hope that good sanitation would prevent an outbreak of fever. The town was under siege. No communication with the outside was permitted— even mail—for fear of contamination by "microbes." The officer in charge of the military barracks offered to supply food to those in need if necessary. The town's depleted treasury sagged further under the burden of supporting the quarantine, even though private citizens contributed money for its support in the hope of preserving the resort town's reputation for health. When the first frost of winter arrived, signaling the end of the fever season, St. Augustine remained free of the disease, but hardly unscathed. In other parts of the state hundreds had died; St. Augustine's losses were mostly financial.

The 1888-1889 winter tourist season was dismal compared to the glorious days of the previous year when Flagler's Hotel

Ponce de Leon had first opened its doors. Many Yankees stayed home in the cold rather than chance the possibility of encountering any lingering threat of fever in Florida. St. Augustine's leaders realized that dependence on the seasonal tourist trade left the city with a built-in boom and bust business cycle. A call was made for new industries. One hope was that the harbor entrance could be deepened and St. Augustine made into a port. The extension of the railroad south and north reinforced this dream that the town might become a trade center. It was suggested that manufacturing be encouraged to come into the area. However, few of these hopes were realized.

One idea did become a reality. Since the days of Manuel Solana and Francisco Xavier Sanchez it had been known that the soil west of town was quite fertile, and a few cracker farmers had long inhabited the area, but it was supposed that large-scale farming was impossible due to the fact that the land was swampy and subject to flooding. Utley J. White, who had come to build railroads and cut timber, studied the land and figured it might be opened up by drainage. He dug a canal from his farm near the railroad's Merrifield station to Deep Creek, which runs into the St. Johns River. In the fall of 1889 he demonstrated that vegetables could be grown on the land and shipped by rail to the north for sale. The next year Thomas Hastings, a relative of the architect, came to the area with Flagler's blessings to grow vegetables for the St. Augustine hotels and for export. Soon St. Johns County was booming as a vegetable and potato farming region, its center the town of Hastings.

The winter season of 1890 witnessed the return of the north's elegant society to Flagler's hotels. The dream of a winter Newport unfolded into opulent reality. Beginning in mid-December the railroad's plush parlor cars, with their blue velvet interiors, disgorged a steady stream of conspicuously rich visitors. Entering the lobby of the Hotel Ponce de Leon beneath the tall dome supported by stout oak caryatids, the Vanderbilts, Rockefellers, Whitneys and their peers experienced the marvels wrought by Flagler's architects and artists. In the grand parlors, where President Cleveland shook hands with his fellow citizens during the 1888 season, the atmosphere was one of gold, gilt, pastels and crystal chandeliers. Balls, the greatest of which was held annually on Washington's birthday, were staged in the vaulted dining room, where tables and chairs were cleared away so that guests could dance beneath the monumental allegorical murals of George W. Maynard. The hotel's own electric generators supplied power for the lights which illuminated the interior and for the fairy lights which twinkled in the trees of the courtyard. During the day the sun's rays filtered into the dining room and lobby through stained glass windows by Louis C. Tiffany. Ornamented but efficient, modern but recalling the glories of the epic past, the Ponce de Leon was a marvel of its age—and remains so today.

Enhancing the renaissance atmosphere of the hotel was a community of noted artists who made St. Augustine their winter home. Flagler accommodated the artists by attaching a row of seven studios to the rear of the hotel. William Aikin Walker, painter of southern genre and one of the first artists to take up residence in town, did not, however, do his work there. The most eminent of those who did was Martin J. Heade, an accomplished landscape artist who had branched out into paintings of exotic flora inhabited by tiny hummingbirds. Others whose works could be inspected in the hotel's studios were Frank H. Shapleigh, George Seavey, W. Staples Drown and Felix de Crano. The weekly receptions held in the artists' quarters were a diversion for hotel guests and an opportunity for the artists to make sales.

Since in those days winter visitors customarily spent most of their time in one town, rather than touring from place to place, a variety of amusements and diversions were required to keep resort patrons entertained. Flagler employed the Alcazar's Casino as the site for popular dances, plays, stage programs and water sports in the pool. Each of the several hotels in town offered card parties and the like to its own patrons and to guests from other hotels. The earliest moving pictures found audiences in the gathering rooms of the hotels. Before the turn of the century cakewalks featuring the Negro employees of the hotels were a standard feature of resort life. Prior to the cakewalk itself there would be exhibitions of dances by blacks and social dancing by the white audience. Then a parade of black couples, men in suits

Tourists have always been drawn to St. Augustine's Castillo de San Marcos. Here a mother and one child (the other refused to come), mount the steps at what was then called Fort Marion.

carrying canes and women in flowing gowns and flowery broad-brimmed hats, would stroll before a panel of distinguished judges from the hotel guests who would determine which couple had "taken the cake."

Outdoor recreation traditionally included sailing on the bay, fishing, hunting, horseback or carriage rides and walking along the seawall. To this were added golf and bicycling in the 1890's. The first links were laid out on the grounds of the fort and incorporated the moat as one of the fairway hazards. Cycling became so popular that the town government was obliged to discuss safety rules to cut down the accident rate. Tennis was played on the courts behind the Casino. The leading spectator sport since the end of the war was baseball. Some of the teams in the state featured professional players from the major leagues who came to Florida during the winter to sharpen their skills.

During the Flagler era more and more visitors discovered the delights of the ocean beaches across the bay from town. Excursions by boat to picnic or hike on the island continued, but more elaborate recreational facilities developed. North Beach could be reached by taking a boat across to a landing on North River and then embarking on a horse-cart ride across a tramway to an ocean-side pavilion. On Anastasia Island the St. Augustine and South Beach Railway ran a similar line across the marsh to the high ground near the new lighthouse. Here the curious could wander through the old coquina quarries and examine the ruins of the old Spanish lighthouse which had tumbled into the ocean when the beach eroded under it. The government had recently built a jetty to protect the area from further erosion. Nearby was the Casa Marina Hotel, designed for those who wanted to sleep within sound of the breakers.

Eventually a little cluster of houses grew up in what was then called Anastasia, but is now known as Lighthouse Park. In 1895 a bridge spanned the bay from the plaza, and the rail line was improved and extended another mile down the beach where a large bathhouse and dance pavilion were erected. South Beach was the scene of evening dances, bicycling on the hard sand, swimming in the surf and parties such as the Fourth of July celebration. Here also was the Museum of Marine Curiosities and

the mysterious Burning Spring, an artesian well whose
combustible nature was attributed to "sulphurated hydrogen,"
but which actually resulted from the more familiar substance,
gasoline, slyly piped into the spring from a tank through a copper
tube. Within a few years the pen of alligators outside the spring
grew into the Alligator Farm, a tourist attraction which would
become one of the town's most popular sights. Unfortunately the
little development at South Beach was doomed to be completely
eroded away by the 1920's, and today only the rusted pipe of the
artesian well stands in the breakers as a reminder of the once-
popular recreation spot. However, the Alligator Farm, relocated
away from the beach, still prospers, a reminder of the days when
the word "Florida" elicited visions of "oranges and alligators" in
the minds of most Americans.

St. Augustine itself was suffering erosion of its tentative
position as the Newport of the south. More quickly than most had
expected—probably including Flagler himself—the Florida
frontier was pushed back by the building of railroads to points
further south on the peninsula where new resort hotels opened.
Henry Plant began inviting guests to his version of a tropical
wonderland, the Tampa Bay Hotel, in 1891. Flagler responded by
extending his railroad down the east coast, first to Ormond Beach
and then to Palm Beach. In Palm Beach he found a virtually
uninhabited wilderness where he built his dream of a complete
resort community all over again; except this time there was no
tradition-bound populace or stubborn city government to
contend with. After 1894 Flagler turned his attention away from
St. Augustine to the southern portion of what was rapidly
becoming his empire.

Although St. Augustine's dull, dingy ways had a great deal to do
with the decline of its fortunes as the ultimate winter resort, some
of the blows to its status cannot be blamed on local conditions and
were unavoidable. In 1893 the whole country fell into one of the
deepest economic depressions in history. In the north thousands
were unemployed; strikes and labor violence in the city streets
and factories led to the calling out of the army. During this time of
hardship even the rich were not spared, and winter visitation at St.
Augustine's hotels dropped. The balls were not so gay as before.

A hurricane which struck St. Augustine in 1894 left debris piled in Charlotte Street, just west of the Matanzas River. At left is the public market.

Nature itself turned against the old city in the winter of 1894-1895 when the worst freeze in memory swept the state. At the Hotel Ponce de Leon water pipes burst, oranges froze solid on the trees, and all the exotic foliage in the courtyard blackened and died.

Toward the end of the decade Anna M. Marcotte, editor of the society magazine *The Tatler*, noted that the town had become a way station for visitors on their journey to Palm Beach and Miami. Passing luxury seekers spent a night or two at the Ponce de Leon, gave the fort and the town's antiquities the once-over, and hastened on to the greener lawns of south Florida. Mrs. Marcotte tirelessly crusaded for cleaning the city streets and sprucing-up the community's image as a resort for the elite, but too many factors in the ancient town dragged down her high aspirations.

From Flagler's arrival there had been some who realized that the town could not rely on his hotels and winter tourism as a sound foundation for the local economy. One of the few successful

A well-dressed crowd watches as workmen install cypress paving blocks in Cathedral Place. The Hotel Ponce de Leon is in the background.

efforts at diversification was the establishment of several small cigar factories in St. Augustine. The influx of Cuban workers employed in these factories re-established the connection between St. Augustine and Cuba which had existed in colonial days. The timing of this development was significant, for in Cuba the movement for independence from Spain had gained momentum. Sympathy for the Cuban revolutionaries ran high in St. Augustine among both the Cuban cigar workers and the general population. When the Cuban patriot José Martí visited St. Augustine in 1892 his cause received a favorable response, leading to the formation of a club dedicated to a free Cuba.

St. Augustine's enthusiasm for Cuban independence was put to the test in 1898 when the United States declared war on Spain. City leaders were suddenly thrown into a panic. Fearing an attack by the Spanish navy on the eastern seaboard of the United States, local politicians drafted a letter to the Secretary of War declaring: "Saint Augustine is in greater peril from attack by hostile force than any city in the country." They reasoned that the Spanish would remember St. Augustine as the most important city in their former North American colonies and would sail directly to bombard the town with the guns of its battle fleet. Doubtless there were sighs of relief shortly thereafter when the Spanish flotilla was bottled up in Santiago, Cuba by the United States Navy.

St. Augustine's young men, like those in thousands of towns across the country, enlisted in the military enthusiastically, hoping for adventure and glory in this "Splendid Little War." Two companies of light infantry were cheered and waved off from the railway depot on their way to Tampa where the army was gathering to invade Cuba. Only a few days later one company returned, having been rejected because Florida had already filled its troop quota. The second was shuttled from Tampa to Fernandina to Huntsville, Alabama, where they were discharged a year later without firing a shot in combat. About the only evidence of the war in St. Augustine itself consisted of the soldiers stationed in Jacksonville who paid visits to town during furloughs.

By the turn of the century the dream of St. Augustine as the winter Newport of America's leisured class had evaporated, but the town had entered a new phase of sustained growth, however modest. After losing population in the decade of the nineties following completion of Flagler's major building projects, St. Augustine began a gentle surge of population growth which would not level off until the Great Depression of the 1930's. The hotels were again full during the winters, but with an older, less wealthy clientele which felt at home in the sedate, calm atmosphere of the old town. The social climate was more relaxed and casual than in the stuffy-formal days of Victorian society's dying blaze of extravagance. The new houses being built were unpretentious bungalows, not gingerbread mansions. This altered state of affairs was reflected in the promotional literature put out by local boosters: "Pictured as the winter playground of the wealthy and fashionable, this city has not been portrayed as a resort with accommodations easily within the reach of people of moderate means." St. Augustine was no longer the "curious antique" village Whitelaw Reid had visited forty years earlier; it was a modern city with streetcars, telephones, electricity, paved streets—all the amenities of 20th-century civilization.

Although the local economy remained pinned to tourism, some further diversification in St. Augustine's business base developed during this time. Increasingly northerners sought out the town as a permanent, year-round retirement home, stimulating home building and a variety of service businesses. The Florida School for the Deaf and Blind, founded back in 1885, grew to become one of the community's major assets. Flagler's Florida East Coast Railway had its offices and maintenance shops in St. Augustine, providing employment for a number of skilled workers. When power fishing boats and refrigerated railroad cars made it possible to ship seafood to northern markets, St. Augustine became the home base of a growing fleet of fishing boats. St. Augustine was by no means a wealthy town, but its inhabitants no longer subsisted on a diet of mullet and sweet potatoes as in former days.

It was to this emerging new town that Henry Flagler, now an old man and already almost an anachronism, returned toward the end of the first decade of the young century. His empire along the Florida east coast was nearing completion with the building of the railroad across the sea to Key West, and he turned from his enterprises to visit again the town where his original dream had taken shape. Each December he and his family would occupy the first floor of the Ponce de Leon's west wing until after Christmas when they would move on to Palm Beach. There were a few grand balls in the dining room, as was the custom in the hotel's heyday, but often social affairs were moved to the more intimate spaces of the parlors. On Christmas day the Flaglers and their friends would gather around a large decorated tree in the rotunda to celebrate and exchange gifts. Flagler found Palm Beach society not entirely to his liking, and St. Augustine offered a respite from Palm Beach's demands on his time and from the jealousy and criticism which he perceived among many of its residents.

This did not mean that Flagler had forgiven St. Augustine for its faults: "The condition of our asphalt streets (made originally by me and given to the City) excites my disgust every time I go to and from the R. R. Depot," he wrote James E. Ingraham of St. Augustine. "I have realized from the beginning that St. Augustine was a dull place, but it does seem as though twenty years would stir up some little measure of public spirit; enough to at least keep the only street we have to the Railroad in decent condition."

Flagler's life had been touched by tragedy during his years in Florida. In 1889 his daughter Jenny Louise had died after childbirth while on her way by ship to St. Augustine. Flagler dedicated the Memorial Presbyterian Church, which he was then building, to her memory and placed her remains in a mausoleum at the side of the church. Shortly thereafter Flagler became estranged from his son because of their vastly different temperaments. Harry Harkness Flagler could not be the sort of businessman that his father expected, and, although Harry did take a try at managing the Hotel Ponce de Leon, he finally broke with his father and lived a separate life in New York. The blow of Harry's "desertion" was compounded by the onset of incurable insanity in Alice Flagler. Always extravagant, red-haired Alice became so erratic in her behavior and lost to reality that she had to be institutionalized. When Flagler later divorced his wife and married Mary Lily Kenan, a young society lady, public opinion ran strongly against Flagler. It was alleged that he had bribed the state legislature to pass a law making insanity grounds for divorce. As it turned out, his life with Mary Lily brought him little happiness.

With advancing age Flagler began to lose his sight and hearing; more and more he was confined to a wheelchair—infirmities which he bore with ill grace. Through force of will, brains and hard work he had triumphed with Standard Oil and in his Florida enterprises, but to his dismay he could not now control his own destiny. In the spring of 1913 he fell and broke a hip on the stairs of Whitehall, his marble palace in Palm Beach. Bedridden and delirious, Flagler clung tenaciously to life as all Florida, as well as much of the business world, waited and read the newspapers for daily bulletins. On May 20 he passed away at the age of eighty-three.

Flagler's body was carried by train from Palm Beach to St. Augustine and placed in the rotunda of the Hotel Ponce de Leon so that citizens could pay their respects to the town's greatest benefactor. On May 30, 1913 the wheels on all Florida East Coast Railway trains stopped around the state while the funeral cortege made the short trip from the hotel to the Memorial Presbyterian Church where Flagler would be put to rest next to his daughter Jenny Louise and his first wife Mary. Businesses were closed all afternoon in St. Augustine, and toward evening it rained.

Henry M. Flagler, Standard Oil magnate and builder of St. Augustine's great hotels, with his wife, Mary Lily Kenan, and friends on the observation platform of one of his Florida East Coast Railway trains.

Chapter Eight

Yesterday and the Day Before
1913 to the present

by

Robert N. Dow, Jr.

The so-called Golden Age of tourism in St. Augustine ended, symbolically at least, with the death of Henry M. Flagler in May 1913. But realistically, the days when St. Augustine was being hailed as the American Riviera and the winter Newport were long past. Oddly enough, the man who had produced the city's Golden Age also contributed to its decline. "Dull, sleepy, unprogressive" St. Augustine by 1914 was subtly and quietly declining as a mecca for the rich and powerful.

The gleaming Flagler trains, which in the early days reached the end of the line in St. Augustine and disgorged all their passengers onto King Street, now were "passing through." They bore names like "Palm Beach Limited" and "Overseas Limited" (destination Key West). Some passengers debarked in familiar St. Augustine, but more and more continued on to glamorous points farther south. More vexing was that few of the magnificent private railway cars of the very rich were any longer seen on St. Augustine sidings.

Some had tried to warn of what lay ahead for St. Augustine. Outspoken Anna M. Marcotte, proprietor of *The Tatler*, put one problem succinctly:

> "St. Augustine must wake to the fact that she is a resort, that if she is not to sink to a village of a few inhabitants, she must stay in the race, grow in cleanliness and beauty, or sit down and see her visitors of former years pass them by on their journey to even newer, more progressive resorts."

William Dean Howells, "an insightful literary gentleman," looked at the change in hotel clientele and contributed another view of St. Augustine's problems:

"People now do not want that series of drawing and
dining rooms which open from the inner patio of the
Ponce de Leon: and if they did they would not have
the form fitly to inhabit them; their short skirts and
their lounge-coats are not for such gracious interiors,
but rather for the golf links."

Winter visitors, for a quarter of a century, had made a major
contribution to the economy of St. Augustine. But in the first
decades of the new century, there was a continuing decline in
tourism.

St. Augustine business and political leaders addressed the
possibility of replacing lost winter season visitors with summer
tourists and in 1915 began planning an active campaign to draw
this clientele to St. Augustine.

At a time when the railroads were siphoning more and more
winter tourists off southward, there was on the St. Augustine
horizon a barely recognized new form of both winter and
summer tourist transportation—the automobile.

In the second decade of the 20th century, it was an ungainly,
noisy, uncomfortable monster. But it already had gone through
its first phase, when it was the toy of the bored city rich. Now it
was escaping the cities and being driven cross-country by
daredevil "automobilists" accompanied by their "mechanicians,"
who coaxed balky engines back to life, changed fragile tires and
arranged extrication from deep sand or mud holes. The quest
was for record times between cities.

St. Augustine had its questers. At 6 a.m. one morning in 1914, a
big Cadillac driven by its owner, Frank J. Parker, accompanied
by his mechanician Harry W. House, headed out of St. Augustine,
its destination Miami 350 miles south. At 11 that night, 17 hours
later, the two pulled into Miami with a new record. They had
averaged better than 20 miles an hour, an astounding speed for
the day. Later that year, the St. Augustine/Tampa record was
lowered by another driving team to 15 hours.

But there were growing indications that the daredevil days
were ending, that a new phase in the maturing of the automobile
was nearing, when ordinary citizens would move by auto from

The hard sand of the beach brought out an impressive line-up of automobiles and passengers for a spin along the shore one chilly day in the early 1900's.

The beach was equally good for bicycles, even the high-wheelers known as "ordinaries." Those and the more common variety of bikes provided transportation and recreation for visitors and townspeople alike.

Roads and automobiles have long been important in St. Augustine's life. By 1916 the brick roads of the area were considered some of the best in the nation—provided an auto didn't run off into the sand bordering the brick.

Forerunner of the trailers and mobile homes of later years, this vehicle was home for one tourist family on its St. Augustine visit in the 1920's.

city to city. On January 14, 1915, the *St. Augustine Record* headlined a thrilling auto trek. The Misses Montgomery of Indiana, regular winter visitors to St. Augustine, had decided to make their annual trip to the city in their auto. Accompanied by a friend, Miss Beyers, and their driver/mechanician C. P. Mathews, they fought their way over "wretched roads" to arrive safely in St. Augustine fifteen days after leaving Indianapolis.

Later in the year, a record-seeking duo on a run from St. Louis to Miami stopped briefly in St. Augustine with an enthusiastic report that they had passed 75 cars on the way "all Florida bound and filled with prosperous looking and apparently well-to-do people." Their record trip covered six and a half days.

A checkpoint on the southern St. Johns County line counted the motorists passing through for the last months of 1915. In November, there were 341 motorists headed north, 752 south for a total of 1,093 for the month.

So automobilists were on the move toward and within Florida. And St. Augustine leaders recognized that if the movement was to grow, one thing had to be done, and quickly. Good roads must be constructed, present roads improved.

They began discussing such improvements in 1914, and in 1915 took action—$650,000 was appropriated to pave 64 miles of St. Johns County roads. And the paving would be brick, not the more popular and less expensive macadam. The decision favoring brick resulted from growing evidence that macadam (in those days a broken stone layer on an earthen roadbed) did not stand up under heavy use by large autos.

The major project in the paving program was a nine-foot-wide brick pavement, bordered on each side by a six-foot-wide grassed berm. The road would cover the entire St. Johns County portion of the Dixie Highway, from the Duval County line though St. Augustine and on to the Volusia County line to the south.

The final brick was laid in early 1916 and immediately the new stretch of roadway was hailed by visiting motorists as the finest in all the eastern United States.

Law enforcement people were a little less enthusiastic. The new road quickly created new problems for them—speeding and accidents. Only a few months before, the police had requested and received their first motorcycle (the city fathers also bought them a speedometer to go on the 'cycle). The request stemmed from the growing number of auto speeders in St. Augustine. As the *St. Augustine Record* put it:

> "And now local automobile drivers of the reckless class—which includes some very prominent citizens— will have to tell it to Judge Goode pretty soon. And the judge has shown in the past the view he takes of the wilful violation of this ordinance."

But the smooth new stretch of the Dixie Highway proved irresistible to speed-demon drivers, regardless of the motorcycle. Within weeks after it opened, almost daily accidents were being reported, injuring and even killing drivers and passengers. At first, a drastically low speed limit was proposed but was rejected after it was found that most accidents were occurring when vehicles, not only autos but also motorcycles and bicycles, were trying to pass each other. Inexperienced drivers were using the unpaved berm and losing control of their vehicles. So an ordinance was drafted limiting the speed of passing vehicles to ten miles per hour.

Now St. Augustine had a spectacular road which would certainly attract auto tourists from throughout the country. But Duval County to the north and Volusia County to the south lagged in improving their portions of the Dixie Highway, despite constant prodding by St. Johns County. All St. Augustine could do was erect a prideful masonry archway where the two roads met at the Duval-St. Johns County line. On the side facing the ruts and mud holes of Duval County was a message "Welcome to St. Johns County" and on the other side was a farewell to motorists venturing from the smooth brick into the Duval mire, "Goodbye, Come Again." Several years were to pass before adjacent counties paved their sections of the highway.

At the time, the beginning trickle of auto tourists in both summer and winter helped somewhat to replace railroad tourists being lost by the city. But ahead lay the Roaring Twenties, the "tin lizzy," the "tin can tourist," a trickle grown to a stream. And then finally as the decades passed, the torrent as the automobile took over, crowding railroads from the passenger scene. America's love affair with the automobile was on, and St. Augustine was to profit greatly along with other Florida resorts.

While St. Augustine's tourist business and life-style were slowly changing, the face of the city was suddenly altered in a single fiery, frightening night. In the early morning hours of April 2, 1914, fire broke out in the wooden Florida House hotel and by daylight, five blocks containing hotels, businesses, residences, historic landmarks were smoking ruins. That day's *St. Augustine Record* reported the extent of the disaster:

> "Sweeping from St. George Street between Treasury and Hypolita, a wide swath through the heart of the city, fire discovered at an early hour this morning caused heavy damage and loss to St. Augustine estimated at $750,000. Today all that remains of four hotels, a big business block, the County Courthouse, many beautiful homes and other buildings is a smouldering heap of ashes. But for heroic work, the entire section from Cordova to Bay and from Cathedral Place to the City Gates would have been lost."

Surprisingly, no one died in the early morning blaze that engulfed hotels full of sleeping and, in some cases, aged guests.

Although St. Augustine had had a series of earlier fires, this was the most disastrous since 1821. It prompted several actions by the city fathers, first to pass a stricter fire code for buildings and secondly, to bring to fruition a project under discussion for some time before the fire, a fully mechanized fire department.

Within a year, horsepower had replaced horses except for one piece of equipment, a horse-drawn engine which was kept as a backup for the new motorized equipment.

A pair of veteran fire horses was retained but all experienced horse drivers were now driving fire trucks. So a city employee was detailed to handle the horses and wagon, which led to a scene that set all St. Augustine laughing. The inexperienced driver was given a quick course in the procedure for getting the wagon under way. First he was to set the brake, then drop the harness from the ceiling of the firehouse onto the horses, then ring the equipment bell to which the horses were trained to respond at full gallop and finally to release the brake when he had control of the horses. On his first run, he failed to set the brake and when the bell sounded the horses went charging out of the firehouse, bits in their teeth, and swung down Hypolita Street toward the bay. Completely out of control, the horses kept straight ahead. The wheels hit the seawall and the wagon stopped, but both horses, with the driver hanging on to the reins, ended up in the bay. It took embarrassed firemen hours to convince the swimming horses to climb up the steps of the seawall to dry land.

The driver was given another lecture on procedure and another chance. On the next run, he made sure he set the brake to keep control of the horses. Again the wagon swung out of the firehouse and headed downtown. But the horses slowed down after a block or two and finally came to a full stop, utterly exhausted. This time the driver forgot to release the brake. He ended up not only wearing down the horses but also the rubber tires on both back wheels—all the way down to the metal rims.

When widespread fighting erupted suddenly in Europe in the hot summer of 1914, marking the start of what was to become World War I, St. Augustine first viewed what was reported daily in black newspaper headlines as something happening in far-away places hardly known to most citizens, and therefore of little real interest.

In the first weeks of fighting, there was a brief period of excitement when observers at St. Augustine Beach and South Beach on two occasions reported sounds of a "great sea battle" off the coast. They claimed hearing gunfire and, in the evening, seeing flashes of light from guns and from searchlights. Rumor had British warships chasing a German raider off the St. Augustine coast. But as time went by, there was no official confirmation and the incidents were written off as overactive imaginations confusing thunderstorms far at sea with the sounds of battle.

The reality of fighting dawned on St. Augustine when stories of St. Augustinians and well-known visitors trapped on the Continent began to filter through. One poignant incident involved a St. Augustine father and daughter—W. H. Chambers, comptroller of the Florida East Coast Railway, and Miss Kathleen Chambers. They were on the Continent at the outbreak of war when Mr. Chambers fell seriously ill, leaving the full burden of escape from the Continent on the shoulders of his daughter. Abandoning their baggage, without funds, she fought for scarce space on railways, finally making it to the coast and aboard a ship for England with her helpless father, who died the next day in London of a heart attack. Quick work by St. Augustine railway officials through business contacts in London finally provided Miss Chambers with aid and funds to return, with her father's body, to the United States.

Actually, the war was something of a bonanza to St. Augustine, since with the Continental spas and resorts closed, more well-to-do tourists than ever headed for the Ancient City and other Florida areas. Activities during "the season" continued full blast. Auction bridge dominated the hotel card rooms, there were picnics on the beach, dancing in the ballrooms and afternoon Japanese musical teas. Operas, plays, minstrel shows and moving pictures attracted large audiences. Outdoor types pedaled bicycles around town, automobiled into the countryside and a few of the more daring tried the latest fad, "aeroplaning."

The movies were great attractions during this period, since many of them contained scenes shot in St. Augustine including local persons as extras. The climate, the outdoor scenery and the picturesqueness of St. Augustine attracted many early moviemakers. Some maintained permanent studios in the city, others moved in for sequences of filming. Glimpses of stars like Mary Garden and Theda Bara were frequent on St. Augustine streets.

A commentary written in 1917 by William Dean Howells, for *Harper's Magazine*, assesses St. Augustine-made movies of the day:

"St. Augustine is indeed the setting of almost any most dramatic fact, as the companies of movie players rehearsing their pantomines everywhere so recurrently testified. No week passed without encountering these genial fellow creatures dismounting from motors at this picturesque point or that, or delaying in them to darken an eye or redden lip or cheek or pull a bodice into shape before alighting to take part in the drama. I talk as if there were no men in these affairs but there were plenty, preferably villains like brigands or smugglers or savages, with consoling cowboys or American cavalrymen for the rescue of ladies in extremity. Seeing the films so much in formation we naturally went a great deal to see them ultimated in the movie theaters, where we found them nearly all bad. In this I do not suppose that they differed from the movie drama elsewhere, or that they were more unfailingly worthless. They were less offensive as they were more romantic. When they tried to be realistic they illustrated the life of crime in the East and the violence in the West. There was very little comedy but one night in the representation of a medieval action, an involuntary stroke of burlesque buried the poetry of love interest when the mechanical piano which had been set to the music of the tango continued that deplorable strain while the funeral of a nun slowly paced through the garden of the convent to the chapel. The general vulgarity and worse, seemed the more the pity because the theaters were always well filled not only with the prouder visitors from the great hotels and the friendly roomers from everywhere, but also with nice-looking townspeople who had brought their children with them."

The combination of movie production, excellent weather and well-heeled visitors attracted another unusual group to the city— the aeronauts. They would head their flimsy machines south as the winter season began and land on the beach, or, in the case of

St. Augustine's unique appearance and fine weather attracted many early movie-making companies. Their stars, such as Theda Bara, could often be seen posing and rehearsing in the Florida sunlight.

one of the early seaplanes, on the bay. Their routines included regular exhibitions of flying prowess: short flights with passengers bold enough to chance the crashes that were a regular part of the flying process, and flights made before cameras for inclusion in the current movie drama in production in St. Augustine.

St. Augustine, during this period, was considered "sports crazy." So many of its visitors liked golf that a new 18-hole course was constructed for them. The Alcazar Hotel's swimming pool, the largest indoor pool in the country, served not only visitors but also the nation's finest swimmers who came to the city to compete in the National Amateur Athletics Union's national tournaments. A special baseball diamond, grandstand and clubhouse complex was built to bring the St. Louis Cardinals to the city for spring training. The country's fastest powerboats

Fragile airplanes appeared in St. Augustine within a few years of
the Wright brothers' flights at Kitty Hawk, N.C.

Daredevils flying planes developed during World War I performed
acts such as acquiring a passenger who climbed to the plane from a
car speeding on the beach.

were attracted to the Matanzas River to compete in races sponsored by the city's Power Boat Club.

For the locals, it was hard to choose between hunting, fishing and baseball. The area was bountifully supplied with quail, dove, duck, squirrel, rabbit and deer for the hunters and a choice of fine saltwater fishing in the ocean and inland waterways, or freshwater fishing in the nearby St. Johns River, for the anglers. Mullet was a favorite saltwater fish and there was always high excitement during the "mullet run" season when the tasty fish gathered in great schools in the inland waterways and along the beaches, easy prey for the cast nets wielded so expertly by the local fishermen.

St. Augustine's interest in baseball was kept at a fever pitch not only by the presence of the major league Cardinals but also by the local team, the Saints, whose season was always highlighted by a series of "for blood" games played against nearby opposing teams such as Palatka.

One such game during a warm weekend afternoon sorely tested the loyalty of St. Augustine's sports fans. Hundreds were in the stands as the St. Augustine team and its opponent went at it in a close, hard-fought game. In a late inning, a local sportsman trotted through the gates to the front of the grandstand and announced in a loud voice, "Mullet on the beach." There was a moment's hesitation, then a general scramble for the exits by the men in the stands. The crowd that saw the end of the game was made up mainly of women and children.

With the entry of the United States in the summer of 1917, the war that had dragged on for years in Europe came home to St. Augustine.

Registration of young men for the draft made the terrible casualty reports that had long flowed in from the faraway front lines of much more immediate concern to St. Augustinians. As in most American cities, patriotic fervor burgeoned. Many rushed to volunteer; the first issue of Liberty Bonds was far over-subscribed; a Red Cross fund drive went well over its goal;

patriotic poems and sayings graced nearly every front page of the daily newspaper.

National Guard units were mobilized and headed off to war along with volunteers and draftees for the regular forces. A County Home Guard was organized to replace the lost Guard units.

The first war casualty notices came not from the trenches, but from the training camps in the U.S., where several St. Augustinians died, not from bullets but by disease.

Gradually letters began to arrive bearing different postmarks— from "over there." Ralph Edwards wrote from London, Milton Fuller cabled his parents of his safe arrival in England, Alva Perkins wrote home using a dateline "U.S. Expeditionary Force in France."

Two more sombre letters were received by the mother of brothers Gene and Walter Clark, who had enlisted in the Marines and who were both in the first big offensives by U.S. troops at Chateau-Thierry. Gene was severely wounded by machine gunfire and, while recovering in a hospital, wrote home:

"It was real war and no mistake this time. But we not only stopped the Germans but drove them back."

Walter supplemented his brother's letter with one saying:

"Gene was in the thick of it. He sure did some scrapping."

As the war reached its climax in the summer of 1918, St. Augustinians contended with food shortages, purchased their Liberty Bonds, wrapped bandages for the front and worried about a new home front menace, the "Spanish influenza." As flu cases mounted and deaths increased, all public gatherings were forbidden, schools were closed, flu victims and their families were isolated in their homes.

With the coming of fall, victory was in sight in the war and the flu epidemic subsided, with the various bans being lifted. St. Augustine was ready to celebrate when November 11 and the Armistice arrived. The *St. Augustine Record* described the scene:

"St. Augustine went wild with patriotic enthusiasm upon hearing the news that the great world war is over. The demonstration began with the blowing of whistles and the ringing of the bells.

At 3:15 a.m., the whistles and bells throughout the city, including the locomotives of the Florida East Coast Railway, announced the glorious news.

As minutes passed, the crowd downtown grew in size until daylight it had assumed enormous proportions.

By 4 a.m., the Plaza presented a wondrous sight, being ablaze with fireworks and red fire. Automobiles and trucks—crowded to the limit—paraded the streets, the occupants sounding horns, sirens and whistles. Up and down St. George Street, local 'cowboys' raced on their fleet ponies, cracking their long whips and adding to the deafening yet joyful noises contributed by the crowds on the streets.

St. Augustine is in true gala attire for the celebration of the great victory that has been won."

Ironically, in that same decade after the death of Henry M. Flagler in 1913, St. Augustine began slowly to change in the direction that Flagler had tried to prod city fathers for nearly twenty-five years after he opened his great tourist hotels. "Quaint" St. Augustine finally was moving toward urban maturity.

One by one, dusty, rutted streets of the city were paved as part of the county-wide "good roads" project, city leaders finally facing a street situation that had irritated Flagler almost from the beginning of his arrival in the city. Better lighting came to dark city streets when a "white way" project saw additional gaslights installed throughout downtown. The necessity for food protection, medical therapy and cool drinks in hot summers prompted the city to construct a municipal ice plant.

Perhaps the greatest impetus to progress came in 1915 when a decision was made to adopt a commission/city manager form of government, the most modern and progressive system of its day.

Building permits started to soar as replacement buildings finally began to be constructed in the area left blighted by the fire of 1914. In addition, "sub-divisions" blossomed in the area just outside the city limits, creating residential suburbs between crowded downtown St. Augustine and surrounding agricultural areas.

As the "decade of progress" continued, it touched every facet of the city's economic life and base. The Flagler railway system added to its office and repair shops. Expanding boat docks, shipyards and seafood packing plants supported a fleet of fishing boats that reached one hundred and kept going. The outlying Hastings farm area was booming. The municipal water and sewer systems were updated and expanded, as was electric service. The latest telephone system now allowed guests in the great hotels to make calls right from their own rooms. As the decade ended in 1924, the city's progress was formally recognized by extending the city limits. In the next few years, downtown began to spread out—and up, with its first "skyscraper," the First National Bank building (now occupied by the Atlantic Bank of St. Augustine).

St. Augustine was in good economic condition and quietly proud of its sound postwar progress when, in the early 1920's, Florida's real estate boom developed in the southern part of the state. A mixed bag of promoters, using every known sales gimmick, took advantage of the state's reputation for sunshine and soft breezes and its wide expanses of open and inexpensive land to launch a series of wild real estate and construction schemes, centered around Miami, Palm Beach and Tampa. Supported by some hard cash and mountains of paper credit, the boom sent land values soaring. Plots of land would change hands almost daily, doubling and tripling in value by the week. Instant millionaires were created—on paper—by the score, then by the hundreds.

St. Augustinians viewed the frenzied buying, selling and building with mixed emotions. The basically conservative banking and business community watched the goings-on with doubt and even fear. But many wished the city could get in on the action, feeling that they were missing golden opportunities to make their fortunes.

Although the boom psychology spread slowly northward to Daytona and Ormond Beach and Jacksonville, St. Augustine won little attention from developers until a homegrown entrepreneur cast his eyes on the city and its surroundings in 1924.

D. P. Davis was born in Green Cove Springs, a St. Johns River town only thirty miles northwest of St. Augustine. The boom in Miami attracted him with his small hoard of cash. On arrival he discovered he was a very small fish in a large school of land sharks, so he moved on to Tampa. Two small marshy islands where the Hillsborough River joins Tampa Bay caught his attention. If he could bulkhead those islands and then pump mud from the bay behind the bulkheads, he could create some spectacular building sites.

With a little cash and a lot of brass, he established a line of credit and went to work on his dream islands. In early 1924 the lots were placed on sale and less than a year later all were gone for total sales of $18,000,000.

Shortly thereafter on a visit to St. Augustine, he noticed the deserted marshy northern end of Anastasia Island, just across the Matanzas River from downtown St. Augustine. Again he saw bulkheads and dredges at work, another spectacular land coup like Davis Islands. Jacksonville institutions bankrolled his dream for a quarter of a million dollars. Davis Shores began to rise from the Anastasia marsh. It was 1925 and the boom had reached St. Augustine.

Though conservatives stood on the sidelines, many St. Augustinians leaped at the chance to get in on the easy money. Other land values around the city started to balloon.

Sales on Davis Shores were promoted in every possible way by Davis, including a controversial mechanical model of the development which he wanted housed in a special building in the plaza. The model featured homes, parks, hotels and a yacht club in miniature. The plan to construct a building 66 feet long, 30 feet wide and 15 feet high in the plaza to display the model was met with outrage by some St. Augustinians. Challenged in

In 1925 land-developer D. P. Davis brought the Florida land boom to St. Augustine. His big dredges sucked mud from the Matanzas River and spewed it out in the marsh off Anastasia Island, across the river from downtown St. Augustine, to create Davis Shores.

the courts, Davis lost, so he settled on erecting a building on Aviles Street, just south of the plaza.

But Davis's St. Augustine venture was sailing against the wind; Florida's boom was turning into a bust. Credit to buy St. Augustine's Davis Shores land and homes disappeared and anyone with cash was holding on to it.

In October 1926 Davis decided he needed a vacation in Europe and boarded the Cunard liner *Majestic* in New York. In the early morning hours of October 11, he disappeared from his stateroom. Though there were many speculations on just what happened and why, the hard fact was that D. P. Davis was "lost at sea."

The news was received with shock in St. Augustine. The death, coupled with increasing financial chaos in south Florida and elsewhere over the state, brought St. Augustine's short-lived boom to an abrupt halt. Though Davis's land company struggled on until it went bankrupt during the 1930's Depression, activity on Davis Shores immediately ceased. A half-dozen forlorn model homes stood for years on the reclaimed land, the only buildings in the vast expanse of dredged-up fill so slow to accept any softening green of weeds and young cedars. It would be a full generation before the development finally reached the proportion of Davis's dream, a lush and attractive residential community, just across the river from the Ancient City.

Across the inlet to the north, the boom had brought a casino, swimming pool and elaborately laid-out streets for the Vilano Beach development, most of which disappeared under the waves as the ocean encroached in the 1930's. While subdivisions north, west and south of the town were not so dramatically destroyed, many of their streets and entrance gates gradually crumbled, overgrown with vines, weeds and bushes.

St. Augustine was not badly scarred by its brief flirtation with boom psychology. But as it settled back into its conservative routine, there were other threatening financial signs on the national horizon that caused concern. Dependent as it was on tourism, the city was sensitive to every fluctuation in the country's economy.

In 1928 and 1929, there were many signs that the economy was sick. Newspapers headlined a growing number of bank failures over the country. As depositors lost confidence in the banking system, runs on banks began with panic withdrawals. St. Augustine banks were caught in the rising tide of fear and two went under. Many local businesses were in financial difficulty. Then the stock market crashed. The Great Depression was upon St. Augustine and the rest of the nation.

X. L. Pellicer, a St. Augustine banker, recalls the reaction as the Depression settled over St. Augustine like a dark cloud:

> "The majority of the town sort of banded together. People said, 'We've got problems—let's help each other.' What happened was inspiring. We got through the hard times pretty good—nothing really catastrophic happened to the city. After all, St. Augustine had faced hard times before during its nearly 400 years of history."

Since the city had no really large industries, there were no mass layoffs to contend with. The Florida East Coast Railway was the largest employer and it survived quite well. Small businesses were hurt and many farmers, highly dependent on credit, lost their farms. The fishing industry stayed strong. Oddly enough, the hard times actually helped tourism in one way. The summer visitors, which the city had sought for a quarter of a century, began to appear. Despite the money crunch, inlanders in Georgia and Mississippi and Alabama found enough for gas to get to the seashore, for food and for cheap lodging. Instead of spending months as winter visitors did in the past, they stayed only a few days until their money ran out. But the Depression years marked, at last, the switch from dependence on a comparative handful of rich, long-staying winter visitors to a swelling flood of dollar-watching summer tourists.

In other more urbanized parts of the nation, the symbols of hard times were bread lines and soup kitchens. There were none in St. Augustine. Small town, "clannish" traditions led St. Augustinians to take care of their own. One example was the sudden emergence in St. Augustine of a branch of the Society of St. Vincent de Paul, a worldwide charity organization of the

Catholic church. The Society grew quickly to some forty prominent citizens, each responsible for eight to ten hard-pressed families. Supported by special church collections, the Society members stayed in weekly contact with their "families," determining their needs and filling them. Neighbors helped neighbors and St. Augustine struggled through the worst of the Depression.

As the grip of hard times began to fade in the middle 1930's, an unfamiliar and exciting word began to show up in the lexicon of St. Augustinians—restoration.

The Flagler era introduced true tourism to the city and in the following years there was a steady growth of places and things to entertain and educate tourists—and, naturally, to extract dollars from their pockets. These over the years included oldest houses, oldest store, oldest drug store, oldest wooden school house, oldest orange grove, oldest mission, old jail, old sugar mill, a fountain of perpetual youth, alligator farms and a multitude of museums from antiques to wax. Many attractions were authentic, but some were created from whole cloth.

Of course, there were historic sites such as the brooding old Spanish fort that dominated the cityscape, the towering coqina city gate, the venerable cathedral, the plaza that dated almost back to the city's founding. But as the city grew and "modernized," more and more historic structures disappeared or were extensively altered. Little overall attention was paid to historic relics though there were individual efforts by some organizations such as the St. Augustine Historical Society, which since the 1880's had been concerned with the history of the town and preservation of historical sites, structures and objects. Unfortunately, its museum collection was virtually destroyed in the 1914 fire, but soon afterward the Society received permission from the U.S. War Department to occupy Castillo de San Marcos (then called Fort Marion) and to provide guide service for visitors. In 1924, the castillo and city gate, along with Fort Matanzas, the "back door" to St. Augustine, were designated national monuments by presidential proclamation. In this achievement the Society played no small role, and it continued operation of the old fort until the 1933 Historic Sites Act transferred national monuments from the War Department to the National Park Service. Meanwhile, beginning in 1918, the Society had purchased the Oldest House and other historic properties whose preservation it assured through restrictive covenants attached to them on resale.

In 1935, the first broad-scale effort with the avowed purpose of preserving and restoring old St. Augustine took shape.

Two men with widely varying backgrounds started it all off. St. Augustine Mayor Walter B. Fraser was an aggressive entrepreneur who owned and operated various attractions in St. Augustine and dreamed of claiming greater historic attention for the city. John C. Merriam was a prominent paleontologist and president of the Carnegie Institution of Washington, D.C., a foundation endowed by industrialist and philanthropist Andrew Carnegie. Merriam visited St. Augustine in March 1936 and was given an instructive and detailed tour of the old town by Herbert E. Kahler, a Park Service historian and superintendent of the castillo. Kahler then introduced the impressed Merriam to the affable Mayor Fraser. The two discussed St. Augustine's future, the mayor proposing a Colonial Williamsburg-type total reconstruction of Spanish St. Augustine using Carnegie money, Merriam countering with a selective restoration program based on in-depth research and possibly Carnegie funds to partially finance the research program. In the days following the meeting, Mayor Fraser crashed ahead, naming a national committee on the restoration of St. Augustine. He proposed, and talked Merriam into hosting, a conference in Washington, D.C. in October 1936, bringing together the top historians and archeologists in the Hispanic-American field. Results of the conference were encouraging. Within a month, Merriam made an historic decision to support a research project with Carnegie Institution money and he selected as head of the program Dr. Verne Chatelain, who had just left the National Park Service after five years as chief historian.

Charles B. Hosmer, Jr., in his two-volume *Preservation Comes of Age*, comments:

"There probably was no better time than the fall of 1936 to undertake the St. Augustine restoration program. Chatelain was able to put together a fine professional staff, including a historian who had grown up in the St. Augustine area and could read Spanish documents, as well as an archeologist who had worked with the National Park Service at Jamestown Island. These two men—Albert Manucy and W. J. Winter— also had help from some capable secretaries."

The national committee spawned a number of subcommittees, advisory committees and project groups, including the St. Augustine Preservation and Restoration Association, Inc., concerned with finances and development.

Using funds from the Carnegie Institution, the City of St. Augustine and the Federal WPA, the groups set to work on a variety of surveys, historic research projects and archeological activities. In 1937, the Florida Legislature passed a special act which gave St. Johns County and cities in it the power of eminent domain to protect historic sites and structures, and, in addition, appropriated $50,000 to acquire, preserve and maintain historical sites in St. Augustine (unfortunately these funds were not released until nearly a decade later). These two actions established an invaluable precedent for later state support for the St. Augustine historical program.

As the ambitious project moved ahead, finances were a continuing problem, and money began to run low in the last years of the 1930's. The final blow came with the onset of World War II, when funds and manpower of governmental units were channeled into new war-oriented priorities.

Committees and groups were disbanded, reports, data and archeological artifacts went into storage in various locations. It would be nearly two decades before the restoration idea would be fully revived.

Sunday, December 7, 1941 was a warm, bright day in St. Augustine.

In mid-afternoon, everything seemed to turn dark. Stunned citizens listened to their radios in consternation as news bulletins announced the Japanese attack on Pearl Harbor. One St. Augustinian summed up the general feeling:

> "I couldn't believe what was happening. How could a country like Japan come thousands of miles and go into a supposedly safely protected area and sink our fleet, do horrible damage?"

St. Augustine, a city which had been born 376 years before as a military stronghold and which over the centuries had seen more than its share of war and its effects, once again had its life turned upside down by war.

In common with most of the country, the city saw many of its young men rush to arms. Older citizens responded by seeking out their own personal ways of supporting the war effort. Businessmen hastily revised their plans for the future, knowing full well that there would be no room for tourism in wartime—and tourism was the main underpinning of the city's economy. Of some help were day trips to St. Augustine arranged for army and navy trainees from nearby facilities such as the big naval air station in Jacksonville and the sprawling army training base at Camp Blanding, fifty miles west of St. Augustine.

Soon shortages of all types began to appear, soon government controls were enacted, soon the first casualty lists were published. War news was dark; St. Augustine could watch billowing clouds of black smoke off the beaches as German submarines torpedoed merchant ships and tankers; more and more young men disappeared from the streets as they came of age. Most businesses were hurting.

One bright spot was the announcement in the fall of 1942 that the U.S. Coast Guard would establish a training station in the city. The Ponce de Leon and other hotels were taken over by the government to house the trainees. It was a shot in the arm for the economy as government money produced a "little boom," replacing the lost tourist revenue.

Entertainment for the recruits brought the city alive. Music was

During World War II, the U.S. Coast Guard selected St. Augustine as a training location. Here a company of Coast Guardsmen marches through the old city gate.

heard once again, sports events took on a new vitality, local girls helped arrange activities for servicemen. The trainees parti-

Photo courtesy of the Florida National Guard

Yet another hurricane. Florida National Guard trucks were the workhorses in the high winds and waters of a 1964 storm.

cipated in precision marching drills, orchestra concerts and made-up "musicals."

The Coast Guard made other contributions to the city. Federal funds were obtained for improvements in the channel and the harbor. And funds were provided for a program to rid the city of mosquito problems.

Later in the war, females in uniform became a common sight on the street as SPARS, the women's Coast Guard, arrived and took over clerking, bookkeeping and switchboard duties for the service.

The war finally ended on September 2, 1945 and again the city's celebration centered on the city's plaza. In almost a repeat of events of November 11, 1918, crowds in cars and afoot gathered there. Horns, bells, whistles and fireworks joined in a deafening cacophony that lasted for hours.

It was time for St. Augustine to prepare for a return to normal. And from an economic standpoint, that return came soon as tourists, long denied the luxury of travel and vacations, showed up in droves. The Ponce de Leon, returned to private ownership in the final days of the war, quickly filled up, as did motels that had replaced the other, now-defunct grand hotels.

The postwar years saw a slow but steady growth for St. Augustine and St. Johns County. Population increased, new businesses appeared and existing ones expanded. "Good roads," as they had a half century past, aided the growth, this time in a spreading network of federally-financed superhighways that lured added millions of tourists into Florida from farther away than ever; many of them stopped to discover and explore the Ancient City.

In the early 1960's, St. Augustine watched almost with detachment the drama of the civil rights movement spreading over the southern states. The white community seemed to feel that there was little racial tension in the city. The black community was not so sure. There were some early rumblings over segregation in

Around the city of Hastings, a few miles southwest of St. Augustine, fertile acres furnished much produce over the years, finally becoming one of the major potato-growing areas in the nation.

hotels, restaurants and recreation facilities, discrimination in medical facilities and employment, "official hostility." But neither side seemed prepared for the whirlwind of hatred and violence that lay just ahead, placing the city in headlines and on TV screens nationwide and bringing on a weeks-long period when St. Augustine would be under a virtual state of siege.

The first signs of trouble came in the summer of 1963 when tensions began to grow and there were small demonstrations marked by sporadic violence. The spring of 1964 saw an escalation of problems, as the traditional invasion of vacationing college students into the state brought an activist group of young people into St. Augustine to protest separation of blacks and

Photo courtesy of The St. Augustine Record

Shrimp boats have sailed from St. Augustine for over a century. The fleet continues to be an important industry of the city, joined in recent years on the San Sebastian River by ship-building companies producing trawlers and other small vessels.

whites in St. Augustine's socio-political system. St. Augustine drew national attention with the arrival in the city of Mrs. Malcolm E. Peabody, activist mother of Massachusetts Governor Endicott Peabody, who became a "Joan of Arc" of the student group. Mrs. Peabody, leading demonstrations and sit-ins, was arrested and jailed on trespass charges. The national press descended on the city to cover the story of a governor's mother behind bars in the nation's oldest city.

Things quieted down in early April as Easter vacations ended, Mrs. Peabody and others were released, and all returned north. But the stage had now been set, attention of national segregation and desegregation leaders had been focused on the city, the national press was interested and the "hot summer" winds were about to blow.

In May 1964 the Reverend Martin Luther King arrived in the city to unite the black efforts. Andrew Young (later to become a congressman, Ambassador to the United Nations and Mayor of Atlanta) joined him as head of the movement in St. Augustine. On May 28, the first planned marches and demonstrations began, and so did the violence and arrests.

A decision by Young to conduct marches through the downtown area at night brought the problems to a peak. City officials tried to impose a curfew, were overruled by a federal judge. Barely controlled violence broke out as racial elements from both sides began to converge on the city. Florida's Governor Farris Bryant considered sending in the Florida National Guard, then settled on a small army of state troopers. In the final weeks of June, St. Augustine was rocked almost nightly by marches by blacks, countermarches by whites, violence and a maelstrom of blind hatred on both sides.

Passage of the Civil Rights Bill by Congress and its signature into law on July 4 signaled the beginning of the end for the St. Augustine demonstrations.

It had been a hard summer for the city. It left physical, emotional and economic scars. And it engendered fears for the next year, 1965, when the Ancient City would hold a year-long celebration of the 400th anniversary of its founding in 1565. There were sporadic demonstrations and scattered violence during the anniversary year but the civil rights spotlight had been shifted elsewhere in the nation and St. Augustine was now a backwater.

Interest in St. Augustine's restoration, halted by World War II, was slow in reviving after the war.

In the early 1950's, with the cooperation of the St. Augustine Historical Society, three colonial buildings were purchased to prevent their destruction, restoration of one historic house was completed. But by the mid-1950's concerted efforts were underway to get restoration back on track, and St. Augustine leaders approached Florida's Governor LeRoy Collins for assistance in reviving the restoration concept of the 1930's and in providing state backing for the program. The governor named a special advisory committee which suggested new legislation creating the St. Augustine Historical Restoration and Preservation Commission. The commission came into being when the governor signed the legislation into law on June 19, 1959. Restoration was back in business.

Picking up where the Carnegie-sponsored efforts of the 1930's left off, the commission (later renamed the Historic St. Augustine Preservation Board) targeted an area of St. Augustine north of the plaza as the site of a program to restore or reconstruct 18th-century structures there. Historical and archeological research located and identified foundations of numerous buildings and provided accurate architectural details for their reconstruction.

The commission, with essential support from the St. Augustine Restoration Foundation, Inc., a privately funded organization headed by Lawrence Lewis, Jr., concentrated on physical restoration, acquiring 34 parcels of land and restoring or reconstructing 29 buildings, centered around St. George Street. This progress was supplemented by interested citizens and businesses undertaking individual restoration projects on their own.

The next phase saw another 20 physical restorations but greater emphasis began to be placed on research, building a vast reservoir of knowledge about historic sites and buildings in the city.

In 1981, looking back over two decades of concentrated physical activity and data gathering, Dr. William R. Adams, director of the Preservation Board, commented that the board's activities "will provide for many decades to come a basis for rational and thoughtful decisions by state and local governments and by private organizations and residents in the management, preservation and conservation of the rich cultural resources in America's oldest city."

Outstanding as always, the three great Flagler hotels have figured prominently in that "management, preservation and conservation."

The Hotel Ponce de Leon in the fall of 1968 became the new Flagler College, which has grown into a successful liberal arts institution.

Earlier that year, the former Cordova hotel, after considerable interior renovation and a new facade, became the St. Johns County Court House.

The Alcazar hotel, closed since 1930, has served for some years as the home of the Lightner Museum and the location of municipal offices.

And so St. Augustinians have rediscovered and are using their historic past—a past which has become the present and the future of the Oldest City.

Major Sources

Chapter One

Bennett, Charles E., translator. *Three Voyages: René Laudonnière.* Gainesville: University Presses of Florida, 1975.

Kerrigan, Anthony, translator. *Barcia's Chronological History of the Continent of Florida.* Gainesville: University Press of Florida, 1951.

Larson, Lewis H. *Aboriginal Subsistence Technology on the Southeastern Coastal Plain during the Late Prehistories Period.* Gainesville: University Presses of Florida, 1980.

Lorant, Stefan. *The New World.* New York: Duell, Sloan and Pearce, 1946.

Lowery, Woodbury. *The Spanish Settlements within the Present Limits of the United States, 1513-1574.* 2 vols. New York: Russell and Russell, 1959.

Milanich, Jerald T. and Charles H. Fairbanks. *Florida Archaeology.* New York: Academic Press, 1980.

Milanich, Jerald T. and Samuel Proctor, eds. *Tacachale: Essays on the Indians of Florida and Southeastern Georgia during the Historic Period.* Gainesville: University Presses of Florida, 1978.

Morison, Samuel Eliot. *The European Discovery of America: The Southern Voyages, 1492-1616.* New York: Oxford University Press, 1974.

Payne, Edward John. *Voyages of the Elizabethan Seamen.* Oxford: Clarendon Press, 1907.

Swanton, John R. *Early History of the Creek Indians and Their Neighbors.* Washington, D.C.: Government Printing Office (Smithsonian Institution), 1922.

Chapter Two

Arnade, Charles W. *Florida on Trial, 1593-1602.* Coral Gables: University of Miami Press, 1959.

Bushnell, Amy. *The King's Coffer: Proprietors of the Spanish Florida Treasury, 1565-1702.* Gainesville: University Presses of Florida, 1981.

Corbett, Theodore G. "Migration to a Spanish Imperial Frontier

in the Seventeenth and Eighteenth Centuries: St. Augustine,"
Hispanic American Historical Review, 54 (August 1974).

Deagan, Kathleen. "Mestizaje in Colonial St. Augustine,"
Ethnohistory, 20 (1973).

Deagan, Kathleen. "St. Augustine: First Urban Enclave in the
United States," *North American Archaeologist*, 3 (1982).

Gannon, Michael V. *The Cross in the Sand: The Early Catholic
Church in Florida, 1513-1870*. Gainesville: University of
Florida Press, 1965.

Hoffman, Paul E. *The Spanish Crown and the Defense of the
Caribbean, 1535-1585: Precedent, Patrimonialism, and Royal
Parsimony*. Baton Rouge: Louisiana State University Press,
1980.

Lyon, Eugene. *The Enterprise of Florida: Pedro Menéndez de
Avilés and the Spanish Conquest of 1565-1568*. Gainesville:
University Presses of Florida, 1976.

Manucy, Albert. "Changing Traditions in St. Augustine Architecture." In *Eighteenth-Century Florida and the Impact of
the American Revolution*, Samuel Proctor, ed. Gainesville:
University Presses of Florida, 1978.

Matter, Robert A. "The Spanish Missions of Florida: The Friars
Versus the Governors in the 'Golden Age,' 1606-1690."
Ph.D. dissertation, University of Washington, 1972.

Reitz, Elizabeth J., and Margaret Scarry. "Reconstructing
Historic Subsistence: Sixteenth-Century St. Augustine."
Ms in progress, 1983.

Chapter Three

Arana, Luis Rafael, and Albert Manucy. *The Building of Castillo
de San Marcos*. (no place): Eastern National Park and
Monument Association, 1977.

Arnade, Charles W. *The Siege of St. Augustine in 1702*. Gainesville: University of Florida Press, 1959.

Bushnell, Amy. *The King's Coffer*. Gainesville: University Presses
of Florida, 1981.

Collections of the Georgia Historical Society, VII, Part 1. "Letters
of Montiano - Siege of St. Augustine." Savannah: Georgia
Historical Society, 1909.

Gold, Robert L. *Borderlands - Empires in Transition.* Carbondale and Edwardsville: Southern Illinois University Press, 1969.

Harman, Joyce Elizabeth. *Trade and Privateering in Spanish Florida, 1732-1763.* St. Augustine: St. Augustine Historical Society, 1969.

Lanning, John Tate. *The Diplomatic History of Georgia.* Chapel Hill: University of North Carolina Press, 1936.

TePaske, John Jay. *The Governorship of Spanish Florida, 1700-1763.* Durham: Duke University Press, 1964.

Torres-Reyes, Ricardo. "The British Siege of St. Augustine in 1740." Historic Resource Study. Castillo de San Marcos National Monument: Denver Service Center, 1972.

Wallace, David Duncan. *South Carolina, a Short History, 1520-1948.* Columbia: University of South Carolina Press, 1961.

Chapter Four

Colonial Office Papers (London). Class 5, volumes 540 to 573.

De Vorsey, Jr., Louis, ed. *De Braham's Report of the General Survey in the Southern District of North America.* Columbia: University of South Carolina Press, 1971.

Forbes, James Grant. *Sketches, Historical and Topographical, of the Floridas; More Particularly of East Florida.* New York: C. S. Van Winkle, 1831.

Grant, Alastair Macpherson. *General James Grant of Ballindalloch, 1720 - 1806.* London: privately published by A. M. Grant, 1930.

Grant, James. The James Grant Papers (unpublished). Ballindalloch Castle Muniments, Ballindalloch, Scotland

Lockey, Joseph Byrne. *East Florida 1783 - 1785: A File of Documents Assembled, and Many of Them Translated.* John Walton Caughey, ed. Berkeley and Los Angeles: University of California Press, 1949.

Mowat, Charles Loch. *East Florida as a British Province, 1763 - 1784.* Berkeley and Los Angeles: University of California Press, 1943. Fasimile edition, Gainesville: University of Florida Press, 1964.

——————————. "St. Augustine Under the British Flag, 1763 -

1775." *Florida Historical Quarterly*, XX (October 1941).

Romans, Bernard. *A Concise Natural History of East and West Florida*. New York, 1775. Reprint, New Orleans: Pelican Publishing Company, 1961.

Siebert, Wilbur H. *Loyalists in East Florida, 1774 - 1785*. 2 vols. Deland: Florida Historical Society, 1929.

Wright, J. Leitch, Jr. *British St. Augustine*. St. Augustine: Historic St. Augustine Preservation Board, 1975.

———————. *Florida in the American Revolution*. Gainesville: University Presses of Florida, 1975.

Chapter Five

Anonymous. *Narrative of a Voyage to the Spanish Main in the Ship "Two Friends."* Gainesville: University Presses of Florida, 1978.

Curley, Michael J. *Church and State in the Spanish Floridas (1783 - 1822)*. Washington, D.C.: Catholic University of America Press, 1940

Griffin, Patricia C. "Mullet on the Beach: The Minorcans of Florida, 1768 - 1788." Master's thesis, University of Florida, 1977.

Harlan, Roger C. "A Military History of East Florida during the Governorship of Enrique White: 1796 - 1811." Master's thesis, Florida State University, 1971.

Lockey, Joseph Byrne. *East Florida, 1783 - 1785: A File of Documents Assembled, and Many of them Translated*. Berkeley: University of California Press, 1949.

Miller, Janice Borton. *Juan Nepomuceno Quesada, Governor of Spanish East Florida, 1790 - 1795*. Washington, D.C.: University Press of America, 1981

Patrick, Rembert W. *Florida Fiasco*. Athens: University of Georgia Press, 1954.

Tanner, Helen Hornbeck. *Zéspedes in East Florida, 1784 - 1790*. Coral Gables: University of Miami Press, 1963.

Whitaker, Arthur Preston. *Documents Relating to the Commercial Policy of Spain in the Floridas*. Deland: Florida State Historical Society, 1931.

Chapter Six

Gannon, Michael V. *The Cross in the Sand.* Gainesville: University of Florida Press, 1965.

Graham, Thomas. *The Awakening of St. Augustine: The Anderson Family and the Oldest City, 1821 - 1924.* St. Augustine: St. Augustine Historical Society, 1978.

Mahon, John K. *History of the Second Seminole War, 1835 - 1842.* Gainesville: University of Florida Press, 1967.

Martin, Sidney Walter. *Florida During the Territorial Days.* Athens: University of Georgia Press.

Upton, Onville. "Letters of Private Onville Upton." Private collection, Niles Schuh, Panama City, Fla.

Chapter Seven

Dewhurst, William W. *History of St. Augustine.* New York: Knickerbocker Press, 1886.

Graham, Thomas. *The Awakening of St. Augustine: The Anderson Family and the Oldest City, 1821 - 1924.* St. Augustine: St. Augustine Historical Society, 1978.

Lanier, Sidney. *Florida: Its Scenery, Climate and History.* Philadelphia: J. B. Lippincott, 1876. Facsimile reprint. Gainesville: University Presses of Florida, 1973.

Martin, Sidney, *Florida's Flagler.* Athens: University of Georgia Press, 1949

Reid, Whitelaw. *After the War: A Southern Tour.* Cincinnati and New York: Moore, Wilstach and Baldwin, 1866.

Shofner, Jerrell. *Nor Is It Over Yet: Florida in the Era of Reconstruction.* Gainesville: University Presses of Florida, 1974.

Chapter Eight

Belasco, Warren James. *Americans on the Road.* Cambridge: Massachusetts Institute of Technology Press, 1979.

Edwards, Virginia. *Stories of Old St. Augustine.* St. Augustine: St. Augustine Historical Society, 1973.

Florida Times Union. Jacksonville, 1914 to date.

Graham, Thomas. *The Awakening of St. Augustine: The*

Anderson Family and the Oldest City, 1821 - 1924. St. Augustine: St. Augustine Historical Society, 1978.

Hanna, A. J. and Kathryn. *Florida's Golden Sands.* Indianapolis: Bobbs Merrill Company, 1950.

Hosmer, Charles B., Jr. *Preservation Comes of Age.* Charlottesville: University Press of Virginia, 1981.

Howells, William Dean. "A Confession of St. Augustine." *Harper's Magazine,* April, May, 1917.

Martin, Sidney Walter. *Florida's Flagler.* Athens: University of Georgia Press, 1949.

Oral Histories. St. Augustine Historical Society, 1940 to date.

St. Augustine Record and *St. Augustine Evening Record.* St. Augustine, 1914 to date.

Index

Abraham (black interpreter), 164
Adams, John Quincy, 149
Adams, William R., 241
Adelantado, 21, 28
Africa (Lincolnville), 188
Agriculture: Indian, beginnings of, 7; Guale, 37; corn raised by Indian laborers, 38; wheat farm, 51; Calderón report, 58; Apalache as granary, 60; poor state of, 92; Moultrie as planter, 95; fund to encourage agriculture, 95; promoted, 99; agricultural "college," 100; 1776 production, 113; new lands cleared for, 120; 1790 potential, 141; 19th-century development, 199; Hastings a major potato producer, 238. *See also* Farming, Plantations and names of individual commodities
Airplanes, 219, 220, 222
Ais, 31
Alabama, 32, 230
Alcazar Hotel, 194, 195, 242
Alexander (slave), 111
Alicia Hospital, 196
Alligator Farm, 203
Alligator Creek bridge, 116
Altamaha River, 116
Altamirano, Juan de las Cabezas, 41
Alvarez, Gerónimo, 131, 133, 134, 149, 159
Amber, 39, 41
Amelia Island, 64, 143
American Riviera, the, 192, 211
Amherst, Jeffrey, 92, 98
Anastasia (Lighthouse Park), 202
Anastasia Island, 82, 104; coquina quarries, 56, 57, 60; D. P. Davis, 227, 228; Fish's plantation, 97, 132; formed, 6; Fort Caroline survivors, 30; Oglethorpe battery, 76; lighthouse, 153, 175; tourism, 202
Ancient City Baptist Church, 196
Andalusia, 55
Anderson, Andrew, (first), 161, 163, 175
Anderson, Andrew, (second), 175, 184, 193
Anglican Church. *See* St. Peter's Church
Apache Indians, 191
Apalache, 53, 59; explorations, 3, 21; missions, 44, 48, 51; rebellion, 50; defense, 52, 69; supplies from, 58, 60, 82; Moore campaign, 68; trail to, 71
Apalache Indians, 50
Apalachicola, 50, 58, 68
Apalachicola River, 60
Arapaho Indians, 189
Archiniegas, Admiral Sancho de, 32

Arkansas, 124
Armistice, World War I, 224, 225
Arnau, Paul, 175, 177
Arredondo, Antonio de, 73, 74
Artists' communities, 200
Assembly, Houses of, 96, 107, 109, 118
Astor, William, 186
Asturias, 28
Atlantic Bank of St. Augustine, 226
Aucilla River, 51
Audubon, John James, 157
Augusta, 22, 115
Automobiles, 219, 225; early years of, 212-217
Aviles Street, 187, 229
Axacán, 33

Bachop, Adam, 99
Bahamas, the, 121, 122, 143
Ballindalloch Castle, 93
Banditti, 115, 127, 133; members of, 120, 121; arrested by Zéspedes, 125
Baptiste (Grant's cook), 110
Baptists. *See* Ancient City Baptist Church
Bara, Theda, 219, 221
Barbados, 44
Barcia, 1
Baseball, 221, 223
Bay. *See* Harbor and inlet
Bay Street, 217
Beans, 7, 40, 43, 81
Beaufort, 178
Bee culture, 141
Bella Vista, 101, 117, 118
Bells, 36, 69, 122; church 27, 36, 105, 122, 145; market, 145; fire, 218; celebrating end of war, 225, 237
Benavides, Antonio de, 69-71, 73, 82
Benet, Isabel, 175
Benet, Laura, 155
Benet, Pedro, 155, 159
Benet, Stephen Vincent (West Point graduate), 155, 175
Benet, Stephen Vincent (writer), 155
Benet, William Rose, 155
Bermuda, 44
Betsy, 112
Beyers, Miss, 215
Bicycles, 202, 213, 216, 219
Bishop for Florida, auxiliary, 68, 73
Bishop of Charleston, 158, 159
Bishop of Cuba, 68, 91, 106
Bisset, Robert, 105, 113, 121
Blacks: free, 54, 125, 126, 147, 165; in militia, 112; in East Florida Rangers,

249

Trinity Episcopal Church, 159
Turnbull, Andrew, 100, 101, 107, 113, 118, 155
Turnbull, Gracia Dura Ben, 100, 101
Tuttle, Stephen, 172
Twenty-First Regiment (British), 102

Union Conservative Party, 184
Union Hotel, 170
United States Army: Corps of Engineers, 172. See also Civil War, First Seminole War, Patriots War, Reconstruction period, Second Seminole War, Spanish-American War, World War I, World War II
United States Coast Guard, 234, 235, 237; SPARS 237
United States Military Academy, 155, 164, 175
United States Navy, 164, 175, 177
United States War Department, 231
Upton, Onville, 178

Valdés, Fernando de, 40
Valdés, Pedro de, 40
Vander Dussen, Alexander, 76, 77, 79
Vanderbilts, the, 199
Vegetables, 145, 147, 199
Vera Cruz, 45, 51, 73
Verot, Augustin, 185
Vespucci, Amerigo, 18
Vilano Beach, 229
Villa Zorayda, 193, 194
Vinton, John Rogers, 166
Virginia, 44, 115, 119, 191
Vizcaya, 28
Volusia County, 215

Waldron, Louisa, 126-127, 132
Walker, William Aikin, 200
Walton and Company, 132
Walton, William, 82, 86, 96, 97
War of 1812, 148
War of Austrian Succession, 93
Washington, George, 119, 136
Washington, D.C., 166, 232
Wattle and daub houses, 33
Wells, barrel, 33; coquina, 145
Wells, John, Jr., 120
Westcott, John, 186
West Florida, 96, 119, 127, 144, 149, 151
West Point. See United States Military Academy
Wheat, 51
White, Enrique, 143

White, Utley, J., 199
Whitehall, 209
Whitney, John F., 188
Whitneys, the, 199
Wickliffe, Charles A., 173
Williams, John Lee, 160
Winter, W. J., 233
Winter Newport, the, 197, 199, 203, 206, 211
Wood's Tavern, 112
Woodward, John Henry, 54
Work Progress Administration (WPA), 233
World War I, 218, 219, 223-225
World War II, 233-237, 240
Worth, William, 171
Worthington, William, 154
Wright, Charles, 106, 118, 120
Wright, Jeremyn, 106, 118
Wright, Orville, 222
Wright, Wilbur, 222
Wyllie, H. S., 167

Ximénez-Fatio House, 162

Yamassee Indians, 71
Ybarra, Pedro de, 41, 43
Yeats, David, 98, 115, 122; Masonic lodge member, 102; correspondence with Grant, 111; practices medicine, 112, 117;
Yonge, Henry, 118
Young, Andrew, 240
Young, Mrs., 103
Yorktown, 119
Yucatan, 33
Yuchi Billy, 168
Yuchi Jack, 168
Yulee, David Levy, 172, 173
Yulee, Margarita Wickliffe, 173

Zéspedes, Dominga, 128, 130
Zéspedes, Vizente Manuel de, 121, 125-137; and Tonyn, 121, 122, 125, 126, 127; arrives as governor, 121, 125; finds Canary Islanders slothful, 131; hopes to develop province, 135; and royal celebration, 137
Zúñiga y Cerda, Josef de, 63-68; royal observances, 63; Moore's attack, 65-67